PORTRAITS OF
AMERICAN PRESIDENTS
VOLUME VII

THE
FORD
PRESIDENCY

TWENTY-TWO INTIMATE
PERSPECTIVES OF
GERALD R. FORD

Edited by

KENNETH W. THOMPSON

Miller Center of Public Affairs
University of Virginia

UNIVERSITY
PRESS OF
AMERICA

Lanham • New York • London

The Miller Center

University of Virginia

Library of Congress Cataloging-in-Publication Data

The Ford presidency : twenty-two intimate perspectives of Gerald R.
Ford / edited by Kenneth W. Thomspon.
p. cm.—(Portraits of American presidents ; v. 7)
1. Ford, Gerald R., 1913–   . 2. United States—Politics and
government—1974–1977. I. Thompson, Kenneth W., 1921–
II. Series.
E176.1.P83   1982 vol. 7 [E866]
973'.09.92 s—dc 19 [973.925'092'4]   88–5586 CIP
ISBN 0–8191–6959–5 (alk. paper)
ISBN 0–8191–6960–9 (pbk. : alk. paper)

Dedicated

to

all those who

strive to heal

and

to rebuild and restore

the fabric of national life

TABLE OF CONTENTS

PREFACE · ix
Kenneth W. Thompson

INTRODUCTION · · · · · · · · · · · · · · · · · · · xi
Kenneth W. Thompson

I. THE MAN AND THE POLITICAL LEADER

THE MAN WHO HAPPENED TO BECOME PRESIDENT · · 3
Senator Robert P. Griffin

REFLECTIONS ON A POLITICIAN'S PRESIDENT · · · · · 27
Philip W. Buchen

THE ACCIDENTAL PRESIDENT · · · · · · · · · · · · 45
Leo Cherne

II. THREE VIEWS OF THE FORD WHITE HOUSE

FORMING AND MANAGING AN ADMINISTRATION · · · 57
Richard B. Cheney

TABLE OF CONTENTS

THE LOYALISTS AND THE PRAETORIAN GUARD · · · 89
Robert T. Hartmann

PRESIDENT FORD AND THE BUDGET · · · · · · · · · 111
Paul H. O'Neill

III. DOMESTIC ISSUES AND THE ECONOMY

FORD AND THE FEDERAL RESERVE · · · · · · · · · 135
Arthur F. Burns

FORD AND THE ECONOMY: NATIONAL
AND INTERNATIONAL · · · · · · · · · · · · · · · 141
Kenneth Rush

DOMESTIC ISSUES AND THE BUDGET · · · · · · · · 159
James M. Cannon

IV. FORD, THE MEDIA AND THE PUBLIC

THE FORD PRESIDENCY AND THE PRESS · · · · · · · 179
Ron Nessen

PRESIDENT FORD AND THE MEDIA · · · · · · · · · 209
Jerald F. terHorst

SPEECHES, HUMOR AND THE PUBLIC · · · · · · · · 231
Robert Orben

TABLE OF CONTENTS

A FOOTNOTE ON FORD AND THE VOICE
  OF AMERICA 255
James Keogh

V. THE DEPARTMENTS AND THE WHITE HOUSE

DECISION-MAKING IN THE FORD PRESIDENCY 261
Senator Charles E. Goodell

THE REESTABLISHMENT OF THE WHITE HOUSE
  SCIENCE OFFICE 279
H. Guyford Stever

HIGHLIGHTS OF A BRIEF TENURE, 1975-76 293
John T. Dunlop

FORD VIEWED FROM AGRICULTURE: A NOTE 303
Secretary of Agriculture Earl Butz

VI. THE FORD PRESIDENCY:
FOREIGN POLICY AND DEFENSE

FORD AS PRESIDENT AND HIS FOREIGN POLICY . . . 309
General Brent Scowcroft

FORD, KISSINGER AND THE NIXON-FORD
  FOREIGN POLICY 319
Joseph J. Sisco

FORD, FOREIGN POLICY AND THE BUREAUCRACY . . 333
Michael Rauol-Duval

TABLE OF CONTENTS

FORD AND THE SONNENFELDT DOCTRINE 343
  Helmut Sonnenfeldt

VII. HISTORY'S JUDGMENT

A PRESIDENT WHO BROUGHT HEALING 349
  Lou Cannon

CONCLUDING OBSERVATIONS 359
  Kenneth W. Thompson

PREFACE

A pattern has emerged in the course of organizing Miller Center Forums which has led to the present volume. We have discovered that the leading authorities on particular presidents have helped the Center to draw others with common background to the University of Virginia. By "word of mouth advertising," they have encouraged their friends to come to Faulkner House. Their help has been of inestimable value to a fledgling public affairs center. It has enabled us to conduct further presidential studies through the contributions of distinguished visitors to the understanding of contemporary presidents.

Partly by accident and partly by design, we have discovered our guests were turning the spotlight on certain American presidents. They were viewing particular administrations with shared values but different perspectives. Their differing experiences each illuminated a dimension that otherwise might have remained obscured. They helped us to understand the President they knew best. The product is a portrait, not a photograph; it helps us see the character and spirit of a leader, not the more or less important details a photograph tends to convey. It tells us what was central to his life and works, not what was peripheral. The photograph reveals what can be seen with the naked eye. The portrait shows one thing the photograph cannot reveal: the human essence of the person portrayed.

With this volume, we continue a series of Miller Center publications, *Portraits of American Presidents*. We are grateful to the University Press of America for making volumes in this series available to a wide audience. We have embarked on similar inquiries into the presidency of Jimmy Carter. We plan to complete the series with volumes on the remaining postwar presidents. In the Introduction which follows, the editor traces the history of the Center's interest in the presidency of Gerald R. Ford.

INTRODUCTION

Every American presidency presents historians with contradictory evidence as they seek to evaluate and assess the historical record. President Gerald R. Ford is no exception as becomes clear in the discussions that follow.

To some participants and observers, Gerald Ford is the President who healed the nation after its long, painful Watergate journey. He was respected and beloved by colleagues in the Congress. He possessed strengths some of which were seldom visible to the public. For example, he mastered the federal budget and could present and analyze it as few of his predecessors or successors could do. Despite the controversy over his presidential pardon of Richard M. Nixon, no one questioned his integrity. Some disputed his political judgment, but those who suggested he struck a political deal with President Nixon before his choice as vice president are not convincing.

At the same time, an aura of hard luck and ill fortune hangs over the Ford presidency. He appeared to the media as an awkward and clumsy person despite the fact he was perhaps the best athlete ever to occupy the White House (He was an All-American football player at the University of Michigan). His fate was to stumble as he disembarked from a plane or to slip on a ski slope whenever the media was present. Although he was as well briefed on foreign policy as any contemporary president and pursued a generally enlightened and moderate policy, he minimized the extent of Soviet influence in Poland and Eastern Europe in a presidential debate with challenger Jimmy Carter thereby losing political support with ethnic voters. (Some observers consider that this lapse contributed to his loss in the 1976 presidential election.) He left an impression that he could not manage opposing forces in his administration, that he lacked the ability to "knock heads." Although some considered his vetoes of legislation that threatened the budget a source of strength, others asked why a former congressman should have had such limited success in forging a consensus with the Congress. Even those to whom he was the model of a good and decent man questioned his ability to govern.

Issues such as these form some of the main lines of discourse of participants in the Ford Presidential Portrait. Senator Robert P. Griffin has been a close friend and associate of Gerald Ford since 1956. Griffin's choice of the theme of his forum was deliberate: "How Gerald R. Ford *happened* to become the thirty-eighth President." He was the first President ever to attain that office without being elected either to the vice presidency or presidency. For Griffin, this sets the Ford presidency apart, although not by comparison with the leadership in Britain where the Prime Minister is elected as a Member of Parliament by the voters of only one district. Senator Griffin traces Ford's rise in the Congress, his emergence as a national political figure, and his problems and strengths as President.

Philip W. Buchen was counsel to President Ford who early in his professional career, had been a member of the law firm of Ford and Buchen. More recently, he has been a partner of Dewey, Ballantine, Bushby, Palmer and Wood. He has served on two national commissions sponsored by the Miller Center: one on presidential transitions and foreign policy, and the other on presidential disability and the 25th amendment. His discussion of controversial issues such as the pardon of Richard Nixon in which he is sometimes assumed to have played a part and his assessment of the strengths and weaknesses of President Ford marks this presentation.

Leo Cherne discusses the Ford presidency with special reference to intelligence matters pushed to the fore in recent times by disclosures in the Iran-Contra hearings and writings about William Casey. Cherne characterizes Ford as an "accidental president" in a double sense. He had not sought the office but was appointed vice president by Richard Nixon on the resignation of Spiro Agnew and then rose to the presidency when Nixon resigned. Cherne offers a strongly sympathetic view of Ford's qualities as leader.

Richard Cheney was, first, deputy chief of staff and then chief of staff in the Ford White House. His measured and well-informed comments on the organization of the Ford White House provide a model of political and administrative analysis. He describes with exceptional clarity Ford's relations with the Congress, his view of Ronald Reagan and the 1976 campaign. A present day leader in the Congress, his candor is refreshing and his political understanding unmatched.

Robert T. Hartmann was a leader of the so-called Ford loyalist group who had served Congressman Ford and then Vice President Ford. He became counsellor in the Ford White House. Hartmann discusses a wide variety of issues: succession under the 25th amendment, problems of an unelected president and vice president, carryover staff from the Nixon administration, Ford's style, his achievements and limitations as a leader and the resistance Ford encountered from the praetorian guard. The president, Hartmann argues, must be a commander and this quality he finds lacking in Ford. "Ford was simply too nice a guy; he boasted that he had adversaries but no enemies" (p. 99).

Hartmann's thesis about Ford is that "Ford could have survived his sudden pardon of former President Nixon if he had coupled it with a dismissal of Nixon's entire court and constituted one of his own" (p. 100). Others who are contributors to this volume don't agree, but pro and con arguments serve to crystallize the issues on this important proposition.

In 1987 Paul O'Neill was chosen chairman and chief executive officer of the Aluminum Company of America (Alcoa). When he made his presentation on the Ford presidency at the Miller Center, he was president of the International Paper Company. We proudly announce that in 1987, he became an Associate of the Center. O'Neill captures the high drama of the transition from Nixon to Ford and the change and confusion that can accompany such a transition. For example, an early speech written for Ford as vice president raised problems when it proved not to have been staffed out for presentation by President Ford. O'Neill offers vignettes of President Ford as political leader and the values that inspired his actions, including his conviction that a decision that was right for the country was better than a political decision that served only his own political ends. O'Neill offers comparisons of the use of the budget process in the Johnson, Nixon and Ford presidencies that he is uniquely qualified to make.

The late Arthur Burns is almost alone among recent public servants in having served successive presidents and played a vital role as chairman of the Federal Reserve. From the vantage point of the Fed, he offers some important comparisons of three presidents , Nixon, Ford and Carter, whom he observed first-hand in their relation with that body. Of the three, Burns writes: "Mr. Nixon's record was by far the worst. Mr. Ford's record was by far the best." President Ford not only praised the independence of the Fed but demonstrated his belief in practice. While his discussion of the Ford presidency is brief, he not only throws light on Ford's relationship with the Fed, but comments on his overall view of the role of the chairman of the Council of Economic Advisers.

Kenneth Rush served in both the Nixon and Ford administrations and is well qualified to discuss "Ford and the economy." He was the chief executive of Union Carbide and a respected business leader. Rush contrasts the personal styles of Ford and Nixon and their attitude toward the social agenda. In his words: "President Ford loved life; he loved the job. He fitted in very well" (p. 143). Rush discusses four important issues in the Ford presidency: the organization of the White House, the Nixon carryovers, the Nixon pardon and the economy. Throughout he compares and contrasts Ford with Nixon. His account touches on the human side of the Ford presidency as well as the economy.

James Cannon was assistant to President Ford and executive director of the Domestic Council. A former journalist and magazine executive, he had earlier been a special assistant to Governor Nelson Rockefeller and director of the Commission of Critical Choices which the Governor headed. Later, he became chief of staff for the majority leader of the United States Senate, Senator Howard Baker. Mr. Cannon views the Ford administration especially from the standpoint of domestic issues, the relationship between departments and the White House and between President Ford and Vice President Rockefeller.

Gerald Ford's relationship with the media remains a puzzling aspect of his presidency. While he was respected, he was also the target of media ridicule and criticism, not least from photographic journalism. Photographers seemed ever present with their lenses when he bumped his head on the door of an airplane or fell on some Rocky Mountain ski slope. Reporters seized on his lapse in the foreign policy debate with Jimmy Carter. They conveyed the image, however deliberately, of a slow thinking and rather heavy-handed leader, an image contested by those who were closest to Ford and who shared his political and administrative life. At least until the Iran-Contra crisis, the media appeared to treat the human frailties of President Ronald Reagan in a quite different way; and thoughtful observers ask why.

Ron Nessen who was an editor for UPI and a radio and TV correspondent for NBC addresses the issue of the Ford image. He joined President Ford as his second press secretary in 1974. He is the author of *It Sure Looks Different From the Inside* and two novels, *The Hour* and *The First Lady*. Nessen reports that the relationship between the White House and the press was difficult and explains some of the reasons. Ford inherited the effects of reporters' suspicion of the president in the aftermath of Watergate. The White House press felt frustration and Nessen explains: "They had been right there, thirty feet from the Oval Office, and they had never gotten a whiff of Watergate" (p. 182-83). Ford had to contend with this underlying attitude in the media, and Nessen chronicles some of his successes and failures. He also analyzes his differences with terHorst over the proper relationship between the president and the press secretary.

Jerald F. terHorst is another good and longtime friend of the Miller Center. He participated in the discussions surrounding the work of the presidential press conference commission. He served for a relatively brief period as President Ford's first press secretary preceding Ron Nessen. As a reporter, he had followed Ford's rise from Navy League housing projects in Michigan to his election to the House to his choice as minority leader to his vice presidency and presidency. Except for Philip Buchen, terHorst knew Ford longer than any of his administration associates. His thesis is that President Nixon should have apologized for Watergate and, failing that, should not have been pardoned. TerHorst attributes his own resignation as press secretary to circumstances surrounding the pardon.

Robert Orben edits Orben's *Current Comedy,* a service for public speakers published in Wilmington, Delaware. He observes that humor warms, amuses, instructs and opens emotional doors. He was the director of President Ford's speech writing department. Earlier he wrote scripts for the Jack Paar Show and the Red Skeleton Hour. Mr. Orben's role in the Ford administration extended to being consultant and special assistant. He traces the beginnings of his association with Ford to an assignment preparing the congressman for the 1968 Gridiron Club and thereafter the organization of a speech writing unit in the Ford administration. One of his most memorable accounts is his description of the role of advance parties in assessing what constitutes humor in a particular community, in this case South Bend in preparing for Ford's Notre Dame speech. The quickie bus for students crossing over into Michigan to purchase refreshments is the symbol a speech writer seeks as a handle on local humor.

A final commentary on the media is "A Footnote on Ford and the Voice of America" by James Keogh, who was director of USIA in the Ford administration. Keogh discloses the pressures which Congressman Wayne Hays sought to impose on him and, when he resisted, that congressman's effort to persuade President Ford to fire him. Keogh's brief reflection is illustrative of the relationship between Congress and at least one official in the Ford administration concerned with international communication. It also provides an insight into Ford's courage in the face of political pressure, a theme that recurs again and again in the Ford oral history.

The next section is concerned with decision-making and focuses on the relation of Cabinet level departments and the White House. The late Charles Goodell was one of two congressman who helped install Ford as minority leader in the House. Senator Goodell argues that Cabinet officers should recover some of the power that has gravitated to the

White House. Vice President Nelson Rockefeller while governor of New York appointed Goodell as successor to Robert Kennedy as a senator from New York. Not surprisingly, Goodell's comments on Rockefeller's role in the Ford administration are especially revealing. He is less kind to another key member of the administration who happens to have assisted the Miller Center in many ways. Historical accuracy requires the inclusion of such comments whatever the editor's own views.

Dr. Guy Stever has held a series of important positions including the presidency of Carnegie Mellon University and as President Ford's Science and Technology Adviser. His discussion of Ford's view of science portrays that leader's recognition of the dangers of the decline in federal support of science. Ford showed serious interest in the organization of science advising and in reinstating of the science adviser in the White House. Stever has the reputation of complete fairness, and his analysis of science advising provides a text for any student of the subject.

Dr. Earl Butz offers a brief and pungent note on the Ford administration viewed from the Agriculture Department. He submits his own case study of Ford's veto of an amendment that congressmen from three tobacco states sought to introduce while administration representatives were absent. Butz's example is but one additional proof of Gerald Ford's strength and integrity, whatever the political price.

Harvard professor and Secretary of Labor in the Ford administration, John Dunlop has shared a report of his stewardship which is valuable in itself, particularly in describing the relationship between the large departments and the White House. It has special value from the standpoint of an oral history of the Ford administration because it deals with the same issue that Richard Cheney singles out for discussion in his chapter and comes to somewhat different conclusions. The two presentations illustrate the unique value of oral history as distinguished from the self-serving political autobiographies that have become so commonplace in an era when public servants reap enormous financial gains from accounts of their years in government, something General George C. Marshall declared no government official should pursue.

INTRODUCTION

Foreign policy and defense loom large in any presidency. General Brent Scowcroft evaluates Ford both as a president and a maker of foreign policy. It is necessary to go back to the time of Truman and Eisenhower to find administrations in which the National Security Council adviser functioned in the style Scowcroft followed within that Ford administration. As with his predecessors in the Truman and Eisenhower administrations, Scowcroft placed emphasis on the coordinating role of the adviser. More recently, he served as a member of the Tower Commission investigating the Iran-Contra episode displaying once again the qualities of detachment, fairness and objectivity which set his term as NSC adviser apart.

Joseph Sisco is one of the nation's most respected and experienced figures in foreign policy. His discussion seeks to link the Ford and Nixon foreign policies by emphasizing the role of Henry Kissinger in both administrations. He provides a searching evaluation of Ford's and Kissinger's strengths and weaknesses. Inasmuch as many of the accounts of Ford's foreign policy have been written by Kissinger and his closest associates, Sisco's more detached and less self-serving appraisal is especially valuable.

A different perspective on the Ford foreign policy comes from Michael Rauol-Duval who was special counsel from 1974 to 1977. He dealt particularly with the energy crisis and with certain issues concerning the intelligence system. His rather pithy comments on President Ford and in particular some of the people around Ford provide yet another perspective on the Ford presidency and foreign policy.

Helmut Sonnenfeldt was Kissinger's close associate and, in the secretary's absence, his comments on the so-called "Sonnenfeldt Doctrine" are particularly helpful in illuminating policy on Eastern Europe.

It has been customary to ask the final witnesses in each presidential oral history to place their president in history and to try to forecast what history's judgment will be. Lou Cannon of the *Washington Post*, who has written extensively on the Reagan presidency but also on Ford, offers some responses to such questions. Some of his answers will come as surprises to many people. Cannon's knowledge of Reagan furnishes a unique background for an objective and perceptive assessment of Ford.

I.

THE MAN
AND
THE POLITICAL LEADER

THE MAN WHO HAPPENED
TO BECOME PRESIDENT

SENATOR ROBERT P. GRIFFIN

NARRATOR: Robert P. Griffin was a United States senator from the state of Michigan from 1966 until 1979. He was a graduate of Central Michigan University and then the University of Michigan Law School. He practiced law in Traverse City, Michigan, for six years before he was elected in 1956 to serve in the 85th Congress from the ninth district of Michigan. He served in the House until May 1966 when he was appointed to the U.S. Senate. He ran and was elected in 1966 and 1972 to six-year terms in the Senate. Since 1956 he has known Gerald Ford as a friend and associate in the Republican party in Michigan and in the nation. Today, he is counsel to the leading Michigan law firm which, appropriately enough at this public affairs center, is Miller, Canfield, Paddock & Stone.

    The Miller Center's relationship with Senator Griffin came about as a result of his role as chairman of the board of the Gerald R. Ford Foundation, the Library and the Center in Ann Arbor and Grand Rapids. He was a model host at a conference that several of us attended which was co-sponsored by the Gerald R. Ford Foundation, the Former Members of Congress and the Atlantic Council. His warmth and interest in the Miller Center led me to approach him about the Gerald R. Ford portrait volume. So, this is a reunion of the Ford Center and the Miller Center and of a person who has been especially gracious to the Miller

3

Center, Senator Robert Griffin. Senator Griffin will discuss Gerald R. Ford's political leadership as he observed it.

SENATOR GRIFFIN: Thank you very much, Ken. I am honored by the turnout of so many distinguished people. I hope that I will be able to provide some information about Gerald Ford and his presidency that you didn't know before. Of course, those of us connected with the Gerald R. Ford Foundation are very interested in the volume that the Miller Center is developing on the Ford presidency, so it is a pleasure to be here.

Much of what I shall say, at least until we get to the question and answer period, will be about how Jerry Ford happened—I guess "happened" is a pretty good word—to become the thirty-eighth President of the United States. I hope I will not appear too immodest if I say that at various critical points and junctures I may have played a role in the chain of events that carried, or indeed propelled, Jerry Ford into the White House—an office that he did not seek and which he did not expect to attain. I assume that how Ford became the first president ever to attain that office without being elected either to the vice presidency or to the office of president, is likely to be of more than just footnote interest to historians. Of course, we have had two vice presidents who were appointed to that office under the Twenty-fifth amendment, and I suspect that there will likely be a number more in the future. But the likelihood that another president will emerge by way of the Twenty-fifth amendment appears considerably more remote.

So, this unique aspect of the Ford presidency—the fact that he attained the position without ever being elected to any office other than congressman from Michigan's Fifth District—does set him apart and almost guarantees that his presidency, though brief, is not likely to be overlooked or forgotten. It is inevitable, I suspect, that some of his critics may find it convenient to point to this aspect of his ascendancy with an implication that somehow it had a bearing on his qualifications or ability to serve as president. Of course, I'm a confessed and biased advocate, and I find it somewhat comforting to recall that the Prime Minister of Great Britain is elected by the voters of only one district, and not by the voters of the entire country. Yet I think we might be willing to concede that some of the Prime

Ministers produced by Great Britain have been very capable leaders.

Of course, the differences are wide and significant, but it is interesting to observe that there are some similarities between the British parliamentary system and the process by which Gerald R. Ford became president. I refer specifically to his appointment and confirmation as vice president. I'll say here that I don't think that Jerry Ford was President Nixon's first choice for vice president. Nixon appointed Ford at the time because of the pressures of Watergate and the overhanging threat of impeachment which left him, in my opinion, with no realistic choice except to designate a person who could quickly and easily become confirmed by the vote of both houses of Congress. I don't wish to leave the impression here that Nixon and Ford were not friends or that Nixon lacked confidence in Ford's ability. The relationship between the two of them goes back a long way.

Perhaps that gives me an excuse for mentioning the first time that I ever met President Nixon and the first time I really became acquainted with Jerry Ford. I was thirty-two and the year was 1956. I had exhibited the audacity to run for Congress against an incumbent Republican in the primary, and I had won the nomination for Congress in Michigan's Ninth District, which stretches along Lake Michigan from the city of Muskegon up to and including Traverse City. My district adjoined the Fifth District which includes Grand Rapids and which was represented then by Congressman Jerry Ford.

Richard Nixon, with the help of Jerry Ford and others in the Chowder and Marching Society, had just survived a "dump Nixon" effort at the Republican convention of 1956. Nixon was coming up to Grand Rapids for a campaign stop. Jerry Ford called and said that Nixon was aware of my primary victory, and he invited me to come over to Grand Rapids and join them on the platform. I may have shaken hands with Jerry Ford before at some of the party functions, but I didn't feel I knew him until this call came. Of course, I was delighted to go to Grand Rapids to be on the platform with Vice President Nixon and Congressman Jerry Ford. At that point, Jerry had been in Congress for almost eight years; he had been first elected in 1948. On the other hand, I was just a young upstart. I was thrilled when they gave me the microphone and I had a chance to say something. Most important for me was the fact that there was television and newspaper coverage which blanketed the state, including my district.

In 1956, Ford campaigned for Republican congressional candidates, not only in Michigan but in other states as well. In Michigan that year four new Republican congressmen were elected and as it happened, all of us were under forty. The press took some note of the "four under forty" from Michigan, and it seemed that we received a bit more attention than most freshmen.

From then on, Ford and I worked very closely together in the House. He was in a different age group and had been around Congress longer; we didn't become fast social friends because he moved in a different circle. I was pretty much in the group that came in the Eighty-Fifth Congress, but nevertheless Jerry and I became close associates in the legislative process.

I recall one incident that may be of interest. It happened after the Landrum-Griffin Bill had been passed in 1959. A fellow named Robert Ingersoll came to Washington and invited the Michigan congressional delegation to breakfast. (This was the same Bob Ingersoll who later became prominent in the Ford administration as deputy secretary of state.) Back in about 1962, though, Ingersoll was an executive of the Borg-Warner Company, and he was interested in getting a certain defense contract. Borg-Warner had designed and was prepared to produce a vehicle of some kind that would be manufactured in Michigan, if Ingersoll could just get the contract. At that point Jerry Ford was the ranking Republican on the defense subcommittee of the Appropriations Committee, a mighty powerful position. At the breakfast with Michigan Republicans Ingersoll's mission was to enlist our support for Borg-Warner and the contract. At one point, Ingersoll turned to me and said, "Who is that fellow over there? The one with the pipe?" My mouth dropped for a minute. Finally, I replied, "Well, he's the only guy in this room who could do you any good; he's Jerry Ford." Obviously, Jerry was not a national figure at that point.

After John Kennedy became President in 1961, some of the younger Republicans in the House of Representatives found being in the minority in the House rather irritating. To some extent, the image of the "Ev and Charlie Show"—Ev Dirksen and Charlie Halleck—made us rather restless.

At that time a young colleague named Charles Goodell, who later became United States Senator from New York, sat next to me on the House Education and Labor Committee. We used to talk a lot about our Republican problems and how we thought things ought to be done, etc. To make a long story short, our conversations about the leadership gradually developed into a minor conspiracy. At the beginning of each new Congress, the members of each party caucus separated to elect their party leaders. In January 1963, shortly before the Republican organizational caucus was to take place, Goodell and I got together and surveyed our Republican leadership group. There was Charlie Halleck, the floor leader, Les Arends, the whip, and Charlie Hoven of Iowa, sixty-seven years old, who was the conference chairman. He had not ingratiated himself with the younger members; in fact, he had stepped on a few toes. We didn't quite dare, at that point, to confront or take on Charlie Halleck for the leadership, but we decided that maybe we should put up a candidate against Hoven. We gathered a few others around us, and decided to approach Jerry Ford and ask him to run against Hoven. Ford was reluctant at first. However, by that time Jerry had made up his mind that his goal in politics was not the presidency or the vice presidency, but to become the speaker of the House of Representatives. He loved the House, and he really wanted, someday, to become the speaker. So, here was a chance for him to take a first step up the ladder, and to his credit he was willing to take the gamble. He ran and won this position, which at that time was the third leadership position in the House of Representatives on the Republican side.

By the time January 1965 came around, after Goldwater's devastating defeat by Johnson, the "Ev and Charlie" leadership didn't look so good. The Goodell-Griffin conspiracy got back together again. At that point, I remember, our group included Tom Curtis, Don Rumsfeld, Al Quie and a number of others. We talked a lot about the leadership and what should happen. We decided that Halleck should be challenged for the leadership. Very quickly, our choice for a candidate narrowed down to Mel Laird, who was forty-two, and Gerald Ford, who was fifty-one.

We were very pragmatic. I felt that Ford had a better chance of winning, and most of the others in our group came to the same conclusion. Laird was admired for many abilities and he was especially articulate. As chairman of the Republican Platform Committee and in other ways, however, he had made a number of important political enemies.

Jerry Ford, by contrast, didn't seem to have any enemies. Everybody liked him; he was a good guy. We concluded that he could get more votes than Laird and that he had a better chance of beating Halleck, so our decision was to go with Ford. If Ford wouldn't run, then we would go with Laird. After talking it over with Betty, Ford agreed to run, and, of course, he won by a narrow margin. In January 1965, then, Jerry Ford became the Republican leader of the House of Representatives and emerged on the Washington scene as a national figure.

Most of you probably know something of the Ford story from there on. My life and my political fortunes naturally continued to be connected with Jerry Ford in many ways. In 1966 I was in Vietnam as part of an investigating committee which happened to include Congressmen Don Rumsfeld and Bo Callaway. Pat MacNamara, our Democratic Senator from Michigan, had died shortly before I left. While I was in Saigon I got a call from George Romney who asked, "Are you willing to take the appointment as United States Senator?" I agreed to do it.

One might wonder whether Jerry Ford would have been a likely appointee for the Senate at that point. I really don't know whether Romney talked with Ford about it or not. In any event, Jerry Ford was interested in becoming the Speaker of the House. He had had opportunities before that to run for the Senate, but he had always preferred to stay in the House.

The Senate vacancy occurred in May, 1966. The appointment would be only until the end of the year, and I would have to stand for election in November. I took the appointment and began to campaign. Incidentally, my opponent in that campaign was G. Mennen "Soapy" Williams, so I had my hands full. It was a very difficult campaign in Michigan; but I managed to win, and I was reelected in 1972. During the time of my Senate service, Jerry Ford was on the other side of the Capitol. It's amazing how great the distance is between the two Houses, even though it is only a short walk. Once in the Senate, I didn't have as much contact with Jerry Ford as before.

In October 1973, when Spiro Agnew finally resigned, I had been the Republican whip of the Senate for a considerable period—since 1969. Of course, the whip is a kind of deputy leader. Hugh Scott had taken over as leader from Ev Dirksen. Watergate hadn't been such a big issue in the 1972 campaign. However, after the campaign was over, and as we got into 1973—and the Irwin Committee got going—the issue became more and more a problem and concern for the Republicans.

I'm not sure that Jerry Ford was Nixon's first choice for vice president after Agnew resigned. I think his first choice may have been John Connally. Nixon admired Connally for his executive and administrative ability, and his ability as a politician. I also think—this is just my opinion—that he would have preferred to keep Jerry Ford in a leadership position in the House as the Watergate cloud became more ominous. Of course, as the whip of the party, I was involved in regular meetings with President Nixon at least once a week, sometimes more often than that. On at least one occasion after the Agnew resignation, I pointedly suggested to the President that he ask for recommendations from the members of Congress as to whom he should appoint for vice president, reminding him that the appointee would have to be approved by the vote of each House and that winning approval would not be easy.

President Nixon did invite each senator and House member to submit his or her recommendation. I collected the envelopes for the Senate and turned them over to Scott who delivered them to the White House. On the slip of paper that I put in my envelope I diplomatically wrote two names: Hugh Scott and Jerry Ford. I knew that Hugh Scott was too old to be seriously considered for vice president, so in effect my nomination was for Jerry Ford. In a separate envelope I wrote a stern letter to President Nixon, referring to Watergate and the developing possibility of impeachment proceedings. I cautioned against appointing anyone other than Scott or Ford because, as I saw it, the climate in the Democratic Congress was such that any outsider—such as John Connally (although I did not mention his name)—would not be approved.

At that time Connally carried some baggage having to do with campaign milk funds or some such matter. In addition, there was the problem that Connally had switched from the Democratic to the Republican party; many

Democrats would not be very happy with someone they regarded as a turncoat.

As the Republican whip in the Senate my job was to count votes. I had earned a pretty good reputation at the White House by that time for some accuracy in assessing the mood and predicting what would happen on a given issue, I believe my counsel had some impact upon Nixon. I have no doubt that when they opened those envelopes at the White House and counted the recommendations, Jerry Ford was out in front.

I was also a member of the Senate Rules Committee which had the responsibility for considering and reporting the nomination of Ford when he was nominated as vice president. Those hearings were televised. I was in an awkward position: I was a member of the committee and I was supposed to be nonpartial, but here was Jerry Ford to be examined by the committee. I made a statement on the record about this; I wanted my colleagues to know that I wasn't going to pretend to be impartial and nonpartisan, that I would indeed operate as a representative of Gerald Ford before the committee and act as his counsel. Everybody on the committee, both Democrats and Republicans, agreed that that was all right. So, together with Phil Buchen, Bill Cramer, and others, I counseled Ford in connection with his confirmation hearings as the first Twenty-fifth amendment vice president.

As we worked to prepare for the televised hearings, some awkward questions came to light. Without going into all of the problems, the most difficult to deal with was the charge by a fellow named Winterberger, who had written in a book, and later had filed an affidavit, charging that Ford had accepted $15,000 from him in exchange for some favors, which were never really identified. That was a sticky issue for a while. Of course, you can deny the charge and say, "No, it didn't happen." But how do you prove it didn't happen? We were fortunate that when Winterberger was required to produce his income tax returns for the years that were relevant, it turned out that he didn't even have an income of $15,000 for any of those years. We were extremely fortunate because when that information came to light, his credibility collapsed.

Jerry Ford was confirmed and became vice president. I have a story or two which might add something to your records.

After being sworn in as vice president, Ford almost immediately began grumbling about the secret service and what they were doing to his house on Quaker Lane in Alexandria, Virginia, where he and Betty had lived for many years. The secret service had taken over his garage; they had built big fences around the property; they had put in bulletproof glass. You can imagine what all this would be like in a cozy suburban neighborhood.

His grumbling stirred me to think why didn't the vice president have a government owned house? I looked into it a bit, because it seemed strange to me that for almost two hundred years no house had been provided for the vice president. Every time there was a turnover in the office we went through the same thing. Agnew complained about it, and Humphrey complained about it. Each time a new vice president came into office, it involved a tremendous expense for the taxpayers to put his private home in the shape required for security. I found that there had been talk for years about a house for the vice president, but no action. Plans had been drawn for a new house. At one time, construction was authorized, but, then the money was not appropriated. Most of the top officers of the military service are provided with homes. It had been mentioned from time to time that the home of the Chief of Naval Operations on Observatory Hill would be a good place for the vice president. Those of you who are familiar with it know that those are nice, spacious grounds. The house sits up on a hill and back from the road. It's a good location in terms of security.

I was on my way to work one morning about that time. (I was just about to pass Observatory Hill on Massachusetts Avenue) when I heard a news report on the radio. President Nixon had announced that he would not reappoint the Chief of Naval Operations, Admiral Zumwalt, when his term expired a few months away. At that very moment a light went on. I thought to myself, if there is ever going to be a home for the vice president, this is the time. I went down to the Hill and took Hubert Humphrey aside and talked to him about it. "Good idea," he said. Then we talked to Mike Mansfield, Bob Byrd, Barry Goldwater, and different people like that. Each one thought it was a good idea. So, in not too long a time we had a bill drafted to turn this into the vice president's house. It didn't go sailing through because the Navy wasn't very happy about what we were trying to do. By the time the bill got over on the House side, it became a little bit more difficult. Eventually, it did pass and a house for the vice president was established. That's not quite the end of the story though for Jerry Ford. On the very day that Ford first learned about the Nixon tapes that would bring about his resignation, Betty was in New York buying furnishings for this house. However, of course, Jerry and Betty never had a chance to live in that house: very soon thereafter he was President.

Then, Nelson Rockefeller became vice president, but he was the first vice president in a long time who didn't need a house. He had a much nicer home in Washington on Foxhall Road. Although he and Happy contributed some furnishings, and held a few social events there, they didn't live in it. So it wasn't until Fritz Mondale came into office that the vice president's house was finally used.

President Nixon would not have resigned and Ford would not have become President, at least when he did, if Nixon had not become convinced that a Senate vote on impeachment charges would go against him. I was convinced of that. I was not only very sad and deeply disappointed, but I was angry when I learned about the taped White House conversations that took place on June 23, 1972, six days after the Watergate break-in these tapes would implicate Nixon directly in the Watergate coverup and make it obvious that he had lied to the American people and to his friends in Congress, including me.

Early in August of 1974 over a long weekend in Traverse City, I discussed this new evidence with my wife, Marge. I was wrestling with my conscience trying to decide where I fit into all of this. What should I do in light of this new evidence and my responsibilities as United States senator and as a leader of the Republican party. Even before this new evidence surfaced, I knew that support for President Nixon in the Senate had been growing soft. Indeed, only a week before, Hugh Scott and I had made our own head count or assessment, which we kept to ourselves. We concluded that if Nixon had been tried then, he could have counted only thirty-six sure votes, just two more than the thirty-four needed to avoid conviction. Now, with this new evidence, I knew the picture would be very different: the House would surely impeach President Nixon, charging him with obstruction of justice. I was sure in my own mind that he could not survive a vote in the Senate. I came to the conclusion that weekend that the best thing for the country and for President Nixon would be for him to resign. I decided to do whatever I could to convince him to take that course.

Richard Nixon's final days in the White House have been reviewed and examined in great detail by a number of authors, and I'm not going to try to retread all of that ground. However, I was involved in events which led to President Nixon's resignation. For example, I may have contributed to the decision-making process at the White House when, on the Monday preceding his resignation, I went before the press as the Republican whip of the Senate and the cameras to publicly call for President Nixon's resignation. Those few minutes were among the saddest, the most difficult, and agonizing moments of my life.

In 1979 on another campus I delivered a speech entitled "The Week That Was" which recalls from my perspective and recounts the events of that last week which culminated in the rise of Gerald R. Ford to the presidency. If you would indulge me, I should like to share with you a few paragraphs from the tail end of that speech:

> It was not until Thursday morning that the situation finally became clear at about ten o'clock in the morning. Nixon called Ford into the Oval Office and said he had decided to go on television that evening to announce his resignation, effective Friday noon. Late that Thursday afternoon, I received a White House message that President Nixon was inviting some of his long-time congressional friends and supporters of both parties to join him for a final get-together in the Cabinet room shortly before his national television address now scheduled for 9:00 p.m.
>
> After my efforts earlier in the week I was surprised—but very pleased—to learn that I was included in the group of senators and congressmen. It was a meeting that I shall never forget. I can't find the words to describe the feeling, the tension, the disappointment, and the compassion that permeated every inch of that

majestic room. Perhaps you can imagine what it must have been like.

I sat next to Congressman Bob Michael of Illinois and he took notes. He was the only one to do so and later he gave me a copy. We were directly across the room, the Cabinet room, from the President who took his seat and then paused for what seemed like an interminable period of time, obviously finding it very difficult to begin. 'You know I'm not a quitter,' he finally said and then he proceeded to tell us about his days at the Whittier High School, how he wanted so badly to play football and be on the track team. But he had not been particularly good at either sport. He rambled on and on at some length, and finally he stopped and suggested that perhaps all of this was irrelevant. He said, 'It's not my nature to quit, but I'll take what is coming to me. My decision to resign,' he continued, 'is based on the premise that the presidency is bigger than any man.'

Yes,' he went on, 'it's even bigger than your personal loyalty.' And he seemed at that point to be looking at Goldwater and me. (Goldwater had all but called publicly for his resignation.) 'Some have counseled me to fight this all the way through,' he went on, 'but I have concluded that this long, debilitating thing called Watergate must come to an end. A lengthy trial in the Senate would be just too much for the country. Therefore I will resign; I shall leave the White House about ten o'clock tomorrow, Friday morning, and Vice President Ford will be sworn in at noon. On the way back to California I will have the little black box with me on the plane up until the moment of transition.' Now his voice cracked as he continued. 'This is my last meeting in this room. I will not be back, but without you in this room I could not have made the tough calls for the country that have been necessary.'

Then Nixon looked down at the table; he paused for a long, long time and tried very, very hard to say the next few words. He would get out a word or two and then he would stop and try to regain his composure. 'I want to say, most of all, that I appreciate your friendship more than ever.' Then standing up he paused again and in a voice choked with emotion that was barely audible, he said, 'I hope you won't feel that I've let you down.' At that moment he broke down completely. Suddenly he was an emotional basket case. His aides rushed to his side, groping and with their assistance he slowly made his way out of the room, barely twenty minutes before he was scheduled to go on national television.

Of course the rest of the story is familiar. Marge and I were there in the Oval Office at noon on Friday as Jerry Ford took the oath and declared our long nightmare is over. Until then he had always been Jerry to me, even while he was vice president. Now, suddenly, he was Mr. President. How did I feel? I suppose I was glad but I was also very, very sad. Events had moved so rapidly that my feelings really didn't catch up with me for a couple of days. On Sunday morning I woke up very early. It was just daylight. Marge was still sleeping when I slipped out the door and took off in the car for a drive by myself. At that early hour very few drivers were on Rock Creek Parkway. The flowers were beautiful; it was a gorgeous day. As I sped along my eyes gradually filled up with tears. Finally I couldn't see; I pulled off the road and stopped and I cried and cried. No, I bawled for the first time in many, many years. I felt better and I went home and as Walter Cronkite might have put it: that's the way it was.

On the scale that ultimately determined the outcome of the 1976 election, probably nothing weighed heavier than the pardoning of Richard Nixon by Ford. I understand that Phil Buchen and others have been here at the Miller Center. Outside of Alexander Haig and Ford himself, I don't know of anybody other than Buchen who would know more about that subject. In reaching his decision, Ford consulted with no one outside of a very tight, small circle at the White House, so far as I know. Somehow, I expected the pardon to come but I, too, was surprised when the announcement was made on that Sunday morning. Perhaps the fact that I was not consulted says something about how things change once a President settles in at the White House and the palace guard, as Bob Hartmann refers to them, take over. If the distance between the House and the Senate seems long, it is nothing compared with the distance between the White House and Capitol Hill.

I still called President Ford occasionally, and he would always take my phone calls, but I tried to keep those calls to a minimum. Once in a while he would call me, but not often. Of course, I was part of the Senate leadership, so I was at the meetings with leaders in the White House. Certainly, I had a lot more contact with, and more access to President Ford than the average member of the Senate or the House. Then, too there was the so-called "kitchen cabinet," of which I was a member. In addition to his regular Cabinet, Jerry Ford had what he referred to as a "kitchen cabinet" throughout most of his administration. This was a group of friends and associates whose judgment he trusted. He called the group together at intervals, usually about a month apart, to sit down in late afternoon for a couple of hours and tell him whatever we wanted to tell him. Bill Scranton, Bryce Harlow, Bill White, Rogers Morton, Jack Marsh, Don Rumsfeld, Bob Hartmann, Mel Laird, and Dave Packard were in this group.

While he was in the White House we continued to be friends. But after one's friend makes it to the White House, nothing is ever quite the same thing. I asked him, however, in early 1975 to come out to Traverse City, where Marge and I lived, for the National Cherry Festival and to play in a Walter Hagen Golf Tournament. He quickly accepted. Although the population of our region grows much larger in the summer, Traverse City is a relatively small town, with a population of about 25,000. It was a rather historic occasion when Air Force One made its first and only landing at our airport. A lot of local stories developed out of that visit, as you can imagine. I'd like to share one with you.

After he rode in the Cherry Festival parade as the Grand Marshal, our schedule had him coming out to our home on Long Lake, seven miles west of town where we gathered a lot of friends, neighbors and prominent Traverse City people for a reception. The Secret Service came in about a week ahead and just about drove Marge nuts with all the things that they had to go through to prepare for the President of the United States in connection with this one little stop. We have a small guest house; they took that over and did all sorts of things. It ended up that there were Secret Service people up in the trees, out in boats, etc., taking care of every possible contingency to protect the President of the United States.

Well, that was fine except that it didn't work out quite as planned. After the reception was over—about four o'clock in the afternoon—the presidential cavalcade started down Long Lake Road and headed back toward town and the airport. As they reached the hill where the Gallagher Farm is, suddenly a procession of Gallagher cows in single file started across the road, bringing the presidential cavalcade, including the leader of the free world, to an abrupt halt. They remained there immobilized for eight or ten minutes, much to the embarrassment and concern of the Secret Service detail. The coverage next day by the *Detroit News* of the President's visit to Traverse City featured a huge front picture showing the presidential party waiting while the Gallagher cows paraded slowly across the road.

Well, that isn't quite all of the story. Later, we found out that our neighbor down the road, Gallagher, had been asked by his children for permission to go into Traverse City to see the Cherry Festival parade that Friday afternoon. But the children had chores to do, so Mr. Gallagher told them, "Now, look, you finish your chores. Don't worry, you'll get to see the President of the United States." So, when the cavalcade stopped the Gallagher children were right there with signs welcoming President Ford. They had a chance to talk with the Fords and even to get their autographs.

Sometime early during the campaign season of 1976 I received a call from President Ford asking me to be his floor manager at the Republican National Convention in Kansas City. Your will recall, of course, that Ronald Reagan challenged President Ford for the Republican nomination. After Ford won the New Hampshire primary, and then the Florida primary, things were looking pretty good. Those in the Ford camp were rather smug. It didn't look like this guy Reagan was going to be much competition after all. Then came North Carolina; from there on Reagan's stock went up and Ford's seemed to go down. By the time the primaries were over and we headed for Kansas

City, it was a very close contest. Ford had the most committed delegates, but he was twenty-eight short of having enough to win the nomination. Reagan was only thirty-nine delegates behind Ford, with ninety-four delegates uncommitted. My job was to be sure that the votes to nominate Ford would be there when the roll was called.

Working with Jim Baker, Ford's campaign manager, we had put together a very good organization. There were regional whips who wore red caps; we had walkie talkies and all kinds of communications equipment.

John Sears was Reagan's campaign manager, and Paul Laxalt, a good friend of mine, was floor manager for Reagan at the Kansas City convention. In addition to being well organized, we had to try to anticipate what John Sears would do to win over delegates to the Reagan column.

I studied the records of previous Republican conventions. The most interesting one was the Eisenhower-Taft convention of 1952, when it appeared that Taft was ahead going in. The Eisenhower forces maneuvered skillfully to set up an early test vote on a question involving credentials. The Eisenhower position was so fair and reasonable that they won the test vote, and the mood and momentum of the convention changed.

We expected that John Sears would try to get an early test vote on an issue that he might be able to win. Our expectations were correct.

The convention began Monday night. There were opening speeches but no real business was transacted. On Tuesday evening the convention would first adopt the rules and then the platform would be presented.

Ironically, Tom Curtis of Missouri, one of my fellow conspirators when we helped to elect Ford as minority leader, was now offering an amendment to the rules at the Kansas City convention. This was the Sears move. It would amend Section 16C of the proposed rules so as to require a candidate for President to announce his choice for vice president by 9:00 a.m. of the day when the convention is scheduled to select its nominee for President. That would be the next day (Wednesday).

Adoption of such an amendment would have put Ford in a box, to say the least. Reagan had earlier announced, as you may recall, that Dick Schweicker, senator from Pennsylvania, was his choice for vice president. This amendment sounded like reform. Theoretically, at least, the vice president would not be selected in a smoke-filled room in the middle of the night. But Ford's strength in a few states was related to the possibility that a favorite son had a good chance to be selected for vice president.

We had a dickens of a time with that amendment. It was necessary to devote a lot of educating of our own troops on the point that this would be the important vote in the convention: "Never mind," I would argue, "don't be carried away about how you feel on the merits of the issue. This *is* the key vote. We have to win if Ford is to be nominated."

I was the windup speaker at the convention on our side of the debate. If you will let me, I'll just read a little bit of my speech from the transcript of the convention:

> Frankly, in addition to other reasons given to reject Section 16C, I see it as a divisive proposal. To adopt 16C would drive the wedge of division in our party and impede and make more difficult the unity that we know we must achieve. If he is nominated, and of course I think he will be, I don't know if President Ford will ask Governor Reagan to be his running mate or not. But I do know this: I want President Ford at least to have that opportunity. I believe Governor Reagan when he says he is not interested in running for vice president. I know he means it, and I'm sure he will continue to feel that same way tomorrow morning at 9:00 a.m., the deadline provided in this amendment. But I also know and believe that Governor Reagan should be in a position and should be able to change his mind on Thursday morning if it should be in the interest of the party and the nation. I see no merit in a proposal that would have the effect of locking Senator Schweiker in and locking Governor Reagan out. I can also say with some authority that President Ford, if nominated, would like to at least consult with Governor Reagan (and will do so) about the selection of the vice president before making any final decision. Such consultation on such an important decision between the heads of two great groups of our party would not only be right and appropriate,

but it would be invaluable and most important in achieving the unity we must achieve.

Of course, we tried to reach the Reagan people and say, "Look, President Ford can't name Governor Reagan now as his choice for vice president. It would be interpreted as insincere."

We finally did win the test vote—the amendment was defeated—but the convention battle was not over at that point.

After the rules were adopted, then the proposed platform of the party was presented to the Convention, section by section. Jesse Helms, who had carried the day for Reagan in North Carolina, had his own strategy with respect to the platform. Some debate had gone on within the Reagan camp as to whether the Helms amendment, which he called "morality in foreign policy," or the Sears maneuver, should be the test vote. The Helms amendment, to the platform was a direct, overt slap at Ford and Kissinger, designed to bring back to the attention of conservatives the fact that Solzhenitsyn had not been invited by Ford to the White House at a time when many thought he should have been. References to the Helsinki Accords, Ford's stand on the Panama Canal Treaty and a few other choice items like that were wrapped up in the Helm's foreign policy plank.

When the reading of the platform reached the foreign policy section, Senator Helms obtained recognition and suddenly we were confronted with the Helms amendment. Kissinger was in a rage; he thought it was terrible, and that we had to beat it down. Rockefeller and others pretty much agreed with Kissinger. They were ready to do battle.

The hour was late; it was moving now toward 11:00 p.m. We introduced a few parliamentary maneuvers to stall for time as a debate went on in our camp. I was very much involved in some heated conversations with Ford, Kissinger, Rockefeller, Hugh Scott, and Jim Baker. I insisted that we should not play into their hands by letting the Helms amendment go to a roll call. If we lost, we would lose the whole ball game. In terms of winning the nomination, we were in a very good position. Headlines for the next morning's newspapers had already been made: "Ford wins test vote on 16C. Ford has nomination wrapped up." If that were followed up later in the night by a defeat on a foreign policy plank, the headlines would be rewritten and it could be disaster. My own gut feeling told me that we would lose on the Helms amendment.

Finally, Ford swallowed hard and made the call. Kissinger didn't like it. But the decision was made, and at the appropriate time our spokesman on the Platform Committee made this announcement: "I wish to say that there has been a conference and deliberation among us. Diverse views were expressed. The conclusion was reached, however, that in the interests of unity, we will not oppose this amendment. I shall vote "aye" for the amendment, and I recommend that the delegates to the convention do likewise."

Of course, we then put the word out to all Ford delegates that if Helms insisted on a roll call, we were to vote for it. By voting for the amendment, we could avoid any appearance that a test vote was involved. When Paul Laxalt saw what we were doing, he knew there was no point in taking the time to call the roll, and he indicated he would be satisfied to have a voice vote. It finished quickly, and the battle for the nomination was over, too.

I'm going to conclude quickly. Ford's loss of the presidency to Carter had an impact, as you can imagine, on a lot of people besides President Ford. In January, 1977, Republican senators caucused to select their leaders. Hugh Scott had retired. It was widely expected that the deputy leader or whip would move up and be the next Republican leader of the Senate. Actually, if you look back through history, you find that the whips have seldom achieved that. Nevertheless, when Ford lost and the Republicans were once again out of the White House, his best friend and spokesman in the Senate could feel a difference in his relations with other Republican senators.

In January 1977, although it wasn't quite the same, I felt a certain kinship with Charlie Halleck. Sure enough, there were others with leadership ability and ambition who began to sniff the territory. Finally, at the very last minute, Howard Baker got into the race for Republican leader of the Senate. When the votes were counted one of my supporters was absent and another had switched without telling me. Howard won by a single vote. Nonetheless, Howard Baker is one of my very good friends, and he has been an outstanding Republican leader of the Senate.

Later, in 1977, there came a point when I decided that I would not seek reelection to the Senate. Then, in early 1978 I was persuaded to change my mind and run. In November 1978, I learned that changing your mind is something you can't do in politics. So we've had the opportunity to enjoy civilian life since January 1979. I've had a pleasant association with the American Enterprise Institute; I've been practicing law; and we've been living a comfortable and enjoyable life in Traverse City where we are close to two of our four children. If you are ever up that way, please come and see us. Thank you very much.

QUESTION: What is your interpretation of why Ford pardoned Nixon? You gave a little bit of it when you said it was made by the "mafia" in the White House. Why was there no input from a leader like you or other leaders?

SENATOR GRIFFIN: I don't know how to answer that question. I was very close to Jerry Ford during the last week before Nixon resigned. If any deal had been made I think I would have known about it. I'm convinced that Ford did not agree to the pardon in advance. As you will recall, Ford later went before a Committee of Congress and testified under oath that no deal was involved. So, personally I put the possibility of a deal aside.

At the point when the pardon was granted, the Special Prosecutor, Jaworski, was about to call for an indictment of Nixon. Jaworski let Ford know that. Reading between the lines, I wonder if Jaworski was also hoping—perhaps even urging—that Ford would pardon Nixon. I'm convinced now that Ford had come to the conclusion that it was the only way to get the Watergate business behind him. Exactly why he decided to make the announcement on that particular weekend, I don't know. Once he made up his mind, it would have been his nature to get it over with.

I understand that you are going to have Jerry terHorst in for a session. It will be interesting to question him on that. He should have quite a bit to say. Phil Buchen probably knows as much about it as anybody other than Ford himself.

QUESTION: What kind of a deal could have been made? Could you give us some examples?

SENATOR GRIFFIN: I suppose some people will always be suspicious that Nixon, either directly or through Haig, asked for assurance in advance that, if he resigned, Ford would pardon him. However, that question was examined very thoroughly by the House Judiciary Committee in open session. President Ford went up to the Hill, he testified under oath, and made a very good and complete record on that point.

QUESTION: You gave us your estimate of the vote in the Senate on impeachment before the tapes, and you indicated that their existence would certainly have changed that vote. Have you an estimate that you could give us on the vote after the tapes were revealed?

SENATOR GRIFFIN: It was my guess that the vote for conviction in the Senate would have been overwhelming. I let Nixon know that I probably would vote for conviction. After the incriminating tapes surfaced, Senator Goldwater made it very plain that he thought Nixon should resign. When Goldwater took that position, it was obvious that Nixon had very little support left in the Senate.

QUESTION: Could the vote have been ninety to ten, or something of that sort?

SENATOR GRIFFIN: It could have been.

QUESTION: I wonder how one could explain the error that President Ford made in the presidential debate with Jimmy Carter when he referred to Poland as an independent democracy and so on. How do you explain that?

SENATOR GRIFFIN: I think in Ford's own mind, he was only saying that the Polish people are not controlled by the Soviets in spirit. The fact that he stuck with that position may be evidence of a trace of stubbornness in Jerry Ford—a characteristic that has sometimes been a problem for him. At the time, he had advisers—I wasn't one of them—who urged him to make a clarifying statement, but he refused to do it.

From time to time, we all make mental goofs. Sometimes we recognize them right away; sometimes we don't. It would be absolutely ridiculous, I suggest, to think that a person with Jerry Ford's experience and long service—which included years as a member of the defense subcommittee of the House Appropriation Committee as well as the foreign assistance subcommittee—would not be thoroughly familiar with the situation in Poland. Of course, he could not imagine that anyone would think otherwise.

QUESTION: Senator Griffin, following the Republican primary, were you or was President Ford satisfied that you received sufficient support from the Reagan party during the presidential election campaign?

SENATOR GRIFFIN: No, I'm sure he wasn't satisfied. Another related question might be: Why didn't Ford take Reagan for a vice president at Kansas City? I was involved in a small group that met with Ford at 3:00 a.m. after he finally won the nomination. We were summoned to help him decide who to name for vice president. Ford writes in his autobiography that he didn't feel that he really knew Ronald Reagan very well. I don't think Ford felt comfortable with Reagan in those days. I'm not sure whether that has changed now or not. Of course, Reagan was not in Washington very much when he was governor of California. Ford was hurt deeply when Reagan decided to run against him for the nomination in 1976. Ford felt that he shouldn't have had that challenge.

When I made the suggestion at Kansas City in the battle on 16C, the reaction of the Reagan people was that Ronald Reagan wouldn't take the vice presidential nomination anyway. As I recall, Reagan had made statements to that effect. When Ford came to the meeting at 3:00 a.m., he said he had been to see Reagan and that Reagan didn't want to be vice president. There was a bit of questioning of Ford on that point but perhaps not enough. As I look back, I wish someone had said, "But did you actually ask him to do it? Did you really try to convince him to do it?"

The situation brings to mind the occasion when Kennedy took Johnson as vice president after a bitter battle with him for the nomination. On the other hand, Kennedy knew Lyndon Johnson very well; they had worked together on the Senate floor every day. Whether Kennedy liked Johnson or not, at least he knew what he was getting. Kennedy also may have had in the back of his mind that as

President he would just as soon not have Lyndon Johnson as the Democratic leader of the Senate. He would rather have someone like Mike Mansfield.

Ford has always been a fellow who gets along with everybody. It's interesting to see how he and Carter get along so well now. I wonder how he really gets along with Reagan now.

QUESTION: One of the questions that everyone else has raised is whether one weakness that Gerald Ford had, as someone put it, was that he couldn't bring himself to knock heads. From where you sat, was this a weakness or an aspect of strength?

SENATOR GRIFFIN: Well, in terms of administrative ability, perhaps it was a weakness. Jerry Ford is such a nice guy that he has always found it very hard to fire anyone. Early in his administration he was being pushed hard by the Kitchen Cabinet to move the Nixon people out as quickly as possible. Of course, he had only a short time—a matter of hours—to get ready to assume the office of president. It was a very short, difficult period of time—much different than the situation of being elected President in November and having until the middle of January to organize things. Under circumstances like those faced by Ford, there is a natural tendency to keep people on, people who already know the ropes, and who can help you with the transition. They stayed on and worked with Jerry, and he came to rely on them and it became even more difficult for him to push them out.

If Jerry Ford's personality—his ability to get along with people—involves any weakness, it also carries with it great strength. He always got along well with people of both political parties, and his personal rapport as President with the leaders of foreign countries was very important. It was just marvelous the way he could, as a leader in Congress and as President, bring divergent points of view together. He is, and was, just the kind of a person we needed to heal the country after the terrible Watergate mess. Providence seems to look out for the United States of America.

It's just too bad that Jerry Ford didn't have a chance to serve the country longer as President of the United States.

NARRATOR: When we were in Michigan a colleague who was with me in the meeting made the comment, "It's too bad we don't have a retired Senator who would work for the Miller Center the way Bob Griffin does for the Ford Center." Maybe that's one of the best tributes anybody can pay to a public servant who is in retirement but who continues to work within the limits of time and energy to help a Center that studies public affairs. Some of the reasons he does this have come through this afternoon. We are very grateful.

REFLECTIONS ON A
POLITICIAN'S PRESIDENT

PHILIP W. BUCHEN

NARRATOR: To put first things first, Philip W. Buchen is a member of the Miller Center Presidential Transition and Foreign Policy Commission. He has been one of the most active and faithful members of that group.

Philip Buchen was born in Sheboygan, Wisconsin. He received his A.B. and J.D. degrees from the University of Michigan. He was a member of several law firms, but in terms of American history the most notable was the law firm of Ford and Buchen. That might have had something to do with the place he was to occupy later in presidential politics. He is currently a partner of a distinguished law firm, Dewey, Ballantine, Bushby, Palmer and Wood in Washington, D.C. He was counsel to President Gerald Ford from 1974 to 1977. The Ford presidency and his participation in it qualify him for discussing the questions that we hoped he might address this morning.

MR. BUCHEN: Thank you, Ken.

I think that one way to summarize Ford as President is to say that he was a politician's President in the best sense of the word. The last full day that he was in office, January 19, 1977, he had a small breakfast at the White House in the family dining room to which he invited several of us from his staff and the four congressional leaders, the leading Republicans and Democrats. No newspaper men were

present, and nothing was ever said about the gathering in
the newspapers.   At the conclusion of the breakfast Bob
Byrd, the majority leader, gave a talk.   He said a few words
about how highly he regarded the departing President.   Bob
is not the most eloquent of speakers, but I've never heard
him as eloquent as he was that morning, and the same with
Tip O'Neill.   Each was lavish in his praise of the President.
They showed warmth and real affection for this man.   It
made me think that these people were not doing it for
effect; they were doing it because they felt deeply about
their former colleague on the Hill.   I think he had the true
respect of the finest political minds in Washington all the
time that he was in the Congress and, of course, during his
presidency.   The day after the election I couldn't find
anybody who hadn't voted for President Ford.   I guess he
had more friends than he had supporters, actually.   Even if
they hadn't voted for him, many people felt badly that he
hadn't survived.

One of the strongest influences obviously on the Ford
presidency, and one that distinguishes his presidency from
that of each of his two successors, is the fact that he did
spend twenty-five years in Congress, much of it as a party
leader.   There are certain qualities which that experience
gave him, some good and some not so good.   One is that he
had strong loyalty to his friends, his colleagues and to the
institutions he served.   I guess you can't be a good
politician without developing a very keen sense of loyalty.
He didn't have a vigorous ideology; he had been through too
many arguments and too many fights in Congress to believe
that he had an answer for every issue.   He had a keen
sense of what was practical; and he, of course, had an
alertness to the political implications of anything he did,
which is another talent one develops during long service in
the Congress.   It was not that he necessarily swayed with
the political winds or took the most politically expedient
course.   He knew that he'd lose a good many of his battles,
as he did on many of the vetoes he exercised against the
Democratic Congress.

He was very realistic about how government works and
the effects of its action; he knew what its limitations were.
He didn't think it could accomplish anywhere near what the
framers of legislation had presupposed was possible.   He was
ready to discount quite a few of the steps taken by
Congress.   As you know, in passing legislation everybody

puts his pet idea into the bill as proposed, whether it is realistic or not. When the law passes, everybody has high expectations, but then it turns out that even the best of bureaucracies can't administer the law. He realized that.

He also had few illusions about what the United States could accomplish in world politics. He did support the Helsinki Accords, but I don't think he ever thought that this formal document really changed the situation very much. He did work very hard to move the Soviet Union and the United States toward arriving at SALT II, although nothing was done while he was in office. But I don't think that he ever anticipated that SALT II or something like it could ever be very helpful in the cause.

He was weak as an administrator and a planner. I think that is also part of spending twenty-five years in the Congress. You don't have to have much administrative ability to run a congressional office compared to a huge executive branch or even a huge White House staff. Nor need you do much planning ahead in Congress; you deal with each problem and each legislative challenge as it comes along. You aren't out there thinking about what you are going to do three years from now or two years from now.

He was always ready to receive advice. As President he functioned with almost the same open door policy that he had as a congressman. It was easy for people to see him. The only difference is that his schedule became very much more burdensome as a President and the scheduling problems kept people out, though his unwillingness to talk to them never did.

His leadership qualities I think showed up best within small groups rather than before large audiences or over televisions. I don't know if you detected it, but his voice was unusually high over television. I was surprised that a large and manly person like that would have such a high voice, especially over television.

He was not good at appealing to the people over the heads of Congress. I think that every president threatens to do that, but maybe only the current President [Reagan] is consistently successful. Ford would do it, but I never figured that he actually got the public behind him in such a way as to scare the daylights out of Congress. He just didn't have that kind of mass appeal.

He was a rather poor campaigner in both his campaigns against challenger Reagan and against his opponent Carter

partly because in Congress the campaigns never had to be
very vigorous.   Once he won the first election, he was
pretty much a shoo-in.   He wasn't used to campaigning,
certainly not on the scale that you had to do in a national
election, by addressing so many different audiences and
dealing with many different constituencies.   I didn't think
he was particularly capable in that respect.

In the two and a half years President Ford was in
office, much of his time was spent in overcoming the
effects of the Nixon downfall, battling the rather
unexpected economic recession and then contending for a
nomination and election.   It proved too short a time to
develop any major policy initiatives.   I think a big
disappointment of those of us around him was that we had
much on the drawing board which we really couldn't start
to present for action.

The policy-making machinery functioned quite well in
the White House, both in national security and domestic
matters.   One of the outstanding examples of policy-making
in the complex economic field was the Economic Policy
Council.   It was the first effort to bring together the
various economic voices: the Treasury, the head of the
Council of Economic Advisers, the Budget Office, and
various other groups that had a strong concern with
domestic and world economics.   It met at least once a week
and had a coordinated staff prepare papers.   It was an
effort to keep everybody working together, and I thought it
was quite successful.   This Council also prepared some long-
range initiatives that never could be implemented.

The President knew how to get policy formulated.   He
took the initiative, requesting answers on this policy or that
policy.   Unlike President Carter and possibly President
Reagan, he tried to shape the work done so that when it
came back to him, it wasn't just a mishmash of fifty
options, twenty-five of which he wasn't in the least bit
interested.   He had shaped it before the work was actually
started.   His background in Congress was such that he
certainly knew what the general parameters of a policy
should be, and he wasn't about to let the staff go off half-
cocked and produce a great variety of material, much of it
useless.

He organized his White House staff in the fashion of a
wheel as he called it.   He was at the hub and his eight or
nine chief advisers were the spokes leading to the center.

He had no person called chief of staff, but he had one adviser called "staff coordinator," which was a fairly innocuous term. Don Rumsfeld was the first staff coordinator, then Dick Cheney came after him. The coordinator chaired the meetings of the White House staff and directed the flow of paperwork to and from the President and the preparation of his schedules. He was not a barrier to access by any other of the key staff members. Although he would try to arrange convenient times for the President to meet with other advisers, the coordinator did not direct the staff efforts to any major degree. I'm sure it is different from what you are seeing in the Reagan White House now. The Carter White House probably was a little closer to the one under Ford, because it too didn't have a staff director with a great deal of authority.

Every President wants to cut back the size of his White House staff, and Ford was no exception. He did get it down to something smaller than it had been under President Nixon, although not by much. One of the problems was that there were carry-overs from the prior administration even after new appointees were brought in. Ford was very careful not to harm people who he didn't think should have been blamed for what the former President had done. He wanted to give them plenty of time to find a niche in the outside world, and the delay on their severance caused some duplication in the beginning.

I think the White House staff is still far too large. It was much larger in the Ford administration than it needed to be, probably because of the situation occurring during the Nixon administration of a "White House pitted against the rest of government." I think there is much talent out there in the bureaucracies that the White House should draw upon. You don't need to have a huge Domestic Policy Council staff. Cabinet departments for all domestic concerns are there. The Domestic Policy Council can draw on the resources of each of these departments. There are some very talented and well-informed people in the bureaucracy—probably more so than those you'd be able to recruit for a short run on the White House staff—who can contribute to the making of presidential policy. The White House staff is always there to put a presidential "spin" on any recommendation. Yet the basic materials upon which a decision is going to have to rest, the basic data and information, certainly can be drawn easily and continuously from the departments themselves. You don't need a huge White House staff to do the research and to do the compiling of information which goes into preparing an options paper. Eventually a president is going to appreciate that and insist that the resources of government as a whole be at his beck and call, using the White House staff only as a means of drawing out the necessary information from the bureaucracy and presenting it to him in a condensed and well-organized fashion.

Ford did replace certain of the Cabinet appointees but not at first. He didn't ask for resignations from Nixon's appointees, but eventually there was enough attrition that he was able to appoint the attorney general, and the secretaries of Health, Education and Welfare (HEW), Labor, Housing and Urban Development (HUD), Transportation, and Defense. Ed Levy was the attorney general; David Matthews, President of the University of Alabama, was the new secretary of HEW; John Dunlop, the secretary of Labor; Carla Hills became the secretary of HUD; Bill Coleman, secretary of transportation and Don Rumsfeld, secretary of defense. I think that's a team of pretty high quality that stands up well, probably better than most Cabinets. In fact, if Ford had gone through and replaced all incumbents, he might have set a new record for quality appointments in his administration.

The hold-overs tended to go their own ways. They had been working under a different boss, although not much of a boss because during the last months of the Nixon administration there hadn't been much control from the White House. So it was a little difficult to persuade those departments to coordinate their efforts with the White House.

In respect to Congress the President's relations were harmonious, but not particularly effective. He didn't persuade the Democrats to do things that the Democrats didn't want to do. He may have tempered some of their behavior, but certainly he never overrode their desires in any dramatic way. Maybe you need someone who engages in a much more combative relationship than Ford who had come out of the Congress and had a high regard for the institution.

How did Ford fill his White House staff? Well, he brought people with him from his former staffs. That posed a problem because people moved up from the congressional office, through the vice president's office, to the president's office, but their abilities didn't rise to the same extent. He wasn't going to let his former staff fall by the wayside. It did create some awkward situations, because there were people who couldn't any longer do the same tasks. They had to be assigned to something less responsible or comprehensive when it came to dealing with matters at the presidential level. For example, a press secretary for a congressman has a pretty simple job, and it is not much more complicated to be press secretary for a vice president, but a press secretary for a president has a very critical job. Ford's congressional press secretary had moved on to the vice president's office, but then he was relieved by someone else when Ford became be president.

In selecting his staff President Ford liked to get people around him whom he knew, whom he could trust and with whom he felt comfortable. I think that is a tendency of every president. You can't fault him for favoritism on that account. On the other hand, when it came to appointing the head of the Council of Economic Advisers, he recruited Alan Greenspan. If it were a position that called for some expertise that wasn't available from among his close friends, he went outside his circle of friends to make the appointment. It wasn't that he was uncomfortable with strangers. It's just that a president always needs some friends close by, people who think as he does or know what he would do in a given situation, and who watch out for his interests. At least he knew that his close friends had his interests at heart and weren't looking out for themselves. Quite often there are some rather ambitious people in the White House whose interests are their own rather than the president's, and Ford had very few, if any, of that type.

I think his Cabinet and sub-Cabinet appointments were generally of a very high quality and based much more on merit than is true of most administrations. That is not wholly a plus for Ford because, after all, he didn't have a whole national campaign that he had gone through which would have forced him to reward the hangers-on. He had a little advantage over anyone who goes to the presidency after a tough election campaign and who has a campaign chairman in every state who is going to want a job, if not for himself, then for his nephew. Ford didn't have that burden and he was quite happy to make merit appointments.

Ford told me himself that to make yourself look good, you put good people around you. I think it does help. Some presidents overlook the fact that they would be better presidents if they had better people around them.

One of the downfalls of the administration was the so-called "WIN" campaign. When Ford came in, he was fighting to deal with inflation. In fact, he went all around the country conducting a series of forums in which he had people from various regions, including academics, businessmen and consumers, explain what they thought he should be doing. The general consensus at the time was that inflation was the number one problem and that we had to lick inflation before we could solve anything else. Then, before he put an end to the forums, all of a sudden the bottom dropped out of the economy and unemployment figures started to take off.

This development was something that threw them off stride. For someone who was a conservative in his views on government spending, borrowing and taxing, there aren't an awful lot of quick-fix remedies you can put through if you don't want to spend more money. He vetoed several jobs bills because he felt that they were so wasteful: public works bills that he knew wouldn't really pick things up because the number employed in relation to the dollars being spent was so small that he didn't think it would help. He was criticized for vetoing bills like that, but as it happened, nothing he did or could do turned the situation around. That was, of course, one of the disabling factors in the 1976 campaign. One of Carter's campaign arguments was that the "misery index" was too high. Well, he probably now wishes he hadn't used that expression because it turned out that in another four years he had made it worse.

Ford did one thing which had an influence on the Carter administration and on the Reagan administration. Ford was the first one to move vigorously in the field of deregulation. He tried to get all the regulatory agencies to simplify their rules, to reduce them in number, and to improve the process by which they settled on the rules they did pass. Carter continued and put many of Ford's ideas into practice, as has the current Reagan administration.

Among the crises during the Ford administration were (1) the need to evacuate Americans from Saigon when that city was about to fall and (2) the need to save the

Americans that the Cambodians captured on an American ship, the *Mayaguez.* The withdrawal from Saigon was handled quite effectively. Ford had all the information he needed; the intelligence information was very good. We had people on the ground who could supply it though in the *Mayaguez* situation, I was appalled at the lack of information. We were acting blindly in that situation and had no way to communicate with the Cambodian government, such as it was. We didn't know if this were an official government action or whether there were some renegades that had done it. All we knew was that Ford was determined to save the American crew; he didn't want to find them victims of whoever had captured them, no matter under whose auspices the piracy had occurred. So he did move quickly but not, I think, on the basis of adequate information. It may have been that moving fast, even without the full information, may have saved lives. As it turned out, of course, we did save the lives of the crew, but the cost in lives of our servicemen was considerable.

About the man himself, he was friendly and straightforward. He had an almost earnest demeanor, and he never showed glibness or arrogance or pompousness. I think he had the reputation for honesty and trust-worthiness, which helped restore the presidency at a time when it needed some restoring. He was probably a fortunate choice at the time for this reason. When you look back over the list of people who might have fit into the role, you'd be hard-pressed to find anyone else who could have done the job or served that purpose at the time as well as he did.

Obtaining high office really did nothing to change his outlook or attitudes. He humanized the presidency after it had gained the reputation of being almost an imperial office. I think that LBJ and Nixon created that impression, which Ford then had to overcome. His old friendships didn't decline, and his interests and loyalties didn't change. He didn't expect people around him to treat him with the awe or deference that is commonly regarded to be due a president.

Yet, I don't think he demeaned the office. I don't think he went out of his way just to be a good fellow. Ford did not carry his own suitcase, but he showed in other, more natural ways that a person in the position of president can act in a very human fashion.

Then again all this goodness showed a certain lack of tough-mindedness. Maybe what is needed in the office of president is someone who isn't quite that good a person. Any man who has gone through the ordeal of a national campaign is going to be tough. It's either going to change him or he has to be a hard-driving and competitive person in the first place. Maybe for all the criticism we've given the campaign process—Lord knows it has its down side—it probably does bring out people who are going to be equipped to handle the toughest job in the world. The campaign process engenders qualities that are necessary to bang heads together and to deal with subordinates somewhat ruthlessly. We have still to understand what effective leadership is in the presidency, but I think it has to be something more than what Ford brought to the office. Yet it can't be an overbearing quality that people pay no attention to or begin to laugh at. We still must define the quality that we are looking for; I think we have not yet done that.

People keep asking me about what role the pardon may have played in Ford's electoral defeat. I think it's probably less the pardon than the fact that Ford didn't get angry enough at the former President. He had intended to get a statement of genuine contrition out of the man, almost a confession of the wrongs he had done, but the man he was dealing with wasn't about to be contrite. Ford didn't want to negotiate any more; he didn't feel it was appropriate. So he had to depend on a theory, which is perfectly good law, but doesn't arouse much sympathy or understanding: if you accept a pardon, you admit your guilt. But that wasn't like having an admission of guilt in black and white, and I think the absence of such an admission may have hurt more than the fact of the pardon itself.

Nevertheless, Ford could have been saved under different consequences; there was a time shortly after the pardon when Nixon's health went into a sharp decline. I remember a newspaper person calling me when it was almost certain that Nixon would not survive. He said, "Well, it looks as though Ford is off the hook." Well, of course it wasn't an outcome about which Ford was thinking, but it was a strong possibility. People forget about how close Nixon came to death. By the time of the campaign he was well again, and people saw a healthy former president out there, and judged Ford's act of pardoning him accordingly.

I think probably historians will view Ford as a very fortunate and a salutary entrant in the line of American presidents coming when he did, particularly when they recall the damage to the morale of the country and to the respect for the presidency that occurred during the Nixon administration. He probably was a better President because his politics were seasoned, and he was not out to put his unique personal mark on the presidency. I thought that Larry Barrett's title for his book several years ago about the presidency of President Reagan, *Gambling with History*, was very perceptive. Ford would never have gambled with history, and I'm not sure we ever should have presidents that gamble with our history as a country.

Ford will get high grades for the quality of government he operated, for the key appointments he made and for the reputation he had of making the White House staff work effectively. He disliked botched-up jobs, and I think we have too much of that in government now where a president lets carelessness or slipshod work go by unchallenged, and lets the press scream without doing anything about the cause for the screams. I think he really appreciated that the White House staff can operate very shabbily or it can operate reasonably well. It's not that there wasn't petty squabbling and quibbling in the White House—there always was and always will be—but the important thing was to get good work out on time without any real slips, and in that respect the Ford White House performed well.

We've had two presidents now who campaigned against the Washington establishment. Maybe we ought to get back to one who decides he can make use of what's there and not try to deny the value of our present government establishment. It is just a matter of making it work better, not condemning it or making people who are in it feel as though they are worth nothing even when they have devoted all their lives to government work. I think it is unfortunate that we have campaigns like that, there is plenty of room to campaign on the merits of particular issues, so to campaign on the ground that the government is inept or poorly staffed or overstaffed is not a good idea. I think Ford is a contrast to the last two presidents in that regard. So I give you the politician's President and invite any questions you may want to ask.

NARRATOR: Well, you've seen evidence of why Mr. Buchen has been such a good member of our Presidential Transition Commission and more recently our Presidential Disability Commission.

QUESTION: Could you tell us a little more about the pardon, which was probably the most controversial action of the Ford presidency? Did it give him a lot of trouble? Was it an independent decision or did he arrive at it as a result of discussions with his counsellors? What was your role? How did he react to the criticism of it?

MR. BUCHEN: It was very much his own decision. When he told his staff what he wanted to do, he didn't invite any discussion. I'm sure he got plenty, but it wasn't anything he wanted. He certainly didn't come to us and say, "Should I do it or shouldn't I?" In my case he gave me the assignment of finding out whether he could do it, not whether he should. I thought that it would be far better if I did not form an opinion on whether he should, because it might prejudice my opinion on whether he could. In my research of the law, I proceeded secretly; I was scared even to get a book out of the library that had a "P" on the front of it. Yet we managed to find enough law that made it fairly clear that a very broad right of pardon, going back into English history, was very much within the power of the chief executive under our Constitution.

There was some question about whether a person could be pardoned before he had been tried or convicted, but there is some precedent for that, too. For example, the amnesty of those forgiven after the Civil War was granted without their having been tried or convicted. At one time there had been no way to give immunity to witnesses who took the Fifth Amendment so as not to testify and convict their co-conspirators. The administration some years ago—in an action having nothing to do with the Ford administration—granted a pardon to a witness so that he could not claim the Fifth Amendment. He couldn't be convicted of any crime for which he had been pardoned, even though he had not been charged or convicted. That was upheld by a court in New Jersey, so we were pretty sure on the point of a pardon before conviction.

Ford, I think, abhorred the idea that the country would have to undergo the trial of a president. He was told that it would be just a matter of days before there might be an indictment of the former President. once there was an indictment, Ford felt that he couldn't move, and that the country would then have to wait out the trial. this was late 1974, and we were coming up to the bicentennial. He had an opinion that because of the adverse publicity, the trial probably would have to be put off for a year. John Osborne, who wrote for the *New Republic*, claims credit for having suggested to Ford that he should give a pardon early on, that there was no sense in waiting; If he was ever going to give one, he should do it at the beginning. I think with a trial we wouldn't have gotten a confession from Nixon, because he probably wouldn't even have gone on the stand. The public would have learned only what was pretty evident from the tapes anyhow.

Incidentally, some of the most vociferous and critical statements came from the ministers of the country. There were some very violent letters from ministers, and Ford used to say, "I thought they understood what mercy is about." I think this bothered Ford more than anything.

QUESTION: What was the attitude of Nelson Rockefeller? I saw a friend of mine the day after the pardon, who had worked very closely with Nelson Rockefeller in 1958. He was just about hitting the ceiling saying that we had a crook in the White House before, now we have an idiot. I'm not sure but he may have been reflecting Mr. Rockefeller's opinion. Do you know what Nelson Rockefeller's attitude was?

MR. BUCHEN: I believe he was sympathetic. I think Rockefeller was nominated after the pardon, if I remember correctly. However, I don't know for certain what Rockefeller's feelings were.

QUESTION: I've always been curious as to why President Ford took so long to relieve Henry Kissinger of his White House position as assistant for national security affairs and to bring Brent Scowcroft into that job. I think it is the only time that a secretary of state has ever held that position as well. What special reasons were there for keeping Kissinger in both jobs, and could you shed any light on why it was that Kissinger had such enormous influence on the President?

MR. BUCHEN: Well, one reason is that he had an enormous influence on President Nixon. Also, the only time that there hasn't been a feud between the national security adviser and the secretary of state was during Kissinger's time. That's one way of solving this perennial problem!

As you know, Henry Kissinger started out as a member of the Eastern establishment, which was not President Nixon's favorite. He began his White House service in fairly humble fashion, and I guess he came to be as powerful as he was because of his own tremendous ability. After the harsh treatment of Bill Rogers by the White House, I don't know whether you could have gotten anyone to take the secretary of state's job when Rogers left except Henry Kissinger.

One of Henry Kissinger's ploys for keeping power was to threaten to resign. Our transition team agreed that his two jobs should be separated, since their purposes were different. But it became obvious that if the President had suggested that, Henry would have said, "Well, I've got to get back to Harvard." I am sure Ford did not want to lose Kissinger at that time or any time in his administration. He was much too valuable to the President.

I don't know any individual who could handle as many complicated and intricate problems at once as Kissinger could; it was a facility that was unbelievable. I don't say that he handled them all well, but at least you knew that someone was in charge.

QUESTION: To your knowledge was there any kind of an understanding between Nixon and Ford at the time Mr. Nixon abdicated?

MR. BUCHEN: No, the answer to that came out in some testimony from Ford. After the pardon that question was asked of Ford in one of the House committees. He testified that he had been approached by people in the White House, Al Haig specifically, who were trying desperately to figure out a way to get Nixon to resign. He did go over the possibility that Ford might pardon Nixon. That was one of several options he talked about, but there was never any indication from Ford that he would do anything along that line. In fact Ford told Haig, "Look, I'm not deciding one way or the other." He didn't preclude the possibility of a pardon, but he didn't say he would do it. For that reason

I'm sure there was nothing that could have gone back to Nixon beyond the advice that President Ford would have the power to pardon him. He certainly would have known that anyhow. Nixon was even thinking of pardoning himself at one time while he remained in office. There clearly was no communication between the Vice President and President on the subject. The communication could only have been through Al Haig, but there was no deal at all. Now some people still think that there was enough to read between the lines of what Ford told Haig that it led Nixon to resign, but I don't think that was the case. Nixon was very reluctant to resign. I think that if he had thought there was a deal for his eventual pardon, he would have been quite willing to resign.

QUESTION: Mr. Buchen, there was speculation that President Ford made the mistake of keeping Kissinger and letting Governor Rockefeller go. Can you explain what the relationship was between Ford and Governor Rockefeller?

MR. BUCHEN: It was fine to begin with. Then when Rockefeller was in the process of being confirmed, he tried to get Ford to give him the chairmanship of the Domestic Policy Council, which was a creature of statute. The Council was parallel to the National Security Council for foreign affairs. When the President and Vice President were together by themselves, that became their agreement. But when the word got back to the White House staff, they realized that some of the staff might not be working in the White House at all if Vice President Rockefeller became head of the Domestic Council or they would be working solely for Nelson Rockefeller. The staff began to protest that such was not the way to run the establishment. So eventually Ford had to back down. I think that Nelson Rockefeller finally realized also that you can't have two people at the head of White House operations, which is what would have happened if he had been in charge of the domestic policy staff. He backed off, but the incident strained the relationship between the two men. Even though they always had cordial relations after that, they were never bound by very close relationships.

The Reagan challenge at the time, and the challenge from his supporters, was much more directed at Rockefeller than at Kissinger. I remember one incident that happened even before Rockefeller had been nominated. Word was getting out that he probably would be the choice. A man came to my office saying that he had absolute proof that there was a connection between the Rockefeller family and the Mafia. He even directed us to a safety deposit box which supposedly contained papers to that effect. Anyhow, it turned out that he really belonged to a very conservative organization and that he was doing everything possible to upset the prospective appointment. So I think there was much more antipathy generally to Rockefeller than to Kissinger among the conservatives in the party. I don't think it would have helped too much politically to get rid of Kissinger. I'm sure it was almost necessary to get rid of Rockefeller.

QUESTION: You spoke of the high caliber of the members of Ford's Cabinet. How did he use his Cabinet?

MR. BUCHEN: Almost the only way you can use it. You can't use it as a board of directors. Presidents always come in and say, "We are going to have Cabinet government." It can't be done. You don't sit around a table with your Cabinet and take a vote on whether you ought to remove tobacco subsidies. The government is departmentalized, and the secretary of the Interior isn't going to know about what the secretary of HEW should do. The policies that the president has to consider are far too complicated to resolve through a group discussion. You'd have to say the Cabinet meetings involve a lot of motion, but not much productive activity; they are done more for effect. Somehow I think that if you didn't have Cabinet meetings, people would think the government wasn't operating, but such meetings really don't accomplish much.

The most interesting ones occurred when Henry Kissinger gave us a scholarly lecture on the state of the world. The lectures were delightful because he presented them so well.

QUESTION: I often wondered, if Ford was such a good politician, why did he not avoid having a second, very close inspection of his finances when he had already gone through that before he was made vice president? It seemed to me this hurt the momentum of his campaign against Carter.

What is the law about that? Why couldn't he have forestalled that special prosecutor?

MR. BUCHEN: Here was a case where someone just came up with what they said was new evidence, namely, an informer from a union who claimed that Ford was given cash payments. After a longer investigation than we hoped would occur, the special prosecutor concluded that there was nothing to it, that there was nothing to back up the charge, no evidence beyond the statement of this one man.

QUESTION: How good was Mr. Ford's grasp of economics and the economy? He wasn't very successful with "WIN" and he was sandbagged by the recession. If he had been reelected and had four more years, do you think he would have had a clear program for dealing with economic problems?

MR. BUCHEN: I think he had some awfully good people around him. I think Bill Simon, Alan Greenspan and Bill Seidman had planned some rather sophisticated economic policy initiatives for after the election. I think Ford personally knew no more about the subject than most people who have been through Congress. It had never been his specialty (he had served on the Armed Services Committee principally), but he had good people around him and the policy was being worked on very carefully.

NARRATOR: This has certainly been one of the most fair-minded and even-handed assessments of a president that we've heard in this room. Phil, thank you very much.

THE ACCIDENTAL PRESIDENT

LEO CHERNE

NARRATOR: I would like, in introducing Mr. Cherne, to read from President Reagan's words, of November 15, 1983, in awarding the Presidential Medal of Freedom, this country's highest civilian award to Leo Cherne, when he said, "In addition to being a humanitarian, Leo has been an economist, political scientist, sculptor, and adviser to presidents for over forty years. His extraordinary service to his country and to mankind are inspiring and deserving of recognition from his fellow citizens."

Leo Cherne helped to found the Research Institute of America and has been its executive director since its creation. He had a major hand in the final drafting of the Army and Navy industrial mobilization plans for World War II. At the close of the war, he served as an economic adviser to General MacArthur and helped to construct the program which revised the Japanese tax structure.

Since 1951 he has served as chairman of the board of the International Rescue Committee, assisting those who flee from totalitarian government. He has been vice chairman of the President's Foreign Intelligence Advisory Board, reporting directly to President Reagan. In the Ford period, he was chairman of that board and also a member of the first Intelligence Oversight Board. The honors and awards he has received are too numerous to mention except to refer to the French Legion of Honor, the Commander's Cross, and the Federal Republic of Germany's Order of Merit. He was a moving spirit in the formation of the so-called Stanton Commission. He had ideas about the development of the country's cultural and educational program and felt that something should be done to restructure and reorganize it. On a flight from New York to Washington, he happened to sit next to Frank Stanton of CBS and asked, "Would you be willing to serve as chairman of the group?" That was the beginning of the Stanton Commission. It is a privilege to have him with us.

MR. CHERNE: Thank you, Ken, for those warm words. I value them very deeply, but I must say they take second place to a unique honor. I hardly thought I would ever be privileged to participate in an activity at Thomas Jefferson's "academical village." And while I've been here before, it takes on a special ambience today.

As Ken Thompson said I've served in one capacity or another, seven presidents and one monarch—Douglas MacArthur. Those associations from Franklin Roosevelt to Ronald Reagan have involved advisory responsibilities of varying character and importance. My association with Gerald Ford is set against that backdrop, which is why I mention it.

I was first appointed a member of the President's Foreign Intelligence Advisory Board by Richard Nixon following his 1972 reelection to the presidency. I was then appointed chairman of that board by Gerald Ford when he instituted an extensive reorganization of the entire intelligence community several months after he suddenly assumed the presidency. During President Ford's term of office, my meetings with him were frequent. And during that same period, my relationship was especially close with the two members of the top White House staff and Ford confidants probably closest and most deeply involved in the intelligence process: former Congressman Jack Marsh, and the President's counsel, Philip Buchen, long-time personal friend and legal associate in Michigan.

Ford's decision to appoint a Democrat as chairman of a revised President's Foreign Intelligence Advisory Board (PFIAB) reflected the fact that the Board is by definition expected to play a non-political role. It is essential, if it is to be the president's eyes and ears in the intelligence community, that it be affected in no way whatever by political considerations. An additional surprise to me was the President's appointment of another, second board to serve in the field of intelligence. That board was the Intelligence Oversight Board, to which he appointed Ambassador Robert Murphy as chairman, and former Secretary of the Army Stephen Ailes and me as members.

Not only were the tasks assigned to each of the boards totally different, but the manner in which they related to President Ford also differed dramatically. In the case of the President's Foreign Intelligence Advisory Board, he arranged for meetings with the complete Board, with a greater frequency than any president before him except John F. Kennedy. During the first months of his presidency, and until the Bay of Pigs, Kennedy didn't meet with his Board at all. The Bay of Pigs changed the picture profoundly. Having been burned by that event, President Kennedy turned to the Board more frequently.

It is clear that two factors which motivated the heavy reliance which President Ford placed upon the President's Foreign Intelligence Advisory Board were the "revelations" contained in a series of articles by Seymour Hersh in the *New York Times*, and the hearings of the Senate Intelligence Committee under the chairmanship of Frank Church, which focused with intensity, and occasional responsibility, on a host of impropriety charges.

The substantial loss of public confidence in government after the Vietnam War, the Watergate period, and the media and congressional assault on U.S. intelligence activities clearly led Gerald Ford to the conclusion that his first responsibility was to restore confidence in the integrity of government. The appointment of the Rockefeller Commission on January 4, 1975, which essentially, but not entirely, focused on the behavior of the intelligence community was a major step in this direction.

Rockefeller himself had been a member of the President's Foreign Intelligence Advisory Board. I quickly learned that he was in fact one of the most effective members of that Board. The fact that the President selected his vice president to head up the Commission on CIA Activities Within the United States, and appointed to that Commission, with Nelson Rockefeller's concurrence, a group of most distinguished citizens, including Ronald Reagan, whose presence showed that this was not an aggregation of Ford sycophants, assured that the conclusions of the Commission would at least enjoy some public credibility. [Editor's note: former University of Virginia

President Edgar F. Shannon, Jr., was also a member.] The conduct of that Commission, under the vice president's guidance, its reach, candor, and complete willingness to examine every asserted aspect of impropriety or questionable behavior or procedure made that Commission's conclusions of historic significance.

Nelson Rockefeller's interest in intelligence was great. After the defeat of the Ford/Dole candidacies, Rockefeller confided to me that not only did he regard his membership on the President's Foreign Intelligence Advisory Board as his most valuable activity in his long history of service to several administrations, but he hoped that he would be reappointed to the Board by the Carter administration. But Carter's decision, though, was to discontinue that body completely.

The frequency with which Gerald Ford met with the full Board, as well as the contacts he maintained with me as chairman, and the occasional presentations which smaller groups of the Board made to him in connection with particular aspects of intelligence they had been studying, coupled with the creation of the Intelligence Oversight Board, clearly marked President Ford's determination that respect for intelligence and a wider understanding of its importance were essential to the healing role in which he saw his presidency. It must be understood that serving the President directly as these Boards did, and dealing with intelligence, much of the work was extremely sensitive and cannot be revealed.

Indeed, the work of the President's Foreign Intelligence Advisory Board has been so leak-proof that some of the most seasoned Washington reporters have periodically questioned whether or not its existence is cosmetic. I can only assert emphatically that the opposite is the case, though I must repeat that the Board functions quite differently under different presidents and consequently the range and magnitude of its contribution to more effective intelligence has varied from administration to administration.

More important than the fact that President Ford met with his Board frequently was the fact that on not one occasion did any matter of the many which were presented to Ford, or on which he actively inquired, ever involve a question that did *not* deal with foreign intelligence. During the Nixon administration the Board was, of course, deeply involved in a number of fundamental intelligence-related questions. Nixon felt equally free to ask its judgment, and express his own views, though, on matters which were not within the normal purview of the Board.

Perhaps the most profound difference which characterized President Ford's relationship to the Board also contributes to understanding the nature of the man and his presidency. I know of no occasion when he had to evaluate a problem facing him as President in which he permitted his ego to affect his judgment. The explanations for this fact are to some extent speculative. Gerald Ford, more than any other president I have known, had a uniquely confident sense of self. Twenty-five years in the Congress undoubtedly helped reinforce that quality.

One other fact unique to Gerald Ford contributed to the remarkable objectivity and absence of ego. Gerald Ford was doubly an accidental President: First, he had not sought the office. There is no substantial indication that he ever aspired to that position. It was the accidental fact of Spiro Agnew's clouded resignation from the vice presidency which led to Richard Nixon's appointing Gerald Ford to that role in the first place, and it was the even more dramatic series of events which led Richard Nixon to resign which automatically elevated Gerald Ford to the presidency.

To this one must add that he could not have been more acutely aware of the urgency to perform as president in a manner which would, as rapidly as possible, assure the public not only of a non-political presidency, but of one which the public would accept as unblemished. It will long be debated whether he best served those purposes by the pardon he granted to Richard Nixon. He has been clear on this subject. In essence, his purpose, as he asserted it, reflected the feeling that it was urgent to put the continuing acrimony behind him and the nation.

It is argued by many that the Nixon pardon, more than one other fact, cost him the presidency in 1976. Whether he perceived that possible consequence at the time is unlikely to be known. I can only advance my own conviction that he would have taken that action even had he clearly foreseen the political consequences for himself.

There are certain attributes of his presidency which seem clear to me. The same objective, warm, eager and inquiring attitudes which consistently guided his relationships with his Foreign Intelligence Advisory Board led him to gather around him, both for policy-making and the execution of the responsibilities of the presidency, highly competent people, but even more, people who would not burden his presidency with the continuous struggle for eminence, attention and primacy most often in evidence in the White House. There have been very few presidencies as devoid of the internal struggles either for the President's attention, or over policy, as occurred during the Ford presidency.

Conflicts between members of the Cabinet on matters of policy are both inevitable and desirable. They were more infrequent and subdued, however, within the Ford administration than one has the right to expect of a presidency. As for his closest personal associates, his counsel Philip Buchen and Jack Marsh, I cannot recall them ever rushing into print. Donald Rumsfeld, not normally given to self-effacement, was the most anonymous White House chief of staff I have known and was extremely effective. The same can be said of Richard Cheney. Absence of drive or the presence of limited ability could be one explanation, yet these individuals were precisely the opposite of that; a number of them have, either in subsequent government activity or in private affairs, achieved substantial eminence.

The quality of Ford's people is illustrated further by his choice of National Security Adviser; Brent Scowcroft, who performed his task with total commitment, held to the view that the President would be best served if his personal role were nearly invisible.

Another key appointment further emphasizes the character of the Ford White House. Alan Greenspan, one of the nation's most respected economists, was the chairman of Ford's Council of Economic Advisers. One of President Ford's speech writers who has written a book on the Ford presidency says, "Greenspan is the eagle who soars above others in the room during economic discussion. His grasp of economic concepts is unequaled." Yet Greenspan's public visibility could hardly have been more contained.

I am not suggesting that Ford, depending so heavily on the experience and judgment of those to whom he turned for advice, invariably followed that advice. I am not free to discuss the particular issues or crises we confronted. There was, however, one intelligence question involving national security which I, as chairman, had assigned to one of the new members, Edward Bennett Williams. Working with him, we not only reached complete agreement, but felt that our conclusion must be brought to the President. The question was of a nature which involved Attorney General Edward J. Levi. After a lengthy debate between the attorney general and the two members of the President's Foreign Intelligence Advisory Board, the President accepted the dissenting and less security-oriented judgment of his attorney general.

On no other subject which confronted us during the months of the Ford presidency were any recommendations we made rejected by the President, though in one instance Director of Central Intelligence William Colby strongly resisted a proposal we made, which led us to suggest an interim study to determine whether or not our proposal was valid. The outcome of that study put to rest any further question about the urgency of our radical proposals, and was then strongly supported by the President. This particular debate led to what may well be the only leak involving the Board which, incidentally, did not emanate from it. Because of the largely accurate journalism of the Washington correspondent of the Boston Globe, the matter is now historic knowledge, and I feel free to refer to it.

The Board, after lengthy study, was dissatisfied with certain conclusions which were part of a basic national estimate prepared by the intelligence community. A "national estimate" is one of the most important responsibilities involving the highest level of "the community." The Board recommended a review of that estimate by a team of experts on the subject not associated with the intelligence community, but cleared to study the identical information which had been available to those who had been involved in the preparation of that estimate. It was, in addition, a means of looking at the effectiveness of the *process which produces national estimates*. That episode has come to be known as "The Experiment in Competitive Estimates," or, more colloquially, "The A and B Team Experiment." At the end of an extensive process involving deep study, followed by debate by both teams of participants before the full board of PFIAB, the original purpose was achieved. A new estimate was prepared reflecting in its major conclusions the judgments of the B Team and validating the concern which had been conveyed to the President by the Board.

Looking at it from President Ford's perspective, he was being asked by his advisory board to authorize an unprecedented course of action. The recommendation and procedure were controversial. It was initially resisted by the President's Director of Central Intelligence. President Ford acted decisively and, upon his instruction, an ambitious effort involving some of the nation's most respected scholars and former government officials, as well as key members of the CIA's analytic staff, began. It is the nearly universal view of those who have been exposed to the results of their work that not only was the particular national estimate under study improved, but the beneficial effects, as we had hoped, extended throughout the subsequent estimating process.

My very first impression of Gerald Ford was of a warm, thoughtful, open-minded and eager-to-learn President. The only change in those initial perceptions was my realization that each of these qualities were deep and consistent. One more important quality became evident. He always sought exposure to a wide range of views; he listened with what seemed to be infinite patience, and then had no reluctance to reach decisions and act. I have known no president as intent on securing every conflicting judgment on the problems he had to resolve. I have known no other President to listen as intently, tirelessly and patiently and with such comprehension.

Another quality was innate and invariable in Gerald Ford: his sensitive and always warm human decency. Perhaps the presidency requires a limit to decency, but stature as a human being does not. I would find it difficult to believe that his fairness and integrity have ever been exceeded in the Oval Office. A small incident which occurred after the disappointment of his defeat by Jimmy Carter is illustrative. Ford personally signed letters of deepest gratitude sent to each Board member who had served him. That same Board, having gone through the formality of submitting their resignations to the newly-elected President Carter, waited for five months before he made his decision to terminate the life of PFIAB. When he did so, though I had seen President Carter's Counsel that very day, it wasn't until I returned to my home in New York that I received a phone call from his Counsel telling me that the President had decided to end the President's Foreign Intelligence Advisory Board's existence. When I inquired whether or not the members of the Board had been so advised, he explained that the news would be in the next morning's newspaper and hoped that I might reach the members between the time of his evening call and their discovery of the Board's demise in the morning news.

Trying to determine what President Ford's main strengths and weaknesses were makes me wonder whether some of the attributes which I have identified as his strengths—the absence of assertive ego, the remarkable openness and nonpolitical objectivity, the warmth and personal thoughtfulness—may not also have been weaknesses in some ways. Most institutions tend to be a reflection of the individual who leads their efforts. The stakes and the tensions in the White House are infinitely greater, and the individuals close to the President are often strong and ambitious. The views they hold are, as they should be, strong ones. The character of President Ford assured that many of those closest to him undoubtedly expressed their strong views to him, as in fact the members of the Board did on occasion.

The President's self-effacement was reflected in the self-effacement of some of his associates. But that was not true of every member of the Ford team. One who made no effort at anonymity, a former newsman, was the President's press chief Ron Nessen, but his role of course was, by definition, an extremely public one. Then, too, there was Henry Kissinger, one of the most gifted men ever to serve his government, and not altogether eager to deny it. I know of no indication that the President suggested or imposed a style on his colleagues, though it is clear, or at least suggested by White House hearsay at the time, that there were those who tested his patience, and at least one who did so to the point that produced that individual's resignation.

How will history judge President Ford? This, of course, is the most elusive of questions. I think historians may judge him to have been too permissive. Yet accompanying that judgment, if indeed it is made, will be the inescapable fact that he was exactly the right president to follow the turbulence which preceded him, and the constitutional crisis which made him president.

I'll end by telling of a personal episode which means a great deal to me. Queen Elizabeth was an official guest of the Ford White House where she was honored at a state dinner. The Queen returned the courtesy at the British Embassy where, after dinner, she and the President made their way down a cleared path on the beautiful lawn of that Embassy so that several hundred invited guests might see them. At one point Gerald Ford, turning to my wife, asked her, "Is Leo as tough at home as he is with me?" She replied that I was actually quite gentle. He responded, and I will always value his generous words, "I want you to know how much I value his services to our country and his total honesty with me."

I have had one opportunity to say something publicly in the presence of Gerald Ford about my feelings towards him, and I'll repeat it now. I have known and worked for seven presidents. Of those presidents, there has been no one I would rather have worked for than Gerald Ford.

QUESTION: How do you account for the fact that the men who served under President Ford were, as you said, reticent in regard to publicity?

MR. CHERNE: I think in corporate life, community life, and university life, people tend to reflect the shadow of the man who is the leader. There is no factor which affects human behavior more than rewards and penalties. If the President praises reticence, he is going to get reticence. If the President seems to applaud louder voices, he is going to get an infinite supply of them.

NARRATOR: I'm sure I speak for all of us in saying that this has been a most stimulating presentation. Thank you very much.

II.

THREE VIEWS
OF
THE FORD WHITE HOUSE

FORMING AND MANAGING
AN ADMINISTRATION

RICHARD B. CHENEY

NARRATOR: In recent months Americans have become well acquainted with Richard Cheney. At age 45, he is a leader in the House of Representatives. Since the 96th Congress he has been a congressman at large from Wyoming. He was chairman of the Republican policy committee in discussions on aid to the contras. Earlier, he was deputy counselor from 1970 to 1971 in the Nixon administration. He left that administration but returned to the executive branch in 1974, first, as a deputy assistant and then as assistant to President Gerald Ford.

We have had discussions on the Ford White House, but surely for the period 1975 to 1977 when he was chief of staff in that White House, no one could speak to us with greater authority or knowledge than Richard Cheney. We are terribly pleased that in the midst of a busy schedule he has come down to participate in this important oral history.

MR. CHENEY: Thank you very much, Ken. Let me first begin with a recounting of my first association with the Ford administration. I did not know Jerry Ford at all until he became President. My original aspirations in life were to be an academic. I was working on my Ph.D. at the University of Wisconsin in political science with a specialty in the Congress. I completed my course work and passed my preliminary exams for the doctorate in 1968 and went

57

off to Washington with a grant to study the Congress. I
was going to spend a year on the Hill as a congressional
fellow, and then return to the academic world to write my
dissertation and teach. However, I got caught up, first,
with Bill Steiger from Wisconsin, a young congressman, and
later with Don Rumsfeld and served in the Nixon
administration for four years. After having served about
four layers down in a couple of the executive branch
agencies and the White House, I left and went into private
business after the 1972 election. I was in Washington on
"the outside" for eighteen months as the Nixon
administration came apart as a result of the Watergate
crisis. I watched all that unfold.

    Then, on the night that President Nixon went on
nationwide television and announced that he was going to
resign at noon the next day, I received a call from Brussels.
Don Rumsfeld, who had been my boss in the Nixon
administration, was there as ambassador to NATO. I got a
phone call from Don's secretary who said that he was en
route to Washington. He was to arrive at Dulles the next
afternoon at 2:00 p.m. and his secretary asked if I could
meet his plane. I agreed to do so.

    In the meantime, between that evening when President
Nixon spoke and the next afternoon, there was the very
emotional ceremony in the east wing where he in effect said
"good-bye" to the staff. Then Nixon left and Ford was
sworn in. I watched all of that on television before I went
out to Dulles airport to meet Don. As he got off the
airplane, he was also met by a White House messenger with
a letter for him. The letter directed him to come straight
to the White House and asked that he consider taking over
as the leader of the transition team for the new President.

    As we rode into town together, Don asked me if I
could get away from my job for a few days and help out
with the transition. I agreed to do so. That was about
2:00 p.m. on the day the President was sworn in. That
afternoon Ford spent virtually the first four or five hours
meeting with ambassadors. He wanted to reassure our
NATO allies that there would be no fundamental change in
policy due to Richard Nixon's resignation and that he would
continue the policies that were in place. He met with the
Soviet ambassador and others because he wanted to reassure
everyone around the world that the political crisis in the
American government would have no impact on policy.

Then, at about 5:00 p.m., he met with the transition team which consisted of Don Rumsfeld, Rogers Morton, Bob Griffin, Jack Marsh and others. His assignment to the transition team said a lot about the problems we faced in the Ford administration. The initial assignment was to look at the entire organization at the White House: the way the White House related to the Cabinet; how the Cabinet was organized; personnel; the Office of Management and Budget and so on. There was one area that was off limits, that we were not to get involved in. That, specifically, was the national security structure; we were not to study or make recommendations about the National Security Council, State, Defense or the CIA.

That complex of national security agencies was basically left untouched by the transition team which was clearly a reflection of the problem the President faced. On the one hand, there was a great need after the strife and turmoil of the Watergate years to reassure everyone, especially our allies and adversaries overseas, that we were going to emphasize continuity. On the other hand, after all of the scandal and turmoil of Watergate, domestically it was very important to emphasize change and the fact that the old crowd was out, that we had had a house cleaning at the White House and that the people who had been responsible for the Watergate scandals were no longer in power.

We lived with these conflicting objectives. We had to emphasize continuity, on one hand, and change, on the other. One of the ways Ford affected that at the outset was to order that we take a good, hard look and thoroughly scrub that whole set of relationships and organizational arrangements that was the domestic side of the White House. Yet he left the foreign policy and national security apparatus alone for the time being. This was partly a reflection of Henry Kissinger's influence. Henry was then head of the NSC and secretary of state, a unique arrangement in American history.

My beginning, then, was during that ten-day transition period. We wrote a report and I left at the end of that time. We were in a hurry to get the transition behind us, and we didn't want the transition team and the White House staff functioning side by side. We thought that would create great confusion. So around the twentieth of August or thereabouts, I left and went back to my business and Rumsfeld left and went back to NATO.

Then, around the second week in September, about a
week after the Nixon pardon, I received another phone call.
It was from Rumsfeld again, who was then in Chicago on a
home visit. I was in Florida on business, and he asked me
to meet him that weekend in Washington. I met him on a
Saturday afternoon and he indicated that he would have a
private meeting with the President the next afternoon. He
believed he was going to be offered the job as White House
chief of staff and he had reason to believe that Al Haig
was going to be asked to leave and take on a new
assignment as commander in chief of NATO and that he
would be asked to take over. He wanted to know what I
thought of that and whether, if he agreed to take the post,
I would agree to sign on as his deputy. We agreed that we
would get together the next afternoon after he had formally
received the offer from the President. He had the meeting
with the President on the following Sunday and we met
again that afternoon. He had agreed to accept the post and
I agreed to become his deputy.

Within two weeks I wrapped up my personal affairs and
by the end of September 1974, we took over at the White
House. We moved in on a weekend and the President
happened to be in the Oval Office on that Sunday. Don
went down to the Oval Office as I recall and got Ford and
brought him back down to the corner office in the west
wing that the chief of staff occupies. At that point he
introduced me to Ford for the first time. I had been in a
couple of larger meetings with him during the transition,
but he didn't know me personally and I didn't know him.

I was always amazed that he was so amenable to
having such a relatively young stranger—I think I was
thirty-three at the time—come in and all of a sudden become
a part of his inner operation. Yet there was never any
hesitancy on his part at all. He was such an open
individual, both privately and publicly, that there was no
concern on his part that I might not be loyal or in any way
less than committed to his success. He just assumed we all
were and I think that was a correct assumption most of the
time.

I served for about a year in that post as deputy and
approximately a year later in the fall of 1975, the President
made a decision to go back and reassess his earlier decision
not to look at the national security apparatus. In the fall
of 1975 he decided to relieve Henry Kissinger of his NSC

role, but leave him as secretary of state and appoint General Brent Scowcroft to run the NSC. He also decided he would fire Jim Schlesinger from his post as secretary of defense and send Rumsfeld over to the Pentagon. Part of that move was his decision to ask me to assume the chief of staff's job which, obviously, I was happy to do. It was a strange kind of thing in the sense that I went from being a subordinate of Don Rumsfeld's one morning to his former position of authority the next.

Decisions had been made a couple of weeks before, but there began to be some leaks on a Saturday, so on that Sunday morning we called Jim Schlesinger and others to the White House to implement the decision. The President had to fire those people who were involved. As difficult as Ford often found it to deal with personnel problems—no president ever finds that very comfortable and the fact is there are very few people who find that situation easy to deal with—for that morning he had made up his mind in no uncertain terms. It was the kind of situation in which he had stored up his dissatisfaction with an individual that had developed over a period of months. I don't mean to be critical of Jim Schlesinger; he's a great man and I'm not sure Ford made the right decision. The point is that it was the course that he wanted to take and finally, when he decided to do it, there was absolutely no way to persuade him to do anything else. It was just a "get him in here so I can fire him" attitude. That's what happened that morning.

Afterwards, we flew to Jacksonville, Florida for a summit meeting with President Sadat of Egypt, who was in the country for a couple of days. As we got ready to land in Jacksonville, the President summoned me to his compartment on Air Force One because we still had one major piece of unfinished business. (I was running the trip that day but Don Rumsfeld had not yet agreed to take the job as secretary of defense. The President assumed he would do it, but Don had never said yes.) My assignment when we landed in Jacksonville, was to get on the telephone and contact Rumsfeld and get a commitment from him to serve as secretary of defense. The day before he had been my boss, but that morning I was doing the President's bidding by trying to get Don to leave the job I was going to have; an interesting situation which actually worked out fairly well.

In terms of organizing the White House the way that
we wanted, we had some difficulties. One of the pieces of
conventional wisdom in Washington the summer of 1974
believed by politicians, the press and everyone else, was
that somehow the organizational arrangements of the Nixon
White House had contributed to Watergate. The theory was
that with a strong centralized chief of staff such as Nixon
had in Bob Haldeman, the president would get into
difficulty. Of course, you have the continuing debate in the
political science profession between the "Roosevelt model"
for organizing the White House with eight or nine senior
aids to the president and no one person in charge versus
the "Eisenhower model," with a strong chief of staff
(Sherman Adams). Nixon clearly operated along the
Eisenhower model, but everybody believed, I think
incorrectly at the time, that organizing the way Nixon had
been organized would very likely lead to the same kind of
scandal that ultimately destroyed his presidency.

When President Ford was asked what his philosophy
and style for organizing the White House was going to be,
he said he had a new concept called "the spokes of the
wheel." It meant that there would be no single individual
in charge, no gatekeeper. There were going to be eight or
nine senior aides, all of whom would report to the
President. We tried that and the fact is that it didn't
work. Within six months we had to scrap it. I recall that
during the transition period after Jimmy Carter was elected
in 1976 he was asked what his philosophy for managing the
White House was. Interestingly enough he said he didn't
believe in the chief of staff concept, but that he had a
brand new idea called "the spokes of the wheel." He used
the exact same phrase. Ford probably had gotten it from
Jack Kennedy or somebody else.

Anyway, there was this belief that the strong
centralized chief of staff was wrong. When I was ready to
leave the White House in January 1977, the staff had a
going away party for me, a sort of roast. They all had a
great time and gave me a number of gifts to commemorate
my service on the Ford staff. One of the things they gave
me was a bicycle wheel mounted on a piece of plywood. It
consisted of the rim and the hub and every single spoke
between the hub and the rim except one had been broken.
There was a little tag at the bottom of the board that said,
"The spokes of the wheel: a rare form of management

artistry devised by Don Rumsfeld and modified by Dick Cheney."

When I left the White House on January 20, 1977, I left that bicycle wheel mounted on a piece of plywood for Hamilton Jordan in the chief of staff's office with a note pinned to it saying, "Dear Hamilton, beware of the spokes of the wheel." The Carter people went through exactly the same process we did. It didn't work for us, and it didn't work for Carter. In terms of my own strongly held views on how you organize the White House, to talk about the Roosevelt model—which may have been appropriate in the thirties—in the 1980s and 1990s is silly. What it means is that no one is in charge. There is no accountability so no one accepts the responsibility for delivering bad news to the president. There has to be a structured system if you are going to have discipline and accountability in a White House staff and we quickly learned the importance of that kind of arrangement.

Early in the Ford administration we had problems with staffing and the decision-making process, partly because we had come to power in an unusual way. The vice president and President had both resigned under scandal within the year before Ford came to power. He had never run a nation-wide campaign. He had been a vice president with a small staff and a congressman with an even smaller staff before that. His own personal style was not at all related to the role of a strong executive and it was in those early days much more the style of a congressman.

I can recall instances in which the President would be in the cabinet room meeting with the National Security Council, working out a position for negotiations with the Soviets on the SALT talks, and a group of Rotarians from Grand Rapids would show up in the west wing lobby for their meeting with "Jerry." Of course he couldn't meet with them because he was meeting with the secretaries of state and defense and others. The system was so fouled up in those early weeks that many people were making commitments about who could see the President and who had access. Of course, somebody from Grand Rapids had called down and said they were going to be in Washington and that they would love to see "Jerry" when they got there. They still thought of him as their congressman instead of President. Whoever they talked to said, "Sure,

come on down." So forty Rotarians showed up in the west
wing office and we had to deal with them.

Eventually, we got away from that type of confusion.
As time went on, the President himself became a much more
efficient manager of his time and the resources available to
him. At first, he was fairly uncritical of the staff and the
briefing papers that were prepared for him. Oftentimes he
would spend too much time in meetings that were going
nowhere. Decisions that should have been made crisply
weren't made crisply. Presentations to him were sloppy and
disorganized. He had the normal congressman's tolerance
for that when he first became president.

I speak as a congressman; I don't mean to malign the
tendency. Congressmen are paid to be close to the people,
to represent their constituents and to see anybody who
wants to see them. Presidents don't have time for that.
Gradually over time President Ford acquired all of those
skills, and by the end of his presidency he was a very
tough customer to deal with. If papers were not prepared
properly and were not in on time, he canceled the meeting.
If the presentations didn't look like they were a wise and
efficient use of his time, he would cancel the meeting and
tell them to leave and come back when they were ready to
talk to him again, because he became much better at that.
There was a learning process and he certainly went through
that.

In terms of our relations with Congress, I think it is
important to remember the context within which those
relationships were played out. Ford had been a member of
Congress for twenty-five years. He was a man who loved
the House and aspired only to be speaker of the House of
Representatives, not president. Nonetheless, he came to
power at a time when the relationships between Congress
and president were probably the lowest they had been in a
hundred years. The only equivalent period was in the 1860s
during the impeachment of Andrew Johnson.

The result was a series of institutional confrontations
during the late Nixon and early Ford years that, in my
opinion, led repeatedly to efforts on the part of the
Congress to impose limitations and restrictions on the
president. It wasn't personal and it wasn't directed at Ford
in that sense. It was institutional in the sense that it was
directed at the presidency. The main concern in the
Congress often seemed to be to find ways to restrict

presidential power so that future presidents would not abuse power the way Lyndon Johnson had allegedly abused power in Vietnam or Richard Nixon had abused presidential power in the Watergate affair. Thus we ended up with things like the Turkish Arms embargo in the summer of 1974 which limited our ability to deal with a key NATO ally because of the Cyprus crisis; the War Powers Act that limited the president's ability to commit troops overseas; the Clark Amendment in late 1975 that prohibited U.S. involvement in Angola; the Budget Reform Act of 1974; legislative vetoes and so forth. The whole series of actions that were taken made life difficult if you worked at the other end of Pennsylvania Avenue.

The President, who had a great warmth and affection for the House, was capable, after he had been in the White House for a few months, of going behind the closed doors of the oval office and saying some very tough things about his former colleagues. It was a very different perspective when he got down to 1600 Pennsylvania Avenue.

There were also a couple of other important factors that need to be kept in mind when we look at presidential-congressional relations. One, of course, was the Nixon pardon itself. That pardon led to the unprecedented Ford testimony before the House Judiciary Committee to explain why he had pardoned Richard Nixon. It was only the second time in history that the president had ever done that. (The first time the President was Abraham Lincoln.) It led also to some extent to the electoral defeat in which we Republicans lost over forty seats in the House in the 1974 election. Almost immediately after the President came to power, as a result of the election in November of 1974, we found ourselves outnumbered about two to one in both the House and the Senate. That in turn meant that we had virtually no options *vis-à-vis* Congress but to pursue a veto strategy. We were not able to operate the way Lyndon Johnson had in his first two years or the way FDR had in the 1930s. Even Ronald Reagan today has an easier time with the Congress. In the mid-1970s, we were down to about 140 seats in the House and were badly outnumbered in the Senate. That shaped our whole strategy. Obviously, the impact of the 1974 election was very important.

In organizing the White House for policy-making purposes, we took the Nixon mechanisms and pretty much adapted them to our own uses, rather than invent new

organizations. The Reagan administration has followed a
very similar pattern. One of the big problems that we had
was the vice president's role generally, and his
responsibilities in the domestic council. President Ford,
because he had been vice president, was bound and
determined to give significant responsibilities to Vice
President Rockefeller and Vice President Rockefeller was not
a bashful man: he was eager to get all the power and
authority he could. I don't mean that in a negative sense,
but the key arrangement that they came to was that
Rockefeller would essentially serve as the President's chief
domestic policy adviser, and that he would have control of
the Domestic Council. He would staff it, decide who those
few people were going to be, etc. In short, he was
responsible for the "Domestic Council."

The basic mission of the Domestic Council is to create
new policy and come up with new initiatives: health,
education, and other such areas. The only problem with
that was that it was in direct contradiction of our veto
strategy on Capitol Hill. It was also unwise in light of the
fact that we were coming out of a recession and that we
had made a judgment in terms of macro-economic policy
that we didn't want any new starts. We built in a major
institutional conflict with Nelson Rockefeller, a strong,
dynamic political leader in his own right. Ford gave him a
mandate to come up with new starts but, on the other hand,
there weren't going to be any new starts. So every time
the Vice President would go into the Oval Office for his
weekly meeting with the President, he would come in with
some new proposal. It might be a new health insurance
scheme or some other kind of package he wanted to pursue
and the President would take it and review it. Ford would
usually sit on it for the rest of the day and when I would
go in for the evening wrap-up session with him he would
hand that to me among all the other things and ask, "What
are we going to do with this?" I'd say, "Well, Mr.
President, we'll staff it out." So I would take it and put it
through the staff mechanism.

The proposal, if it dealt with energy, for example,
would go to the Energy Department, then to the Council of
Economic Advisers and to all those agencies with anything
to say about it. Then their comments would come back in
so that we could go to the President for a decision. Of
course, what we always got from the staff in this process

was word that this recommendation was inconsistent with our basic policy of no new starts.

The Vice President came to a point that he was absolutely convinced that Don Rumsfeld and I were out to scuttle whatever new initiatives he could come up with. In terms of the relationship between Ford and Rockefeller, it never caused serious problems. They got along very well, even after they left the White House. Ford used to be able to get financial advice from Nelson Rockefeller—not a bad arrangement—and their relationship was very good. The friction between the White House staff and the vice president's office focused specifically on that early decision that Nelson Rockefeller would in fact be in charge of domestic policy. It was an institutional problem. I don't know any way to clean it up. There was a rumor (though I've never been able to confirm it) that Vice President Rockefeller told President Ford that he would not serve as vice president in the second Ford administration unless he could also be White House chief of staff. He could then do what he wanted.

I have another brief anecdote on the Vice President. I was not at all critical of Vice President Rockefeller; in fact, I was a fan of his. I will always remember his appearance before the San Francisco Republican convention in 1964. It was a great moment of political drama. However, he and I inevitably developed a very strained relationship which probably hit bottom when they opened the new vice president's residence in Washington. When Ford was vice president, the government acquired an official residence for the vice president for the first time. It was the old chief of naval operations' house on Observatory Hill and Ford never got a chance to move in because he became president first. So Rockefeller inherited the responsibility of fixing up the residence. After it was all completed, renovated, furnished and so forth he had a series of parties for virtually everybody in Washington. He had all the press, congressmen and administration over. Essentially, everyone in Washington over GS12 got invited to the vice president's residence—except me. I was never to attend a function there until Walter Mondale was vice president. It wasn't a personal conflict as far as I was concerned, but it was a friction inherent in our positions.

In terms of relationships between the White House staff and the Cabinet, I would generally give them fairly high marks. What happened to us improved as we moved through the administration. We started like all administrations do, with a Cabinet meeting every week. Of course, by the end of the term we probably had one a month, because cabinet meetings are basically irrelevant to the function of the government.

The Cabinet is not a viable entity from the standpoint of the president's daily operations. Subcommittees of the Cabinet are very important but you really don't care what the secretary of Housing and Urban Development has to say about the conflict between North and South Yemen in the Red Sea. He has nothing to contribute and he has got other things to worry about. The secretary of state has his interests but doesn't care a lot about the corn prices in Iowa. Getting that collection of people together once a week provides a nice "show and tell" time, but it is basically a group that doesn't have any relevance for policy-making. You must break the cabinet down into smaller groups, which is what all administrations do in the end and what we did.

On the foreign policy side, obviously, Secretary Kissinger was a dominant figure throughout the administration. That broadened a little bit later on, as the President became more experienced and confident in his own judgments in foreign policy. He would reach out to include a larger number of people in the process. In the economic policy arena, we used the Economic Policy Board concept, which is similar to the vehicle that is used now for Reagan. It was a subcommittee of the cabinet comprised of all those people who had economic policy responsibilities. This system established a formal mechanism for everybody to get a shot at the staff papers before they went to the President.

Ford would thoroughly discuss the issues around the table in the Cabinet room before he made a decision. Often, he would not make a decision at the meeting. Once the meeting was over he would go back into the Oval Office and then maybe have a private chat with Arthur Burns. Ford and Burns had great respect for one another and used to talk a lot privately in the Oval Office on a regular basis. He would also consult Alan Greenspan, chairman of the Council of Economic Advisers, and Jim Lynn. It was not unusual after a major meeting on some major policy, for the President to go back into the Oval Office and then maybe later in the day, ask me to get Greenspan and Lynn over. Then we would sit down and he would talk to the two of them. That's where he really decided what he was going to do. Of course, he had been briefed and everybody else had had the opportunity to give him advice and input at the beginning.

There were some fairly typical problems with the Cabinet. There is a natural tendency for the Cabinet to believe that the White House staff is interfering with the relationship between Cabinet and President. It is true. The fact of the matter is that everybody in the Cabinet represents a parochial interest; even Henry Kissinger did. He may have worried about the world; he may have had a global perspective, but he had loyalty to the State Department. He didn't have a Defense Department perspective or CIA perspective when it came to talking to the President. Everybody in the Cabinet is a special interest pleader in that sense. I don't mean that in a negative sense, but they are there because they have expertise in particular policy areas. There are really only a handful of people around the president who can truly be described as generalists in that their jobs are to worry not only about the foreign policy considerations, but also about economic policy implications. These people are on board to see to it that all of a president's units are pulled together.

Cabinet members, left to their own devices, want wide-open access to the president. They want to be able to walk in and talk to him face to face about their problem, to get a decision from him and then implement it. If they are good executives and strong advocates in their areas, that's the way they want to operate. However, that scenario is the last thing you want to have if you are a staff member of the president. This isn't due to jealously; rather it is because it is absolutely vital that the president get a broader perspective, and not just the opinion of the advocate of a particular course of action. If only the advocate is allowed in the Oval Office and the contrary point of view isn't presented, the president is going to get blind-sided; he's going to make an ill-informed decision.

A classic example, and the story I like to tell to illustrate this, involved John Dunlop. John, our labor secretary, noted labor expert, professor at Harvard, and a very strong member of our cabinet, got us involved in what I like to call an "oh-by-the-way" decision. An "oh-by-the-way" decision was something the White House staff people feared. It would bring cold terror to your heart to think about an "oh-by-the-way" decision. That's what would happen when somebody would go into the Oval Office to talk to the president about the issue they had asked to discuss in that meeting. They would deal with that piece of business, which was all right, since we would prepare him. But, the cabinet member would get up, and as he headed out the door he would turn to the President and say, "Oh, by the way, Mr. President," and he then would bring up a totally unrelated issue to try to get some kind of guidance from the President on it. (See Dunlop, p. 299).

Well, John Dunlop did that one day. John went in and did the business he was there for, got ready to leave and on his way out said, "Oh, by the way Mr. President, there is this issue coming up called 'common *situs* picketing.'" Common *situs* picketing is an issue that had been around Washington for a long time. It is a legal term that refers to the power of a labor union to shut down a construction site. It's a very controversial issue that had been around Washington at that point for twenty-five years. Labor was always pushing to broaden their authority to shut down construction sites with strikes and Congress had never granted it. Well, it was coming up again and John Dunlop had to go testify. So he said, "Mr. President, I think we ought to support common *situs* picketing. I think that would be a very useful thing for us to do." The President said, "Fine, John, sounds okay to me." So John left and went to Capitol Hill and testified. He put the administration four-square behind 'common *situs* picketing' legislation. For twenty-five years it had been around and nothing had ever happened to it. Lo and behold, we couldn't get anything else passed, but they passed common *situs* picketing. It went all the way through the Congress and landed on the President's desk.

Now, when we first endorsed it, the business community went wild. We were buried in mail. By the time the bill had passed, he had all of the political arguments against it, as well as some substantive arguments. So after a great deal of agonizing, he decided to veto the bill. Well then labor went wild. We got more mail on common *situs* picketing than we got on the Nixon pardon.

After we had antagonized business, antagonized labor and, incidentally given our political opponents a great device for raising money against us, John Dunlop came in and said "You know, Mr. President, I went up there in good faith and you told me I could support common *situs* picketing. My credibility is at stake. I quit." So we lost a labor secretary as well. All of that for thirty seconds in the Oval Office from an "oh-by-the-way" decision. It is the best example I have for showing the constant inevitable friction between the White House staff and cabinet members. It also clearly points out why it is important to have White House staff that are going to say to the cabinet member before he goes in, "Look, we know you are for it John, but it is in the interest of the President to have those who are against it in there at the same time so that he hears both views before he makes a decision." That was one basis for occasional conflicts in our administration.

The worst conflicts in terms of personal relationships were inside the White House. There is no question about it. We had conflicts between the old Nixon carryovers, and the new Ford staffers. The Nixon hands who were there when President Ford arrived knew how the White House ought to operate. Most of them were absolutely first-rate people untainted by Watergate in any shape or form. The old Ford people had been with President Ford either when he was a congressman on the Hill or since he joined the administration as vice president. We had to meld those two groups together and it wasn't very easy to do. There were those of us, like myself and Rumsfeld, who had worked in the Nixon administration and then left. We were brought back and I suppose we were probably better able to bridge that gulf between the old Ford aides and the old Nixon aides than anyone else.

My own impression of it is that the staff came together in reasonably good shape. There were isolated problems throughout the administration, but, as a general proposition, a great many very able and talented people who had worked for President Nixon became the heart and soul of the Ford administration. It wouldn't have been possible to run the administration without them. I would include in that group everyone from Henry Kissinger to Paul O'Neill to Frank Zarb to the core of the White House staff. A lot of the people who worked directly for me, for example, served in the Nixon administration and then continued under President Ford. That tension did create some problems, however. I think there were old Ford staffers who resented the Nixon staff people's influence. Still, it wasn't so much two camps as it was a few isolated problems.

Among the main crises or problems, I would include the assumption of office. When the vice president suddenly is asked to be president of the United States and his predecessor is on the verge of impeachment by the Congress, that's a crisis. The pardon itself was a major exigency which ultimately led to the congressional testimony. I always felt the pardon was the right thing to do, although the way in which it was done, I thought, was inappropriate. I thought it should have been delayed until after the 1974 elections because I think it did cost us seats. If you say that that is a political judgment, it's true, but then, the presidency is a political office. If we had had twenty or thirty more House Republicans during the two years of the Ford presidency, we would have been in much better shape than we were from a legislative standpoint.

The pardon was also handled poorly in terms of notifying other players. We could have gone to Capitol Hill and to other prominent Americans and talked about the Nixon pardon before it was done. That way, we might have built some support and understanding for it around the country. When we totally surprised everybody, it generated the kind of reaction that obviously created big problems for us. It really was unheard of that a president would go to Capitol Hill and put himself in a position where he was subject to interrogation by members of the Judiciary Committee. It had to be done to dampen the criticism that had boiled up over the pardon itself. I think the pardon decision was correct, though that's easy for me to say because I wasn't there when it happened.

In terms of other issues, the whole collapse of our position in Southeast Asia in the spring of 1975 was a major setback. We really appeared in the final act, if you will, of a decade-long U.S. involvement in South Vietnam. We had to preside over the final demise and it was not at all a pleasant or an easy task. I think today we still are wrestling with the legacy of Vietnam. The *Mayaguez* incident was another crisis. It was a short-term kind of problem that was significant symbolically partly because of all the focus that it got at the time. Substantively, it is only a footnote in history. Lebanon was a crucial issue too. It is interesting to compare Reagan's approach in Lebanon with Ford's approach ten years earlier. I thought the Ford approach was far more effective. When things started to get nasty inside Lebanon—we lost our ambassador at one point—we sent in the navy and evacuated all Americans. I think that was the right response then and I think probably would have been the right response in 1982.

I would also identify two other areas that were of continuing concern from the policy standpoint. The economy fluctuated in 1974-75, first because of very high inflation and then a very severe recession followed by the energy crisis throughout that period. Finally the 1976 campaign was in many respects a series of crises all the way from New Hampshire in February of 1976 when we won by 1,300 votes, to the convention in Kansas City with a lot of wins and losses in between, to the final outcome in November.

If I were to cite two problems that I feel in hindsight that Ford had, one was his lack of executive experience when he became president, although that was corrected over time. It's difficult to find any appropriate training ground for the presidency. Secondly, in terms of loyalty to subordinates, I felt that on balance there were times when certain people on the staff should have been fired and weren't. One of those things we all liked about Ford was that he is a kind, warm man. Most of us today, if he picked up the telephone and called, would do absolutely anything he asked. We all loved him because of his warmth and character. At the same time, it meant that people did things that they should have been chastised for and weren't.

In terms of his strengths, I would cite his personal growth during the time he was president as an important strength. Another is that he was a very good decision-maker. He was a man who was able to sit down and listen to debates. He never cut off an individual's access because that person disagreed with him. He relished the give and take of political dialogue. I think that's very important. Having listened to everybody else agonize over a problem, he was then very good at making the decision and not worrying about it and at moving on to the next step. There were moments in crises I can recall when everybody else was losing their heads and he was just as solid as a rock, following through on a decision he had made earlier.

I would also give him high marks for his very wide knowledge of government. Oftentimes I don't think this quality came through to the public, because he was not a man who was especially articulate. There were times when President Ford did not speak effectively enough to convey his impressive ideas.

His knowledge and grasp of government and political issues was just enormous. He spent a great deal of time on the budget, and he knew a great deal more about it than anybody else in government. In 1976 he briefed the press on the budget all by himself. Not since Harry Truman thirty years before had a president been able to stand up in front of the Washington press corps and give a briefing on the entire budget without a note and without any help from the cabinet and the head of the OMB sitting behind him. It was a masterful performance on his part, and showed his enormous depth and grasp of the government. But occasionally he was not as effective verbally at articulating his keen understanding.

Finally, the nation was fortunate to have a man of Ford's character in office. I can't think of another man who has become president under such adverse or difficult circumstances (with the possible exception perhaps of Abraham Lincoln a hundred years before), who by virtue of who he was, the way he carried himself and the way he operated was able to restore the integrity of the presidency. When history ultimately judges and evaluates Ford, the calming, therapeutic nature of his tenure will be praised. He was there when the country most needed him and was especially effective at binding up the wounds and restoring the most important institution of our society.

QUESTION: It is quite clear that graduate work at two institutions and the congressional fellowship of the American Political Science Association has established Dick Cheney for all time as a teacher in the political field. If the voters of Wyoming get at all restless, he ought to let Virginia know.

What isn't so clear is what in his background—the Governor Knowles episode, the Congressman Steiger episode, the price control period, the OEO or any of the other things he did—prepared him best for the post of chief of staff. Is there any part of your experience that you would recommend to others who at some point might have that responsibility?

MR. CHENEY: Well, I'm not sure what I would highlight in that regard. Obviously, I developed a love for politics in those earlier experiences. If you were to have sent out a search team to look for a chief of staff when President Ford was trying to replace Don Rumsfield in the fall of 1975, you would not have picked a thirty-four year old graduate school drop-out for the job.

I think probably the thing that best qualified me for the job, and the reason he offered it to me, was my work the previous year. I had had the good fortune to serve as Rumsfeld's deputy for a year. To Don's great credit, he was the kind of man, as was Jerry Ford, who was perfectly happy to give me a big piece of the action. A lot of executives and their senior advisers or assistants—I think this may well be true in the present case with Reagan, and I know it was true in the Nixon administration with Haldeman—would never have allowed a subordinate in the Oval Office by himself. Shortly after I had started working there, Don and I had worked out an arrangement. Part of the understanding when I took the job was that I would get access to the President and that I would be Rumsfeld's surrogate. When he wasn't around, I would be in a position to make decisions for him and to operate as though I had his job. We agreed at the outset that we would alternate trips. He would take one presidential trip and I would stay in the White House and run it; the next time I'd go on the trip and he'd stay at the White House. This gave me a great opportunity to get to know the President.

To the President's credit, he was willing to have somebody that had never been around him and never served on his staff before have close contact. He didn't know me personally until the day he walked into that corner office and met me for the first time, yet he let me come in and deal with the most sensitive political and national security issues, or whatever it was that we had to cope with. He was just as comfortable with me walking into the office as with Don. That experience for a year meant that by the time he wanted to send Rumsfeld over to the Pentagon, it was a logical and normal thing for me to step in because I had already been doing a significant part of the job for a year. As I said, I can think of other administrations where it simply wouldn't have worked.

For example, during the Nixon administration, there was a colonel from the military office who used to get the presidential summary or schedule every day. Shortly after President Ford was sworn in and I came on board in

October 1974, my name started to show up on the schedule.
Entries read, "Cheney in the Oval Office for thirty minutes."
This military aide received a copy of the schedule one day
and he sent it to the guy who occupied the office that I
had taken over during the Nixon years. He evidently told
his secretary to send this schedule to George somebody.
His secretary didn't know that that guy was gone and I was
now in the office, so I got this schedule by accident. He
had circled my name on the schedule and in a note to his
old friend, wrote beside it, "Can you believe this?" I saved
that for about six months and then I went to see him to let
him know I had received it. He was very cooperative from
then on.

QUESTION: Allow me to invoke the caricature that the
popular press presents of any complex person like a
president whom it must oversimplify. The simplified image
of Ford was perhaps not very flattering; oftentimes the
press presented him as a very clumsy, inarticulate person. I
wonder if you would elaborate a bit on the relationship to
the press, your attempts to relate to it, manipulate it, use
it, and the role of that image. How did you relate to that
image as you did the job?

MR. CHENEY: The image was a problem, and I must say
that Lyndon Johnson had contributed to its being rather
negative. Lyndon Johnson was the original source of the
quote that Jerry Ford couldn't walk and chew gum at the
same time. It was a cheap shot but it stuck. (Actually,
"walk and chew gum at the same time" is not what Lyndon
Johnson said, but you can't repeat his words in polite
company!) That false image was strong enough so that
when Ford came on board, it was something we had to deal
with on a regular basis. I think it was accentuated by the
President's speaking style. On occasion his remarks may
have sounded less than articulate and I think that
contributed to his problem.

Sometimes we were just plain unlucky. I can remember
a trip in which Ford went out to California and spoke to a
large group. He was upstairs in the room they had set
aside for him after the speech and was getting ready to
leave to go to the airport. The secret service likes to move
the president on the freight elevators because they are more
secure and in this instance, it was one of these elevators

with doors that open vertically instead of horizontally.
Well, he was on that elevator and as the elevator landed on
the main floor, the top door went up and the President
started to step out. (He had a secret service agent on each
side of him, both of them shorter than he was.) The door
went up, caught and then bounced back down and hit him
right across the top of the head, knocking him to his knees.
We got him back on the elevator and took him back upstairs
to the suite.   I still have a picture of Dr. Lukash, his
personal physician, holding an ice bag on the President's
head to stop the bleeding.   We took care of that incident,
got back on the elevator, went back downstairs to the
ground floor, walked outside on the street and Sara Jane
Moore took a shot at him.   It was all in the same day
within about thirty minutes. Now that was just a bum day.

     He was very active athletically.   He was the first
president to ski since Teddy Roosevelt; he played tennis,
swam and golfed very aggressively.   Nonetheless, the press
oftentimes—and this is more aggravating than anything
else—would get a shot of him falling down in the snow.
You know, I ski all the time; I love it but I've never been
on a mountain that I haven't fallen down at least once.
Nobody on the press corps could ski. They couldn't follow
him down the mountain.   They had to stand down at the
bottom to catch him but they would still peddle any mishap
as an indication of clumsiness.

     It was the combination of that, the rap from Lyndon
Johnson, and occasional policy problems that led to this
notion of a bungling, stumbling, Jerry Ford.   Of course
Chevy Chase on "Saturday Night Live" didn't help either.
Once you get to the point at which something becomes a
stock gag on Johnny Carson's "Tonight Show" or one of
those kinds of TV shows, that label sticks and you can't get
rid of it.   I reiterate that it is very hard to get rid of,
though we did try sometimes very successfully to deal with
that problem.

     One of the things we did was the budget briefing I
mentioned earlier.   It was the beginning of the 1976
campaign and one of the raps on Jerry Ford was that he
just wasn't very smart or a very good manager.   We very
consciously set up this briefing and had the President brief
the entire press corps on the budget because there wasn't
anybody else in town that could do it.   That really helped
dissipate the negative image.   We were successful through

most of the 1976 campaign in avoiding that. However, one of the reasons the second debate with Carter in San Francisco on foreign policy hurt so much was because it raised again the question of intellectual competence. The statement by the President that Poland is not dominated by the Soviet Union was at the heart of the problem. It wasn't the content of what he said so much as this impression that it created once again that he didn't know Poland was dominated by the Soviet Union.

Right after the event that night, we tried to focus the White House press corps on who won the debate in hopes of getting our spin on the story. As soon as we got Ford home that night after the debate, Stu Spencer, General Scowcroft and I went down to the hotel in San Francisco where the White House press and campaign corps were assembled. There were about two hundred reporters, all with their cameras set up, ready to go. As we walked up on the podium, Lou Cannon of the *Washington Post* who was a good friend, yelled at me from the back of the room. He said, "Hey Cheney, how many Soviet divisions are there in Poland?" We knew immediately that was going to be the word on that story. We did try to cope with that specific image and I think oftentimes we were successful, but never completely. It did haunt us throughout his time in the White House.

QUESTION: If there are so many inconsistencies in our current President, contradicting statements week after week with seemingly no impact on his image, would you fault the press corp for being less than intellectually honest, or would you fault yourself for not understanding the intricacies of the game? How do you account for this difference?

MR. CHENEY: Luck. No, it's more than that. On my part the immediate reaction is one of envy. All politicians wish they could operate the way Ronald Reagan does and get away with it. He's the ablest manipulator of the symbolic aspects of the presidency I've seen in a long time. It's one of his great strengths and successes. We were never able to do that. We tried very hard. Many times I think it had to do with problems and conflicts we had internally about who was going to write a speech and what they would say. In part, I think it has to do with the fact that President

Ford was clearly oriented toward the substance of policy, the nitty gritty detail of what our negotiating position was going to be on SALT or something like that. At a press conference he rarely failed to deal with the crucial issues. If you go back and look, the Ford press conferences are substantively very good.

Reagan's press conferences are a disaster. I'm nervous every time I watch him do it; I'm always disappointed in the quality of his responses. It's kind of hesitant, kind of fuzzy, and sometimes it's completely wrong and has to be corrected later. Maybe this is his acting background, and again I think he does it unconsciously, but Reagan has this enormous capacity to represent the basic fundamental spirit in the American people. He appeals to them in ways that they understand, ways that keep emphasizing fundamental things. There is no question that you may have some trouble getting him to describe for you in any great detail, the substance of his policy. He's for tax reform, but he can't tell you about how his bill treats capital gains or investment tax credits or anything else. Up there on that broad plane of those who favor tax reform though, there is no question about where Ronald Reagan stands. He operates at that level in a way that many of us who spend our professional lives in Washington don't.

I think Jerry Ford's strength, his enormous knowledge of government, was a product of the same system of which I'm a product. Reagan isn't bound down by all of that detail. While sometimes it's frustrating and occasionally it's a weakness, it is also a strength.

QUESTION: I was in the U.N. General Assembly in 1974 when President Ford appeared and spoke. Dr. Kissinger was there and, in fact, I thought President Ford was the politest head of state that we in the U.N. ever saw. He was always praising Dr. Kissinger and trying to promote his secretary of state in the General Assembly forum. I would like to know if there was a foreign policy decision-making process, whether President Ford and Dr. Kissinger had some diversion of views, and in that case, whether you, Mr. Cheney, or Secretary Rumsfeld effectively intervened in favor of the President?

MR. CHENEY: I think the Kissinger example you mentioned is interesting. One of the things President Ford did when he first took over was to show that he wanted to emphasize the continuity of government and thereby reassure people based upon the way he dealt with Kissinger. He kept Kissinger on board and talked about Henry Kissinger all the time when he went to the United Nations. He did all this primarily because he assumed the rest of the world didn't know who Jerry Ford was and that was a correct assumption at the time. After all, he was a congressman from the fifth district of Michigan. Thus, in the selection of these key slots and in his decision to keep Kissinger and give him such a prominent role, he sent a message of reassurance to the rest of the world. They also knew who Nelson Rockefeller was: he was an international figure in his own right; he had been a presidential candidate and governor of one of our larger states. There was an effort to convey a sense that everything was going to be okay, that this man makes wise decisions and selects people with weight.

In terms of the way foreign policy was made, it would be fair to say that at the outset it was strictly a Ford/Kissinger kind of operation. Kissinger functioned oftentimes as a tutor, which a good national security adviser will do. Very few presidents ever come into office with the expertise and knowledge in foreign policy they need. If they have a good national security adviser, those early months are almost a tutorial for the president in what he needs to know to be an effective foreign policy leader of the country.

Later on, I think, it would be fair to say that the circle was broadened a bit. There was some criticism of that decision, both in the press and internally as well. The idea was that Henry Kissinger was basically making all foreign policy decisions and the President was making none. The President to some extent fed it by the kind of behavior he exhibited at the United Nations. It did create problems from time to time because there were occasional difficulties with other cabinet members who disagreed with the Kissinger point of view or who disliked the perception that somehow Henry Kissinger was in charge and Jerry Ford was not.

There were occasional staff conflicts. I can remember a particularly bad situation in the 1976 campaign shortly before the Texas primary. Henry Kissinger was off in South Africa trying to deal with the South African problem. We got advice from the political side of the shop that that was not a good thing to be doing just before the Texas primary. President Ford sat down, considered it and in this case made, I think, the appropriate decision. He said, "Look, we have to deal with the South African problem one way or the other and I'm not going to let my desire to deal with South Africa be interfered with by alleged racism in Texas in connection with the upcoming primary." So Henry went off to South Africa and we lost Texas one hundred percent. We didn't get a single delegate out of Texas, in part because of that decision.

The President made the right foreign policy decision in that case, not the "political" decision. At the time of the *Mayaguez* incident a decision had been made to launch air strikes on the port of Sihanoukville and to land Marines on an island of the Cambodian coast. The height of the crisis occurred during a state dinner in the White House for the Dutch prime minister. It was a black tie affair and periodically the President would have to step out while we briefed him on what was going on or to make some last minute decision. As we wound down towards the end of the crisis, after having already made these decisions, deployed the resources and ordered the air strikes, Secretary Kissinger suddenly became very nervous. Henry was a great strategic thinker; he was not very good at the moment of truth in a crisis. He became very nervous and upset all of a sudden and very uncertain about the decisions that had been made. He wanted to back off and reconsider it again. President Ford was the one who was as solid as a rock and said, "No, Henry, we've made the decision. It's the right thing to do and we're going to do it full speed ahead."

I can think of another example in connection with the SALT talks, probably one of our most contentious foreign policy issues. There were repeated sessions of the National Security Council as we went through the negotiating process. We had been to Vladivostok in the Fall of 1974 and made that major breakthrough with Brezhnev on the Vladivostok Accord. We met with Brezhnev again in Helsinki in the Summer of 1975 and had several bilateral meetings with him there again in connection with the arms control talks.

By late 1975 and early 1976 we were coming up on the campaign at home and we knew that foreign policy might be an issue in the Republican primaries. We knew that Reagan was likely to attack Ford over detente and Kissinger, which he did. We had not been able to resolve the differences within the administration to reach an agreement. In January of 1976, Kissinger went off to Moscow for one last effort to resolve these differences. We had several meetings at the National Security Council with messages back and forth. That was the case in which, in the final analysis, though I don't think the President liked it very much, Ford bought the Defense Department's position that what Kissinger could get from the Russians at that point was inadequate, that we should not close the deal on SALT. That stopped the SALT negotiations partly because we didn't want it to become an issue in that campaign. So there was a case in fact, where he didn't go along with Henry but went along with his other advisers.

QUESTION: Since President Ford was investigated before he was approved by the Senate on his finances, what was his reason for permitting this special prosecutor, whom I think he could have controlled, to investigate him during the campaign with Carter? To what extent do you think this slowed his momentum in that election?

MR. CHENEY: That's a good question that very few people ever ask; it was a key event. The allegation that appeared first in the *Wall Street Journal* was that Ford had received illicit money from labor unions—maritime unions specifically—funneled to him under the table while he was a member of Congress. The allegations had been thoroughly investigated by the FBI before he was confirmed. He underwent the most massive full field investigation in history before he became vice president. Nelson Rockefeller was the only other man who has been under that kind of microscope before the House and Senate would confirm him as vice president.

That allegation had been checked out and found to be false. But the special prosecutor was still in existence. That was part of the legacy of Watergate. With the special prosecutor there, we couldn't abolish the position without resolving the allegation. It would have been a terrible political problem. It would be the Saturday night massacre all over again. If we had tried to tamper with that process at all, word would have gotten out immediately, so we were stuck with it. The allegation arose and became public around the time of the second debate. If you remember the campaign events of 1976, we had a long struggle for the nomination. We finally won it from Reagan in August in Kansas City. But in July, Carter was nominated and at the end of July there was a Gallup poll that showed Ford was thirty-three points behind Jimmy Carter. There was a massive gulf we had to close. And then we started to roll.

After the August convention, we made major progress and then on Labor Day we hit the ground running, challenged Carter to the debates and did well on the first debate. We really had things going for us in September up to mid-October. Then, a couple of things happened. One was the second debate, which hurt us. The main thing, I think, was that suddenly here was a question about the ethics of Jerry Ford. For ten days the story ran in the *Wall Street Journal* and CBS hit it hard too. Some of the others played it much more softly, but they hit it hard enough. We were in a situation where all we could do was demand a very rapid resolution to this question from the special prosecutor. We didn't tell him how to resolve it, we didn't tell him what he ought to come up with, and we didn't control him. Given the Nixon experience just two years before, we had no choice but just to sit back and take it. For ten days we were dead in the water until that was finally resolved and the report was ultimately issued. Of course it said there was nothing to the charges and that it had been checked out before. But the report didn't come out in twenty-four hours; it took ten days and it certainly did hurt.

QUESTION: Would you have been more comfortable with someone other than Nelson Rockefeller as vice president and what, if any, do you think Rockefeller's contributions were while he was in office?

MR. CHENEY: I think Nelson Rockefeller made a considerable contribution. He did exactly what Ford wanted to have done. He was a man of great reputation and stature and Ford needed that in his vice president and Nelson Rockefeller gave him that.

Secondly, he was extremely loyal to Jerry Ford in spite of all the difficulties internally with the staff and the fact that he was not going to be vice president in the second Ford term. He submitted his letter of resignation in the fall of 1975. As we went through the struggle with Ronald Reagan there was a time when it appeared we were falling behind. We lost five primaries in a row, and we were in big trouble in terms of capturing the nomination. We won those early primaries and then we were beaten in North Carolina and came back and won Wisconsin on the first of April. Then we had a hiatus when we went down to Texas. But Texas, Indiana—there was a series of five primaries in which we were absolutely hammered. We had to have a big chunk of delegates committed to the President so that we could regain some momentum and stay ahead of Reagan. We got them out of New York, and we got them with Nelson Rockefeller's help. He said, "Anytime you want them, Mr. President, they are yours." He delivered one hundred and eight delegates to us. Even though he himself wasn't going to be on the ticket, he was intensely loyal to Jerry Ford, and I would always give him very high marks in that regard.

Under different circumstances he would have been very good in the domestic policy area but Ford to some extent created that conflict. Ford made both the decision to give Nelson Rockefeller a mandate to create new programs and also made the decision, a correct one I think, that there weren't going to be any new programs. That's what created the internal difficulties that we were faced with.

Would I have picked somebody else? Perhaps. If you think back to August 1974, you recognize that the very first job Jerry Ford had when he became President of the United States was to pick a vice president, a potential successor. It is perfectly normal and understandable why he did what he did, which was to look for the man with the most stature. Bryce Harlow helped him make that decision. Bryce is, in my opinion, one of the great men in Washington and has been there a lot of times over the years when very important things have happened. In 1976, when we got ready to pick a vice president at the convention, the President pulled out of his desk drawer in the Oval Office this long chart with all the pluses and minuses laid out on all the people he considered in 1974. The guy who put the chart together for him was Bryce Harlow.

I talked to Bryce about the whole operation. Bryce emphasized the theme that Ford wanted to reassure people by picking a man of stature. If, on the other hand he had been thinking in cold, hard-headed political terms in August of 1974, he would have known a couple of things: that Ronald Reagan was going to be his challenger for the nomination in 1976; that Reagan was likely to run against him. Reagan was already, at that point, in his last year of the governorship and everybody assumed that he was going to run for president in 1976. He would have known he was going to have problems with the right of the party and that the last thing he needed was Nelson Rockefeller who was anathema to the conservative wing of the Republican party. But I don't think any of those thoughts entered Ford's head. I don't think when he made that decision the first week or two that he was in office that he gave any thought at all to the 1976 election. He was looking to reassure the country and the world that he was a man who was capable of being president and that would be reflected in the quality of the person he picked for the job.

QUESTION: Could he have ever thought of Reagan as vice president?

MR. CHENEY: He should have thought of Reagan as vice president in the summer of 1974, if you are talking strictly in political terms. That was the move, to go to Reagan in August of 1974. Put Reagan on the ticket and then you don't have any problem.

There actually was a discussion about Reagan as vice president in 1976. There was a meeting at Camp David a few weeks before the convention that I attended with Stu Spencer and Bob Teeter and one or two others. We talked with the President about his vice presidential selections. At this point Rockefeller was off the ticket and the vice presidency had become a very important issue. I remember Reagan tried to use it against Ford in Kansas City. The big fight in Kansas City was over a change in the convention rules that would have required the President to name his vice presidential candidate before he got the nomination instead of after. It was a ploy to try to force Ford to make a choice because they knew that as soon as he made his choice, whichever way he went, he was going to lose delegates. So in the middle of that fight we had to spend a weekend at Camp David. We went over some research that we had Bob Teeter do which showed that Ronald Reagan was the best person you could put on the ticket in 1976. Nobody wanted to believe that at the time. The thought was that you had to go back to the Rockefeller wing or move so that you didn't antagonize them. We had some pretty good research that in light of what has happened subsequently showed that Reagan was the right place for us to go. Ford would not hear of it. The fact is that by the

time we got to the convention in Kansas City, the tension
was so high on both sides that Reagan agreed to meet with
us after the vote only on condition that we not offer him
the vice presidency. Ford was only too happy to say,
"Absolutely right. I don't want to offer him the vice
presidency."

Part of that was also Ford's loyalty to Rockefeller.
Rockefeller would have been irate if he had gotten off the
ticket so that the President could put Ronald Reagan on.
The Reagan/Rockefeller rivalry went way back to their days
as governors. It was very intense and very emotional.
Kissinger was a part of that, too. Rockefeller was there in
Kansas City as the outgoing vice president and he would
have been extremely unhappy, to say the least, if Ford had
gone with Reagan in 1976, so it never came close to being
put together. If you think about it now, if everybody had
been able to overcome their emotions and the personalities
involved, it was absolutely the best thing he could have
done and might have won us the election.

QUESTION: Was Bob Dole then a compromise between
Reagan and Rockefeller?

MR. CHENEY: Well, Rockefeller was off and Reagan was
off. What had occurred with respect to the Reagan choice
was that when we were getting close to the convention at
Kansas City, we reached an understanding with the Reagan
people that whoever won the nomination in Kansas City
would that same night go to the Hotel suite of the loser.
They would have a unity meeting and, subsequent to that, a
press conference as a way of starting to bind up the
wounds.

When in Kansas City we won the rules fight on
Tuesday we knew at that point that we were going to win.
We had it nailed down and the next night was to be the
vote on the presidency and then the meeting. So on
Tuesday I gave Bill Timmons, who was running the
convention for us, instructions to contact John Sears who
was running the convention for Reagan to implement this
earlier agreement. He did. He went to Sears and came
back to me the next morning and said, "Sears agrees to
carry through on their earlier commitment. There will be a
meeting after the voting tonight. You can come to Reagan's
suite over at the Alameda Plaza Hotel. But, there are two
conditions. The meeting has to be one on one with nobody

else present. No wives." Relations between Betty and Nancy were not very good. "Secondly, you have to promise in advance that you will not offer the vice presidency." That's the message that came back to me.

So I went to the President and said, "We've got a deal for the meeting the night after the balloting if I can go back and commit to Sears on these two points." We had no problem with the first point. The second point, not to offer the vice presidency, was Sears' statement to me. I got instructions from the President to agree to that, which was my recommendation anyway. At that point we were beyond asking Reagan, and Ford was delighted to have that situation. It relieved him of the need to make the offer.

Then we went to the meeting that night. I called Sears after the balloting and said, "John, we're rolling. In about thirty minutes we will be at your Hotel." He reiterated, "Okay, but again I want your commitment you will not offer the vice presidency." I said, "Done. We won't do it." So we had the meeting with Reagan. During the course of that meeting Dole came up. Ford had a list of eight or ten potential running mates. Dole was on that list and Ford asked Reagan about Dole and some other names on the list specifically. Reagan responded most affirmatively where Bob Dole was concerned.

Ford had another problem, and that was a developing insurgency among the Republican state chairmen at the convention. There had been a meeting early that morning and about twenty-five of them had gotten together and decided that the right thing to do was to put Ford and Reagan together on the ticket and that Ford had to offer the job to Reagan. We already knew that Reagan wouldn't take it when he made us promise that we wouldn't even offer it to him. Even so, we had this insurgency developing and we had to decide fairly quickly on somebody. We wanted somebody who had credibility in the party. Bob Dole had it because he had been chairman of the Republican National Committee. It was one of his major assets when we decided to pick him in 1976. So we went with Dole, announced it quickly and put out the pro-Reagan fires.

In retrospect, it would have helped if we had had a couple more days and we could have let tempers cool off a bit and gone back, because I still think the right choice was Reagan in 1976, but it was just not an option because of the personalities.

NARRATOR: This forum, like one we had nine or ten years ago when Herbert Storing was with us, is a high point in the history of the Miller Center from at least two standpoints. First, I can't imagine a clearer, more candid, and more honest portrayal of a particular presidency or a better informed one. And, second, I can't think of another instance where someone who is still at the center of our national political life would speak as openly and as authoritatively as Congressman Cheney has. We hope he will come back often and we thank him for his visit.

THE LOYALISTS AND
THE PRAETORIAN GUARD

ROBERT T. HARTMANN

NARRATOR: Mr. Hartmann was born in Rapid City, South Dakota and he is a graduate of Stanford University; he began his journalistic and literary career in 1939 as a reporter for the *Los Angeles Times*. He went on to become an editorial and special writer. Later he was Washington bureau chief for nine years and finally in charge of the Mediterranean and Middle East bureau of the paper. He served on the House Republican Conference staff, and as Minority Sergeant-at-Arms, he accompanied the House Leadership on its first trip in 1972 to mainland China. He was chief of staff for Vice President Ford and then counsellor to the President with Cabinet rank in the Ford White House. In World War II he rose from ensign to lieutenant commander in the United States Navy. He has received numerous journalistic awards from the English Speaking Union, from Sigma Delta Chi, the Professional Society of Journalists for Washington correspondence, and professional groups. His book, *Palace Politics: An Inside Account of the Ford Years*, adds a whole other dimension to our understanding of the Ford presidency, a presidency that increasingly challenges the interest and imagination of presidential scholars. We have heard from several of his colleagues about both the opportunities and achievements of the Ford presidency and also some of the problems as they saw them—problems in the leadership area and problems with staff. I am sure, knowing his book, that Mr. Hartmann will talk about both of those aspects of the Ford presidency. It is a great pleasure to welcome him to the Miller Center.

MR. HARTMANN: Thank you, Dr. Thompson. I am very honored to be here at the University of Virginia and the Miller Center. First of all, Virginia has provided one-fifth of all the Presidents of the United States and, best of all, was the only state of the old Confederacy that voted right in 1976.

I want to talk a little bit today about my boss during fifteen years of my life; they weren't invariably happy years, but they were fun on the whole. Gerald R. Ford was a very unusual president, a unique one you might say, in that he was the first president who was unelected as president and unelected as vice president. All of this came about, as you know, through the adoption of the Twenty-fifth Amendment, which was a result of President Eisenhower's heart attack and several other crises in health. It was also a by-product of the atomic age in which it became quite conceivable that both the president and vice president might be killed simultaneously. We had to have some way of rapidly determining a legitimate succession. This amendment had never been used until the sudden falling star of Spiro Agnew lit up the skies like Halley's comet and we had to use its provisions (really just minor provisions of an amendment designed for other purposes) to get a new vice president.

In the situation of the day it was obvious almost from the beginning that the new vice president was going to become president. Ford refused to admit this to himself until the very last, but to everybody else it was clear that President Nixon was not going to finish his term, one way or another. Thus, the Congress was not merely choosing a replacement vice president, but a replacement for the President also. The Senate always elects a president pro-tem and has put the president pro-tem in the chair several times. But this time, under an untried amendment, the Congress really was choosing the next president. To do this they went through long and arduous hearings, not one but two. Each of the two houses, of course, had to conduct its own investigation. They investigated Gerald Ford's past like nobody has ever been investigated before, but they were unable to come up with anything very terrible. I think the worst thing they found out about him was that when he was chairman of the Republican Convention in Miami in August he charged off his light-weight suits as a business expense. He was forced to repay the IRS, of course, and he's still mad about that.

He suddenly found himself vice president without having had much serious reflection, and then he suddenly found himself president. Needless to say, he came to enjoy it and wanted to continue it. But the public does sometimes make mistakes and so he was denied that opportunity.

The two cases in which a vice president has been chosen under the Twenty-fifth Amendment, Ford and Rockefeller, don't necessarily make an axiom. Yet it does seem to me on the strength of what we have observed that anyone who rises to the office of president without going through a national nomination and election process, at least as the vice presidential candidate, is going to have a hard time remaining in the White House. First and foremost, the Twenty-fifth Amendment gives members of Congress *of the other party* a decisive voice in the choice of a vice president. That isn't true when most vice presidents are chosen by party nomination. Members of the other party will never knowingly pick the strongest possible presidential candidate in the opposition. At best they will pick someone they see as a competent caretaker until the next election, when they hope to come back. Second, any person who is so nominated and confirmed by the Congress is bound to lack the ready and waiting national political constituency and close-knit presidential cadres that he needs to be reelected. He will never be permitted by his president to create such a group while serving as vice president.

Considering these handicaps, I think it is remarkable that Gerald Ford came as close to winning as he did. Every president and every presidential contender is surrounded by a trusted staff which, if he wins, becomes the nucleus of his White House staff. Ronald Reagan's primary challenge to Ford was almost successful because he had such a committed, loyal personal staff. Jimmy Carter's narrow victory was a tribute to his fellow Georgians and their dedication to him; it also proved, incidentally, that people who can win elections are not necessarily people who can run the country.

President Ford had only a handful of close subordinates when he became President. Among them I would include myself, Phil Buchen, and Jack Marsh, secretary of the army and a Virginian. Ford, having only a handful of staff people, not really enough to staff a government, first attempted to take over Nixon's personal staff and impose his own concept of leadership on it. Failing this, as he inevitably did, he tried belatedly to revert to the Nixonian discipline which was foreign to his true nature and which he could not enforce effectively.

It is easy to be objective about those we care little or nothing about. It is harder to be objective about yourself. But the hardest thing is to be objective about someone you love and admire and with whom you have worked for years, sharing hopes, triumphs and disappointments. So how should I sum up Jerry Ford as President of the United States? It would be casuistry to claim that he was a man for all seasons; I cannot say that he was the man for all seasons. I *can* say that he was the man for *that* season when he restored the faith of a troubled people in their constitutional government and in the honor and decency of the presidency. Still this determination "to heal our land" falls far short of what he deserves from history. We have forgotten how desperate the true State of the Union was when he took office. It was not, as in 1860, a case of certain states threatening to secede and defy the federal government in Washington. It was worse; a threat of millions of individual Americans—young and old, black and white, rich and poor, urban and rural—threatening to secede from the social compact which binds us together as a nation. This unspoken understanding had been twice shattered, first by the duplicities of Vietnam and later by the deceptions of Watergate. The fundamental consent of the governed had been rudely overridden, not once but twice. The contract of confidence between ordinary Americans and their leaders in Washington was almost abrogated.

Jerry Ford, simply by being what he was, turned this trend around. He was not a Lincoln or a Washington or a Roosevelt or a Truman or an Eisenhower. He was and is a regular guy—a decent, honest, hard working, God-fearing, patriotic, and proud American who really believed such shibboleths as "right makes might" and "my country, right or wrong." If I heard it once, I heard it one hundred times in confidential talks with the President: "I don't care what the polls say; it's the *right* thing to do." Or, "however the

election turns out, I think this is best for the country."
Whether he was correct or not in those decisions makes no
difference. He never stopped trying to be, as he promised,
the President of all the people. He restored to the
presidency the respect at home and abroad it had not
enjoyed since Eisenhower and Kennedy. He reestablished, in
the hearts of Americans, the full measure of pride and
purpose we had not known since Roosevelt and Truman.

To be a caretaker of the Constitution is no mean
glory. Jerry Ford was a far better president than he was a
politician, though he had been in politics most of his adult
life. In this way he was more like Herbert Hoover than his
professed favorites—Ike and "give'em Hell Harry." What
links Ford and Hoover in my mind is that we Americans
never quite appreciate our former presidents until after they
have left the White House. Take former President Truman
or former President Eisenhower. In their latter years they
became revered elder statesmen, all their sins and
shortcomings forgiven, beloved by most of their fellow
countrymen. I would be last to deny this consolation to Mr.
Carter and Mr. Reagan.

Every president takes office under the illusion that he
is breaking new ground, that things are going to be
different, that there will be some changes made. This is
what they tell the voters and this is what they tell
themselves.

Lincoln asked his countrymen to think anew and act
anew, to disenthrall themselves. His successors proclaimed
New Deals and New Frontiers and we in the Ford years
played with the phrase "New Directions," which I am quite
prepared to forgive you for having forgotten.

In January 1979 the Carter people came up with "New
Foundations," a clear case of going us one worse. Now, as
all women know, New Foundations don't really give you
anything new; they just rearrange what you already have.
It's the same with the problems that a president has: the
redistribution of our national wealth, of our energy
resources, of our tax dollars, and of our global interests and
commitments.

Another persistent illusion is that presidents are better
able to make difficult decisions because they have all the
facts, all of the knowledge that other people don't have.
Actually presidents make hard decisions, but not because
they know more or because they are wiser than the rest of

us. They make them for one reason only: because they
have to and we don't.

Americans expect their presidents to do what no
monarch of Divine Right could ever do: resolve for them
all the contradictions and complexities of life.   Those who
seek the presidency invariably promise, and perhaps really
believe, that they can handle our problems for us at least
better than the other guy.

It is interesting that since Franklin D. Roosevelt only
three Presidents—all of the minority party—have been elected
twice.   Television is certainly a factor; it focuses on
stumbles and fumbles and other trivia instead of a
candidate's real philosophy and performance.   People get
tired of the same old presidential face as quickly as they do
of last year's top-rated television show.   But "the fault,
dear Brutus, is not in our stars but in ourselves."   The
founding fathers had little first-hand experience of anything
except a monarchy limited by an elected parliament.   They
created in the American presidency a republican king,
checked even further by two national legislatures and by
considerable local sovereignty.   The people were to make
the basic decisions and live with them.   The main purpose
of the president, as Washington saw it, was to preside and
to counsel, but to command only in dire emergencies.

Now—without tracing this process in any great
detail—we have shifted most of the onus of hard decision-
making to the president.   The people have to pick him and
then second-guess him.   All Congress has to do is give him,
or deny him, what he proposes.   So the president today has
too much responsibility and too little final authority for
these basic decisions.   It has become an almost impossible
job.   Yet there are always scores of otherwise smart, sane,
and intelligent people who are dying to have it or to keep
it or to get it back.

When President Ford took the oath on August 9, 1974,
proclaiming that "our long national nightmare is over," he
was the first chief executive since Washington who could
honestly say, "I have not sought this enormous responsibility, but I will not shirk it."   He promised his fellow-
countrymen nothing except "to uphold the Constitution, to
do what is right as God gives me to see the right, and to
do the best I can for America."

When you come down to it that is really all any
president can do, and all any president should promise.   We

have heard so long, especially since the dawn of the atomic age, that the President of the United States is the most powerful man in the world. You would be amazed at the things that a President *cannot* do. He cannot control the affairs of other nations, though we spend billions, and sometimes a lot of blood, trying to do so. He cannot control the cloud cover over Cuba or the rains for which he is always blamed, but never praised, in the farm belt. He cannot do a lot of things without the consent of a majority, sometimes a two-thirds majority, of the Senate, the House, and the Supreme Court. He commands five million civilians and military personnel in the executive branch, but when his dog becomes over-excited on a White House rug he finds it simpler to clean it up himself.

Though all Democrats and most Republicans try every election year, no president can fine-tune the American economy on which most of our elections turn. It would be supremely dangerous if a president were to believe in his own omnipotence. Fortunately, a new president is soon disabused.

Let me tell you a little story about that. At the end of the day Ford was sworn in as President, everybody in the White House disappeared except the President and me. I hung around as I had been doing for years up on Capitol Hill to watch him pack his battered briefcase and take off. I went in to say good night and we began talking a little bit; he didn't seem in any great hurry to go home. I looked around and said, "You know, Mr. President, wouldn't it be a good idea to change the portraits in the Cabinet room for your first meeting? It would show that some changes are already being made and this is now the Ford administration, not the Nixon administration." He seemed a little bit puzzled. (Having been a White House reporter during the Eisenhower and Kennedy years, I knew what the press looks for—little signs. The president's heroes are a clue to his own concept of the presidency.) So I said, "Well, every President puts up pictures of his favorite predecessors. Of course George Washington always stays here in the Oval Office, but in the Cabinet room they change. Now come on, let's take a look."

Suddenly it occurred to me whether I should be talking like that to the President of the United States. But he unwound his long legs and followed me into the Cabinet room and we fumbled for the light switch. (That's how new

the place was to us.) When we got the lights on, there was
President Eisenhower smiling down at us from above the
mantle where Nixon had put him, and I said, "Kennedy had
Jefferson up there, and LBJ replaced him with FDR. I think
Ike had Lincoln up there—I can't remember who Truman had.
But most of them kept Lincoln around somewhere. For
some reason Nixon dumped Lincoln and hung Teddy
Roosevelt and Woodrow Wilson at the other end of the
room." President Ford looked around and then said, "I
think we should leave Ike where he is." I said, "Well, I
never heard you talk much about Wilson or Teddy, so who
would you like to have down here at this end?" "Well,
what's your recommendation?" he asked. "Well," I said, "I
think we ought to bring old Abe back," and he nodded.
Then I said, "Now the other one might be a Democrat; how
about Andy Jackson?" "No," he said, "Harry Truman." I
was kind of surprised at this and I said, "Are you sure?"
and he said, "Absolutely!"

As we walked back to the Oval Office, he started
telling me about his first encounter as a junior congressman
with President Truman. Ford had just happened to be on
the Public Works Committee, and he had been invited down
by the President to be lobbied on behalf of the new
balcony, in fact the whole redoing of the White House, after
Margaret's piano fell through the floor, and so forth.

I began to understand that the peppery Missourian had
been drafted as a substitute for a vice president who had
fallen from grace in the same way as Ford. Truman
confounded his critics and won a full term on his own. He
was no orator, no intellectual; he was a plain man, a family
man, a midwestern politician, a fighter, and a patriot, and
nobody liked him except the people and the historians.
Ford was really foretelling his own hopes.

So as we said goodnight, I felt it was a little corny,
but I said, "Mr. President"—and those words still sounded a
bit strange to me—"you are going to be a *great* president."
"Well, thanks, Bob," he said, "I don't know about that, but I
do want to be a *good* president."

I left a note for Al Haig who, because nobody else
knew how, was still running things around there to change
the portraits of TR and Wilson to those of Truman and
Lincoln. The President wanted it done before his first
Cabinet meeting the next morning. But when we gathered
around the long oval table, the faces around it were all the

same: Nixon's Cabinet and the heroes on the walls were all the same; they were Nixon's heroes. The praetorian guard had encountered insurmountable difficulties in locating a portrait of Mr. Truman. Saturday passed, and Sunday, and the following Thursday I noticed the portraits were still unchanged. I spoke to Haig and they were still looking. He asked, "What's the big rush?" Of course he knew what the big rush was, but his purpose was to show that there was no change, that the Nixon-Ford White House was carrying on without Nixon.

This was only a minor test of will. I bit my tongue—it got bloody after a while—and suggested to the President that he'd better tell Haig himself to get a move on—or words to that effect. Well, the President did and this produced a passable likeness of Harry Truman from the National Portrait Gallery down the street where it had been all the time. But somehow it still didn't get hung up, even after I had telephoned Margaret Truman Daniel and made sure that that painting was all right with her and her mother.

Another weekend passed. On the nineteenth of August, ten days after his order to Haig, the President was going to fly out to Chicago to address the national convention of the Veterans of Foreign Wars. He had decided to make an announcement of conditional amnesty for Vietnam draft dodgers and deserters before that superpatriotic crowd. He was going to mention that Lincoln and Truman, after earlier wars, had granted amnesties to help bind up the nation's wounds. Now, nobody knew about this except the President, myself, and Jack Marsh. Haig, who had been a combat general in Vietnam, was violently opposed to the idea just as Nixon had been, and Haig knew nothing about the amnesty at all. So I wrote another memo to Haig and said that the Truman and Lincoln pictures had better be hanging in the Cabinet Room when President Ford got back from Chicago. They wouldn't signal exactly what we originally wanted them to say, but they would still say something.

Well, eventually the President of the United States got his way about the pictures, but the drama was gone. The story was lost in the news of Ford's appointment of Rockefeller to the vice presidency. There was no appreciative murmur from birthright Democrats as there had been from Republicans when Mr. Truman welcomed Mr. Hoover back to the White House.

In this little episode the old Nixon praetorian guard was testing the new President—and testing me too. It is interesting for me to speculate how previous presidents would have handled this case of low-key insubordination. Harry Truman, I am sure, would have fired everybody involved, including me, on the second day. President Eisenhower would have fired me, the man to whom he gave the original order, and scared the hell out of everybody else. Jack Kennedy would have told Bobby to do it and it would have been done. Lyndon Johnson would have fired Haig and then gone to the attic and dusted off a portrait and hung it up himself. Richard Nixon would have denied he ever gave such an order, praised me and Haig as two of the finest public servants he ever knew, and then fired both of us and John Dean to boot. Jimmy Carter, I suppose, would have expressed love and compassion for all concerned and decided there were some other presidents he'd rather have anyway. And Ronald Reagan? Well, he might have said, "Oh shucks, Hartmann—you are Hartmann, aren't you? Now that fellow Haig just wants to have his own picture up there. I'll tell you what, we'll put Nancy above the fireplace. You know, my other two favorite presidents have always been Darryl Zanuck and Louis B. Mayer."

Well, what did Ford do? He simply let things work themselves out. He would not choose between two senior subordinates; he made a firm and instant decision, issued a clear and instant directive—not once but twice—but he would not insist on instant obedience. This tells us a lot about the Ford presidency. It goes to the essential difference between leadership and command. Jerry Ford was a great *leader*, as we use the term in football or on board an aircraft carrier or in the Congress, but *command* is something else. It requires an element of ruthlessness, the toughness that is required to send thousands of fellow human beings to death, the cold-bloodedness that sacrifices old and dear friendships, the iron determination to reach a fixed objective no matter what.

Tomes have been written on presidential leadership, but *command* is what the presidency is all about. Decisiveness is essential in a president; Jerry Ford was decisive about great and small matters. His instincts, his intuition, his powers of reasoning and reconciling divergent interests were very good indeed. But the place where the president must exercise the final decision a hundred times a day is *between people.* Persuading people to work together is leadership; when this fails, deciding between people is the essence of command. A president must be born a great leader and a great commander, but above all he must command, for *only he can.* To put it more simply, a president must be something of an SOB. It's not enough to surround himself with them; he must at times be *the* SOB and he must, however secretly, rather relish it.

Ford was simply too nice a guy; he boasted that he had adversaries but no enemies, and he really meant it. Sometimes he hurt people, but he hated it. Not for nothing was he called "good old Jerry." Can you imagine, though, anybody ever calling our first President "good old George." A commander has to be capable of shooting his own mutinous troops.

George Reedy, who was one of LBJ's associates until he got sick of it, wrote in his book *The Twilight of the Presidency*: "the White House does not provide an atmosphere in which idealism and devotion can flourish. Below the president is a mass of intrigue, posturing, strutting, cringing, and pious windbaggery. For the very young, the process is demoralizing. It is possible for a president to assemble a staff of mature men who are past the period of inordinate ambition which characterizes the courtier, but this rarely if ever happens; the White House *is* a court. Inevitably, in a battle between courtiers and advisers, the courtiers will win out."

But Reedy stopped short of telling the full story of "the twilight of the *Ford* Presidency." However sinister a praetorian guard may become, at least most presidents have their own. Ford simply took over President Nixon's. He made this decision knowingly, over the unanimous advice of his closest personal and political friends who urged him to take a firm grip on his new broom and sweep clean right from the start. He'd never get a second chance. I suppose I attended ninety-nine percent of all the Cabinet and senior staff meetings President Ford had during his two and a half years in office and I made a point of noting the faces around the table. Never once, until he left the White House were there more new Ford faces than there were old Nixon faces. This was a major reason, I think, why President Ford lost the election he wanted so badly to win.

Betty Ford says that both she and her husband blamed the Nixon pardon for his loss. Jerry Ford has refused to engage in postmortems. There are always a dozen alibis in any contest that close, but I will give you mine.

I believe President Ford could have survived his sudden pardon of former President Nixon if he had coupled it with the dismissal of Nixon's entire court and constituted one of his own. Everyone expected him to do so; that's the first thing any new president does. Harry Truman got rid of FDR's praetorian guard in short order; Lyndon Johnson hung on to Kennedy's and lived to regret it. President Ford boldly took the first step and I believe that pardoning Nixon was right and spared the country endless agony which would still be going on. But he didn't take the second step which would really have put Watergate behind us where the American people wanted it to be. Instead, he left it for Jimmy Carter to change the guard, and for Ronald Reagan to reorder the priorities of America, for better or for worse. The American people wanted new faces and they got them. President Ford got his wish—he was a *good* President. Like John F. Kennedy, though, his presidency was too short for us to know whether he would have become a great President.

One of the quotations he liked best was from John Steinbeck, one I think some people in this room are old enough to remember: "Unlike any other thing in the Universe, man grows beyond his work, walks up the stairs of his concepts, and emerges ahead of his accomplishments." I hope that will be history's verdict on Gerald R. Ford, thirty-eighth President of the United States.

NARRATOR: You all know what Mr. Hartmann thinks about the Ford presidency both from his writing and from this fascinating account. That ought to invite a lively and good discussion. Who'd like to raise the first question?

QUESTION: It is clear since Mr. Ford has been out of the White House that he misses it terribly. How about you? Do you miss it?

MR. HARTMANN: Well, there are two parts in my answer to that question. I'm not sure I agree with you that he misses it terribly. I think that for the first few years after he left the White House, he thought he could do a better job than the guy who was there. I'm not sure he would like to go back now. He is having too good a time, although he probably still thinks he could do a better job than the guy who is there.

As for myself, the answer is that the experience was something like being in World War II: I'm glad I went, but I don't want to go again. It was a marvelous experience. If I'd had four more years of it, I probably wouldn't be alive now. It was the hardest work I've ever done and the most exciting. But the one thing I really miss, and I have to confess, is the president's helicopter! That's really the only way to get to Charlottesville!

NARRATOR: Jack Valenti was asked the same question and his answer was that after such an experience, all of life is anticlimax. You wouldn't say that?

MR. HARTMANN: No, not at all. I've had an awful lot of fun since 1977. As I said about the war, I like to talk about it and I'm glad I was there, but I'm not sure I'd want to do it again.

QUESTION: Mr. Hartmann, wouldn't President Ford have had an almost impossible job of rebuilding a staff if he let the Nixon people go without having a cadre of people that he had been working with? Might that not have made for even more disruption and more of a problem than continuing along the path that he did?

MR. HARTMANN: Well, you have a point, and I'm sure that was the point that influenced his thinking. On the other hand, every time we change presidents, along with a change of parties we have an instant turnover and a bunch of completely untrained people.

QUESTION: In normal circumstances, though, it would have been a group of people who had been associated with the new president in a campaign and over a period of transition.

MR. HARTMANN: That's true. On the other hand, Ford had not failed to develop a group of close and trusted people over all the years he had been in Congress before he went to the White House. He could have picked a dozen members of the Cabinet out of that group who would have probably done just about as well as the guys already there. Certainly they would have been much more loyal to Ford's interests than the guys already there and not because they were bad people. Many of them were very fine people, but they had a vested interest in justifying all that had gone before; they were not inclined to move out into new directions in any area.

There is one other point I have to make on the other side of this question. Ford felt very keenly that he had no mandate except the mandate of Nixon's 1972 reelection, which was a rather powerful mandate. Nixon, aside from the fact that he was running against someone from South Dakota, had won a real landslide. This vote of the people, even though Watergate had not yet blossomed into its full glory, was pretty hard to override, especially by a vice president with no mandate at all, especially not in foreign policy. Therefore, Ford was quite determined to carry on the main lines of the Nixon-Kissinger foreign policy. I learned later that he had promised Nixon he would keep Kissinger on, even before Nixon told him he was definitely resigning. The first thing he did when he learned that Nixon was going to resign was to get hold of Henry and twist his arm—he didn't have to twist it very hard—to stay on. I think this was good, although I think that the time would have come when Ford's own secretary of state could have been eased in. However, Kissinger did much better with foreign policy than we've been doing ever since. I can't quibble much about that.

It's not in that area that I was concerned. Ford's economic philosophy was not much different from Nixon's, but Ford's attitudes on how you deal with people, and in particular his appreciation of the role which Congress plays in the government of this country was quite different from Nixon's. Nixon had an ill-disguised contempt of Congress. I don't know if it was because he had served in both Houses, but he really was not very good in cajoling and trading with the members of Congress to bring about some purpose that he wanted. Ford was very good at this. Ford had a large Democratic majority in both Houses of Congress. They were a little hand-tied by the fact that they had all voted to confirm him. With the exception of 38 people out of 535, all had voted for Ford in the first place. Still, he had no control over these Democratic majorities except the close, intimate associations he had with many on both sides of the aisle, and the veto, which he used very adroitly. As Minority Leader in the House, he had been involved in many a veto battle, saving Nixon from being overridden, or trying to override Johnson. He understood the mechanism of the veto. The veto is the one legislative power that is put in the hands of the president, and it's a very powerful one because it requires a two-thirds majority to be overridden.

I can't remember exactly now how many vetoes Ford cast, but it was the largest number since FDR and he was only overridden a handful of times. So between personal persuasion and the threat and actual use of the veto, this was the way he handled the Congress. He spent endless hours with the members of Congress, singly and in groups, and on the telephone, trying to get things done that he thought had to be done. He didn't always succeed but he did a lot better than his successors have.

QUESTION: I wonder if you'd share some of your thoughts with us on having been in the palace guard, or as it is sometimes called, "the unelected government."

MR. HARTMANN: I was in it, but not *of* it.

QUESTION: Well, you were pretty close to it. One of the points you made is that the president's job is becoming almost impossible. My layman's interpretation is that he is turning too much of the government over to the White House staff.

MR. HARTMANN: Well, I think that is a trend that has been going on for some time. Consider the numbers now in comparison to the approximately twenty people FDR had on his White House staff. Now, there are around 500, maybe more technically. There must be several hundred who have frequent, direct access to the president. This is due to the great complexity of things that a president must deal with. I do think, though, that the more it grows, the more responsibility is diffused and the more a president loses control of things. What the staff does is bring in two-page "decision memos" which say at the bottom, "approved," "disapproved," or "see me," and the president initials one of these. Sometimes, of course, the memo lists three dogs and one outstanding candidate for an appointment, and then the president is supposed to pick the outstanding candidate. (Who all the other candidates were before he got that piece of paper we'll never know.) The same thing happens with substantive decisions. It takes a rare bird—and I've never seen one—to prepare such documents for a president without injecting any of his personal beliefs or the collective thinking of the staff as to what the president really ought to do after he finishes reading it. I've written some of these papers myself and I certainly never neglected to lean heavily on my own argument.

So I think that the sheer volume of things that go across the president's desk has weakened his power of command. Still, there are some presidents who are happier with this isolation and some who simply cannot tolerate isolation. Nixon didn't want to see anybody except Haldeman. President Reagan (although I haven't really been invited down to the Oval Office to watch this in person) seems to prefer dealing with a limited number of staff people, or with great masses of cheering crowds. (They all like that.) Presidents Ford, Johnson and Truman were more gregarious.

The influence of a presidential staff depends on the president. Some presidents can resist it and make the best use of it, and others are simply carried away with it.

QUESTION: Do you think Ford would have been elected if Reagan had supported him?

MR. HARTMANN: Yes. I wouldn't say that's the only reason he lost, but I think it was a big one. That's all water over the dam. Still, within a political party, you don't try to dump an incumbent president if you can possibly help it.

QUESTION: I wonder if you'd care to amplify your remarks on the Nixon pardon. You mentioned it only in passing and only made the point that the pardon seemed correct to you because it saved the country a great deal of stress and strain. I'm wondering if you'd care to explain why, at that time, the important principle of equality before the law didn't seem worth defending.

MR. HARTMANN: The point I made is that it spared the country turmoil and strain, not necessarily that it was uppermost in Ford's mind. I can't read his mind; I can guess it better than most people, but I can't read it. There was a fundamental reason, I believe, that caused him to issue the pardon when he did, rather than waiting a month or so until Nixon was lying at death's door; when everybody would have cheered and said, "Oh, what a great and compassionate thing to do." The reason that he did it so early and in contradiction to his previous statements, was (in my thinking anyway) that he simply got fed up with not being able to do anything around the White House except answer questions about the fate of Richard Nixon. In every press conference that he had, nine out of ten questions had to do with Nixon. He was faced with a lot of litigation in which he was called upon, as President of the United States, to produce certain documents or to do this or that. He couldn't put in eight hours in the Oval Office without seven of them being involved with this carryover that had to do with Nixon, Watergate, and so forth. He got impatient with all of it and decided to sweep it off the table. I think it was a selfish act; I don't think it was based on his long-standing friendship with Nixon or their association or any debt he felt he owed Nixon because Nixon had named him vice president. He knew very well he wasn't Nixon's first choice; John Connally was Nixon's first choice. Ford was shoved down Nixon's throat by Speaker Carl Albert and by Mel Laird and others who told Nixon they couldn't get anybody else confirmed.

The Twenty-fifth Amendment, mind you, is lacking in one respect; it doesn't set any deadline on how soon the Congress shall approve the nomination of a vice president. They could have debated it until the end of Nixon's term, if they wanted to, and we would have gotten along without a vice president as we have a dozen times before in our history.

No, it wasn't friendship or indebtedness, or even the compassion he felt, particularly for Pat and the girls. I think it was simply a selfish act; he wanted to be shed of all of this and to go on, to get on with the business of the Ford presidency. He has never admitted that but he has never argued with me about what I wrote in my book about it.

QUESTION: Perhaps you could refresh our recollection. In one of the earlier Miller Center studies of the press secretaries, Jerry terHorst, was quoted as saying the following: "The first thing I obviously had to do, and I thought I had to do because that was what the President wanted done, (and I could see he was on the right track) was to help him make a sharp break between himself and Richard Nixon. But Ford definitely wanted to make the change himself. And in the press area he fussed at me and charged me with making the changes that were created in private." Was he an exception to the general rule in that he was a new man on board, and lasted such a short time? Was he successful with the role in creating a break with the press?

MR. HARTMANN: His statement that he thought what the President wanted to do was to make a sharp break with the Nixon White House was more hope than reality. I perfectly agreed with him, and although I don't know what Philip Buchen said down here I think he and a number of others also agreed that we had to start right away by putting Ford's stamp on the administration and, conversely, taking Nixon's stamp off. I think that Jerry terHorst had the notion, and perhaps was given the notion when he was recruited by Ford, that that was his mandate. The fact is, though, he had the devil's own time firing half of Nixon's people, including this ex-priest, John McLaughlin, and several others who just wouldn't go. I know how he felt because I set off on day number two to fire all of Nixon's speech writers. It wasn't because they were bad guys; I just didn't want Ford's speeches to sound like Nixon's speeches, and I didn't want Nixon's favorite phrases to come popping out of Ford's mouth. I fired Dave Gergen (but he came bouncing back in later generations, hopefully wiser), and I fired all the rest of them. We tried, of course, to make it look like they resigned and to wait until they found a place to land, but the fact is, I cleaned house and terHorst cleaned his house, and that's about as far as it went. After Buchen came in, there was a measure of house cleaning in the Legal Counsel Department too, but not in the operational end of the White House staff. There wasn't very much change because Ford didn't insist upon it. In fact, he was ambivalent about it. When he finally decided that he really wanted to make a big change and fired Schlesinger (which he should have done on the second day—everybody knew he wanted to, including Schlesinger), it looked like an act of desperation rather than an act of resolution.

NARRATOR: Can we push you just a little more on this business of getting rid of people? What is it about the White House and the politics of governance that makes this so vital? We used to say in the Rockefeller Foundation that nobody was any good to the Foundation until they had been there two or three years. We are going through a transition at the University of Virginia. A new president has asked a senior vice president to stay on a year past retirement because only he knows anything about the problems. You'd think that on the face of it, government is so much more complicated than a university or a foundation that the experience factor would be even more important. Yet, there must be another element that you saw firsthand in terms of loyalty and initiative that make this as vital as you say it is.

MR. HARTMANN: Well, I should think that our built-in career civil service system provides the element of continuity, more than enough of it in most areas of the federal government. They have tenure that makes their dismissal nearly impossible. But the problem that faces every president is how to get this huge, complicated machine of government to execute what the chief executive wants executed. They have a million ways of dragging their feet, from studying things to death to keeping things just the way we've always had them. So every president-elect has some commission of experts to look into how he is going to get a handle on the government. The only way to do that, it seems to me, is for the president's closest and most senior subordinates to have their futures wrapped up in the president's future. It is hard for presidents to find that many close, intimate and completely trustworthy people. That's why so many of them use their sons or their wives for the most sensitive message transmissions and so forth. Jimmy Roosevelt, John Eisenhower are examples; some presidents even use their brothers. Some use their wives as confidants and counsellors, because there are not too many people they can really unburden themselves to and not too many people whose judgment they feel is totally at their disposal and in their interest.

One of the things I'm sure that others have told you in these sessions is that the worst thing a president can have around him is somebody who always agrees with him. Yet life is rather precarious for the naysayer. One has to learn how to go about it and when. You don't just rush in and say, "Mr. President, you are full of whatever." You have to work it in such a way that he begins to think it was his own idea.

Ford was particularly good at tolerating people who disagreed with him, and listening to the reasons why. Yet even he didn't really like it; deep down in his soul he didn't really like to be opposed, although sometimes it did change his final decision.

One of the questions I noted in a comment was, how did he change from being a legislative leader to being President? On Capitol Hill you have a true collective leadership. They are all colleagues; they are all peers. They elect a leader, a majority leader, a minority leader, like a football team elects a captain, but they are all equally important, they all have one vote and they all have a different constituency to please. In exercising his role as a minority leader in the House (in which the minority had about 180-190 troops), Ford had to do what he could to influence the decisions of a 435 member body. Ford always had everybody in and listened at great length to a lot of boring dissents and extraneous arguments. He reserved his own opinions, usually to the last, and then said, "Suppose we do this." Everybody would nod and would all go out more or less united on their strategy for the next day's calendar.

Well, as President he continued this habit of collective discussion and finding a strategy. The difference was that, as President, he had a different constituency. He was the President. He was not a peer and they were not his equals. He was the President and the congressmen had their interests and he had his. His constituency was the sum of all theirs, and he never announced what his decision was going to be. He went through the same motions but when he got to the end of the meeting, he would say, "Well, thank you all; I'll think it over." Then, when he made his decision, he announced it without telling anybody—except maybe one or two people—what it was going to be.

For instance, he did this in his choice of Rockefeller as his nominee for vice president, and in his pardon decision. When he made that decision, perhaps there were five people in the White House and maybe three or four on the Hill who knew what he was going to do before he did it. In his nomination of Rockefeller even fewer people knew.   He made it clear that it was the President's decision.   He listened to people in advance, but when a president makes a decision, he can't float it around or it gets out of hand.   It winds up in the *New York Times*.

QUESTION: Mr. Hartmann, I'd like to revert to your animadversions on the Twenty-fifth Amendment.   I certainly share your concern for many of the details of its operation, and even more for the mechanics of the choice of the vice president.   Moreover, as far as I know, there has not been an open convention since 1956.   The vice president has been chosen by the presidential nominee more or less on whim.   Can you suggest anything that could be done to improve this selection process for a vice president, both regularly and in the special circumstances contemplated by the Twenty-fifth Amendment?

MR. HARTMANN: Well, I went through the history of the Twenty-fifth Amendment in as much detail as I could in the course of preparing Mr. Ford for all the hearings that were going to take place upon his confirmation, so, I know some of the ideas that were rejected.   There is not a whole lot of legislative history there because they were dealing with the inability of the president to perform his duties.   The one sentence about choosing a substitute vice president was kind of an afterthought and there wasn't much debate about it.

The convention method of picking someone out of the blue to balance the ticket, as they say, isn't very good.   On the other hand, the vice presidents it has produced have not been bad.   Those whom fate gave an opportunity to show what they could do as president have not turned out badly. We have had worse presidents who were never vice president than we have had presidents who had been vice presidents.   Frankly, I can't think of any other way to do it.   We have a government in which the primary goal is to get nominated by your own political party, and that's the biggest obstacle for anybody rising to the presidency.   The rest is just more or less a crap game.   It depends on the fates and the political climate and the gaffes you make in the campaign.   Getting the nomination is the important thing, and to deny the guy who gets the nomination the opportunity to pick whoever he thinks will help him most, seems to me a dangerous thing to change. As Churchill said, "It's the least worst system."

NARRATOR: One of our tasks at the Miller Center has been to look the Twenty-fifth Amendment. In that area as well as in all that he has told us about the Ford presidency, Bob Hartmann has more than fulfilled his advance notices. We are terribly glad you came, Bob, and we hope you will come back to help us in other areas in which we are trying to study the presidency.

MR. HARTMANN: Thank you, Ken. I'd just like to leave one word with you. The first time I was here was in a presidential helicopter. We went out to Monticello on the fifth of July, 1976, for the last of eight Bicentennial appearances President Ford had to make. He spoke to a small crowd of new citizens who had just taken the oath of allegiance administered by Mr. Justice Powell. (Incidentally, I wonder if you know presidents can't administer oaths. I wanted President Ford to administer mine but we found out he couldn't.) The most memorable lines that Ford spoke in 1976 were in the last of his Bicentennial addresses here at Monticello. He said:

> Remember that none of us are more than care-takers of this great country. Remember that the more freedom you give to others, the more you will have for yourself. Remember that without law there can be no liberty.

PRESIDENT FORD AND THE BUDGET

PAUL H. O'NEILL

NARRATOR: Paul O'Neill's career refutes two misconceptions about our society. One is that there can be no effective movement back and forth between the private and the public sector. He has received great recognition in the private sector. Wilson Newman has described him as one of the most respected and trusted executives in the field of business today. But he also has had awards in the public sector: the Jump Meritorious Award, the National Institute of Public Affairs Award for Public Service, and other prestigious awards. He is a member of the John F. Kennedy School board of advisers at Harvard and a member of the board of the Gerald Ford Foundation; in short a person with unique experience in public affairs.

He was born in St. Louis. He holds an A.B. degree from Fresno State College, was a Haynes Foundation Fellow at Claremont College, did work at George Washington University, and got his M.P.A. at Indiana. He has served as a systems analyst in the Veterans Administration and a site engineer in Anchorage for the Morrison-Knudsen Company. In other words, he has proven his competence in technical fields. That's the other refutation to which I want to call attention. It is said that people who are specialists are unlikely to be capable of generalist administrative roles, and yet his whole career proves this is not necessarily the case. He was budget examiner early in his career, head of the Human Resources Division of the Bureau of the Budget, first assistant then associate, and thereafter deputy director of

111

the Office of Management and Budget in the Ford administration.

Thus Paul O'Neill has carved out a niche for himself in both the private and public sector that is outstanding and respected. We are pleased to have him to talk about the Ford presidency. When we began these discussions we thought this was going to be much simpler than the Nixon presidency or the Johnson presidency, because after all Gerald Ford was a much beloved figure, in the mold of Dwight Eisenhower. Surely, we thought, there were no problems that were of the magnitude of those in the previous presidencies we had explored. As we've listened, Mr. O'Neill, to some of your predecessors, it has become clear that the Ford administration had administrative issues with which to deal. So we are delighted to have your perspective on the budget process, but also your impressions and comments on the Ford presidency generally. It is an honor to have you with us.

MR. O'NEILL: I've had the great pleasure over the last few months of reading the volumes that you've already published, and I must say they are fascinating reading to anyone who has had the opportunity to be part of any administration. It is interesting to see how other people from other times viewed their service with a president or a presidency. I jumped at the chance when it was extended to me to come and share with you my thoughts and recollections about the Ford presidency. Hopefully I can also respond to questions you might have about my own experiences or perceptions of that important time.

You asked in my invitation to speak that I reflect on the first time I had a personal contact with President Ford. I think the first time that I had a direct business dealing with President Ford was in 1971 or 1972 when he was the minority leader in the House and I was an assistant director at the Office of Management and Budget. I have forgotten what the issue was, but I still have a vivid recollection of that meeting and I think it bears telling. It was a meeting held in the minority leader's office in the Capitol, and there must have been ten or fifteen people there. I remember particularly Mel Laird, who was then secretary of defense, and Les Arends, who was one of the House whips and Bob Michel being there. My vivid recollection of that particular meeting was of a group seated in an oval circle like this one is, and President Ford with his ever-present pipe puffing away as various people around the room expressed, with one degree of passion or another, their particular view of whatever the public policy issue was at that point. He was relatively quiet as he listened to the proceedings. From time to time he would interrupt to ask a question or ask someone to explain more fully what was behind the position they were taking. And as this kind of meeting tends to do—as I'm sure you know from your own experiences—the arguments began eventually to recycle. When we got to that point, the President ended the conversation, indicating what he thought was a consensus of the meeting, what each of the participants were to do as a consequence of the decision, and that was it. He was a reflective, thoughtful person drawing out a conversation, not steering it to his own point but listening carefully and then coming to a decision with which people could live. That picture comes to mind because it was so true to my general experience with President Ford as I came to know him more thoroughly by working with him on a day-to-day basis when he became vice president and then president.

I have been doing a little rereading of things in preparation for coming down and visiting with you. Last night I reviewed two volumes, the 1974 volume of the Nixon Presidential Papers and the 1974 volume of the Ford Presidential Papers. I got them out because I was trying to recapture the feeling of what it was like in August of 1974 when President Nixon resigned and Ford became President. Those readings brought to mind a vivid scene which you probably saw on television: The White House staff assembled in the East Room of the White House at 9:30 a.m. on August 9, and President Nixon came down with his family, stood on a raised platform and spoke about his regard for the staff and the grief that he had in leaving the presidency. It was a very touching, emotional and difficult scene. At about 10:00 a.m. he finished his remarks. You probably have a mental image of the President walking out to the helicopter and Vice President Ford saying goodbye to him.

Two hours later the East Room had been reorganized; the chairs had been changed and the platform had been moved. At just about 12:00 p.m. Ford was sworn in as President. You may recall that he said at that time, "I've not been confirmed by your votes, so I hope you will

confirm me with your prayers." I've raised that and remind
you of it because to me it is the tone and the values of
Gerald Ford that rings most true to me in that first speech
when he accepted the responsibility of being president.

It also says something else that is very important: we
found we could bridge the gap of very difficult
constitutional questions. Those of you who have served in
government, know that public issues and affairs of the times
don't stop even for cataclysmic events like the assassination
of President Kennedy or the resignation of President Nixon.
The striking thing about the time immediately after August
9, is that there was a lot of business with which to deal.

There wasn't a lot of time to think about what we
should do or what events we should address. The economy
was rapidly coming apart. Many people thought that
inflation was the issue of the day and that we had to have
a major tax increase. The economy was overheated and
that certainly needed attention. There had been work going
on behind the scenes toward the first SALT talks and there
was an opportunity to do something about strategic arms
limitations. There was a legislative program to produce;
there was one in the making that needed to be dealt with
and there was a budgetary program that needed putting
together. So my recollection of the time is that it was like
all times in the White House and the Executive Office
Building with enormous pressures to do things and to deal
with the affairs of the day.

In looking at some of your earlier volumes and reading
once more the transcript of the meeting we had here in
1977, I'm reminded again of the issue of the risk that is
present in a new administration. A startling example of
that is the Bay of Pigs incident. Clearly, we did not have
that kind of issue early in the Ford administration. Yet I
remember at the time being struck by what I observed in
the Ford administration and in the Ford presidency in the
early days; that is, even a man who had been involved in
government for twenty-five years and who had served as
vice president for a time, had a period when the idea of
putting on the mantle of the presidency was uncomfortable.
It wasn't natural and there was a lack of self-awareness, if
you will. I'll illustrate the point with a trivial example
which I still think is important because it illustrates that
there is a risky time in government when administrations

are beginning. Whatever staff structures may exist are untested by the events and issues of the time.

Before he became President, Mr. Ford had agreed to give a speech, a commencement address, at Ohio State University at the end of August 1974. He went to Ohio State on the thirtieth of August and gave the commencement address. One of the things he spoke about was the need to draw the worlds of business and education closer together. You may remember his words about what he characterized as a "cooperative education." He said we needed to have more interaction of business and education so that education was more carefully producing the skills and requirements that were necessary to make our economy go. The interesting thing is that this speech never went through the White House process; it never was staffed. The President gave the speech at noon. The university audience liked it a lot and they appreciated the warmth of his presentation. At 1:30 p.m., while he was still in the air coming back on Air Force One to Washington, the media began ringing the telephones off the wall at the OMB and the White House wanting to know the details of this "cooperative education program."

I was supposed to be the expert in human resources and community development programs and I knew a lot of people in the media, so my telephone was lit up with red lights everywhere. I had my secretary tell them I'd get back to them and I went banging around in the Executive Office Building trying to find out where this had come from. I finally went down to the speech-writing operation and found the person who had written the speech. I said, "What are the details of this program? Who has staffed it out? How much money do you think we are going to spend on it? Does the President have in mind a particular organization like the Labor Department or HEW or some place where he thinks it should be run?" And the speech writer looked at me as though I were from another planet. He said, "For goodness sake, it's only a speech."

Not just for the speech writer but also, I suspect, for President Ford in those early days, there was a lack of understanding that every word was going to be scrutinized, every fact was going to be tested. I must say that when I recounted this same story in 1977, I felt more certain about the importance of every word and fact, or supposed fact, that a president says than I feel comfortable saying now, because our current president seems to be able to say all kinds of things. I don't say that in any derogatory way, but you must understand that I came of age in the era of the Bureau of the Budget, before there was an Office of Management and Budget. There the standard was that we should never, ever let the president do anything or say anything without at least having the best facts available to him and the best analysis that the mind of man could create. That is not to say he had to use it or that he had to pay attention to it, but it was our responsibility to make sure he had it. Therefore, it was shattering to find a president making speeches about programs none of us knew anything about. Parenthetically, it is interesting that in the period after that, as we tried to define a program and bring together the experts from the Labor Department and HEW, we were never able to create a program of cooperative education, partly, I suspect, because it wasn't the idea the staff had developed.

This is a minor story, but I think it illustrates an important point about the presidency and about our government: even people who have had years, even decades of experience have difficulty grasping the notion of their own importance. This was true especially, I think, of someone like President Ford, who didn't have a large ego and didn't walk around with a perception that everything he said and did should be scrutinized with a microscope. This was a telling event early in the Ford administration. There were other events like that, and as you talk with others, perhaps you'd like to draw it out in a discussion. Some of those early experiences, I think, resulted in the President changing his view of administration in the presidency and the White House. For example, I believe they led to his asking Don Rumsfeld to return from NATO and be chief of staff in order to bring more organization and coordination to the presidency than he first thought he could live with.

The other thing that I would like to emphasize to you as I think back on the Ford presidency, was the feeling of a person operating from a very strong sense of values. Again I'll illustrate it with a story or perhaps with a few stories that make the proposition more concrete. Early in the Ford presidency—it must have been September of 1974—Congress finished work on a bill that it had been developing for some time which was a major benefit increase for the Railroad Retirement System. The bill was passed by massive majorities in both Houses. When it came to the White House, we put it through the staff process and I wrote our recommendations to the President. It was fairly clear that it was not a fiscally sound thing to do. It created a future obligation without any source of funds for eighteen billion dollars for railroad retirement benefits. Along with that observation was a report to the President on the votes and a recommendation that he veto the bill. It was clear from the outset that he wasn't going to be successful in vetoing the bill, but he vetoed the bill nevertheless. As I recall, the vote in the House to override had maybe six votes on his side, and the other four hundred odd members voted to override the President. It went through the Senate, I think, with a voice vote; it was so overwhelming that they didn't even have a recorded vote. But he never looked back on that. I think that was one time when he made a wrong political decision because he thought it was a right substantive decision for the country. I saw that as a repeated pattern in what President Ford did in his administration; it was the standard he set for his administration.

Let me remind you of a few similar events during this time. You may recall after the fall of Vietnam, when we began to receive refugees from Vietnam in this country, that there was not a unanimous view that it was a good idea to bring Vietnamese refugees to the United States. There were even a fair number, I think, among political advisers and members of Congress and maybe even a few people in the administration, who urged the President not to permit this inflow of Vietnamese refugees on the grounds that it was bad politics. You may not recall, but President Ford went out on the hustings and gave speeches for a couple of months to the effect that we were going to do this because it was the right thing to do, because it was consistent with the tradition of the United States that we accept hurting people from other countries.

At the same time—and in a way this points to the administrative characteristic of his presidency—he did not disregard the need to deal skillfully with potential criticism generated by bringing people into the country and potentially having massive numbers of people added to the welfare rolls, roaming the streets and even creating civil discord. So as he was out on the hustings, enunciating his values and principles, he was also being very direct in saying, "We have to do this right."

In other forums I've used this as an example of what, on the administrative side of the Ford presidency, has not been told very well. You may not remember that the Vietnamese Refugee Resettlement Program was a great success. That explains why you do not find today major outposts of criticism for having brought in the Vietnamese refugees. They were brought in without a great deal of fanfare and assimilated into our society. At least those one hears about and reads about are doing exceptionally well. The credit goes to the kind of people who were involved in the resettlement effort. Julia Taft—her name may not ring a bell but she was at the State Department at that time—had both a caring spirit and the administrative savvy to understand how the State Department and HEW could work together to do this resettlement job so that it was a success. And it was in keeping with our traditions and principles.

Perhaps a couple of other examples may illustrate that point—some not very fond recollections—one being the swine flu program. (I hope none of you had aftereffects from the swine flu shots.) This is an issue that cropped up at a very unfortunate time. The wheels were beginning to turn on a presidential election when it came out that seven soldiers, if I remember right, at Fort Dix, New Jersey had the Swine Flu virus and several had died. The medical historians dug out the books and showed us that we had lost thousands, maybe a half million people, in 1918 and 1919 when we'd had a previous occurrence of swine flu.

There were a lot of people urging the President to figure out a way to duck the issue, but again let me recall that he did not duck the issue. What he did was to recruit twenty-five, if I remember rightly, preeminent scientists from around the country, including both Sabin and Salk, (which in a way was a first in its own right: you may not know but they are not too crazy about each other for a strategy session). He got the two of them, noted immunologists and epidemiologists and the other special medical people together in the Cabinet room for a briefing on the indications of the spread of the flu, and a discussion of the options. The twenty-five sitting around the table agreed: we needed to have a crash program to develop a vaccine and a vaccination program. In spite of all the advice he was getting to figure out a way to duck this issue, he decided to go ahead. In the aftermath of the program there were deaths from the vaccine and that was a very, very difficult time. There were commentators and scientists who second-guessed the President endlessly.

Again this I think speaks to the question of the value orientation of a president. The most important thing about Gerald Ford and his presidency was a basic set of values and principles that guided what he did on a day-to-day basis in his administration of the government. While you may not agree with his judgment, he was, in the aftermath of Vietnam, for instance, willing to put himself on the line for the need to rebuild the basic structure of the defense mechanisms which had fallen into disrepair over the years because of the inordinate emphasis on supplying a lifeline to Vietnam. It wasn't a popular time, if you remember, to be recommending real increases for defense programs in the aftermath of Vietnam. Yet he felt very strongly about it and, I think, had a greater knowledge of the issue than most other people because of his more than twenty years of service on the Armed Services Committee in the House. So in his first budget in 1974, and his subsequent budgets in 1975 and 1976, he was out in front arguing for the rebuilding of the undergirding base of our defense establishment because he thought it was the right thing to do. He knew it wasn't good politics in the narrow sense of how you get yourself reelected, but he thought it was the right thing to do.

You asked in your paper how President Ford staffed the organization of the Cabinet and of the Executive branch. In going back and looking through the papers, I have another note on the Ford presidency. He did a substantial amount of restaffing of his Cabinet and his administrative structure, but he did it in a very gentle way. I don't believe that the people who left from the Nixon administration and were replaced (by David Matthews at HEW, for example, and Bill Coleman in the Transportation Department, and Ed Levy who came from Chicago to be the attorney general), had a sense of hard feelings or unhappiness about President Ford's putting his own team in place. The people who had served under President Nixon, I think, left pretty uniformly with a sense of respect and fair dealing.

Perhaps there are two other thoughts that I would like
to give you that are in a way different from conventional
wisdom. I think one would find, if he asked a straphanger
on the subway in New York his or her reflections or
impressions of the Ford presidency, that there are lots of
images of Saturday Night Live characterizations of President
Ford, including the Lyndon Johnson comment about not
being able to do two things at the same time. If I could
have one wish granted it would be that the historians who
look at this time very carefully and at what President Ford
said both orally and in his written statements, to the extent
they can, would delve into some of the videotape records
that are available of his time in the presidency.

As you know, I went to what was then the Bureau of
the Budget in January of 1967, when Lyndon Johnson was
President, and served through the end of his administration,
Nixon's and Ford's. As Ken has indicated, I spent some
time in scholarly pursuits with an interest in the presidency
and our government and how it operates. As a matter of
fact, the reason I went to government is, that having
received a degree in economics and spending a year at the
Claremont Graduate School studying economics, I decided
that there was only one place to apply that knowledge.
That was in the federal government which deals with
macroeconomics issues and major sectors of our economy.

Looking back over the history of presidents and their
involvement in the details of government, I would submit to
you that at least in our time, President Ford was the best
informed President with regard to the document that
represented his budget and legislative program. Not since
President Truman did any President have the audacity to
take open questions from the press about his own budget.
And for those of you who study it on a regular basis that
probably is not a surprise. Even for those who spend a
lifetime studying it, it is crammed full of details and
nuances in areas where one could get tripped up. But I
would say that President Ford's deep understanding was no
accident. He spent literally hours—perhaps a hundred
hours—in each of the years that he was President, between
October and the first of January, going through and
listening to the detailed arguments on the composition of
the legislative and budgetary program, and it was capped off
nicely, I thought, in January of 1976. It has been a
practice for some time that a President's budget be

disclosed in a meeting in the State Department auditorium a few days before it is sent to the Congress and made available to the general public. Those of you who have been there know it is a very large auditorium, holding, perhaps, fifteen hundred people. And there are more television cameras than you can count. All the famous media representatives, and some not so famous, have an opportunity to ask questions about the President's program.

In all of the previous years of my experience in the Executive Office, it was general practice for a President to come and give a three-minute speech about the high points of his budget, then leave, and the budget director, the secretary of the treasury and their associates would answer questions on the details of the budget and the legislative program.

In 1976 President Ford decided that he wanted to do it the way Harry Truman did it. So he assembled on this large stage of the State Department the Cabinet secretaries, the heads of all of the major executive departments, and other key officials, including the vice president. They were stretched out so far you could hardly see the other end of the dais. He gave his three-minute speech and then opened himself up to questions. He answered questions for an hour and a half without reference to any of the rest of us. It was an incredible performance.

I think this incident makes another point about the Ford administration. The tapes and the conversations of this press conference were all embargoed until the materials were actually released. It has become a practice in government affairs these days that nothing survives an embargo stamp, even though it is supposed to, so details of the budget begin to leak out. So all the public ever saw of Gerald Ford's truly remarkable performance was a picture of him standing in front of a podium with the key commentators. I guess it was still Walter Cronkite at that time, Dan Rather, and Sam Donaldson, saying, "The President had a briefing today but his comments are embargoed." The public never saw the Gerald Ford who knew everything there was to know about the government and the reasons for his program proposals.

In a way, I think, that says something very important and it creates a paradoxical problem in our government's practice these days; at least it does for me. From the point of view of insider in three administrations, I continue to be frustrated by a sense that perhaps a president with a value system most easy, for me at least, to associate with, was never able to communicate that in a way which the general public could understand and respect. I would submit to you that's a problem of our time. I don't have a solution, but to me it is a very real problem. Our communications processes don't allow well-grounded politicians to communicate their thoughts and their grasp in a competitive way—that's the important point—so that the people can understand that, while they have no simple solutions, they can identify the problem.

Now, I would be delighted to reflect on experiences, issues of the times, structure of the organization, personalities or whatever else you might wish to pursue.

QUESTION: You mentioned, Mr. O'Neill, that Mr. Ford was our only unelected president, and you also mentioned that he was gentle in making staff changes. Some who have come before you in this oral history felt that he was too gentle and that it slowed down the process of putting his own stamp on his administration. I wondered whether you thought that someone with his characteristic of being gentle and not having too much ego, but having a great deal of integrity, could ever be elected?

MR. O'NEILL: It's a fair question. As a matter of fact I had an opportunity to spend a few hours with Elliot Richardson in the past couple of weeks and we were talking about this very thing. He was reflecting on his own unsuccessful run for the Massachusetts state Senate. He was remarking that there are three levels of abstraction, if you will. One is the value structure level of abstraction; the second is, the analytic layer: facts and thoughts; and the third level is stories. As he made his run for the Senate in Massachusetts, his political advisers kept saying to him, "Elliot, don't get stuck in between. People don't want to hear about how you got there. It's o.k. for you to illustrate your values, but illustrate them with stories like welfare queens and things like that because people can relate to that simple stuff." And he was agonizing about not wanting to deal with important public policy issues in that symbolic, shorthand kind of way, but really wanting to engage the minds of people in sharing with them the thought process that gets you from values to specific judgments about things.

It isn't so clear to me that we as a people have the patience to listen to the analysis. I don't know that we ever did, but I wonder now if we have the patience to listen to the analysis. We do seem to like very much a President who has a rock sense of basic values and can illustrate his points with touches that reach us emotionally, but we don't seem to have very much patience with the in-between layer. For my vote I don't care much for that but I think that's where we are.

To answer your question more directly, I suspect that Gerald Ford or someone like Gerald Ford couldn't be elected president in his own right.

QUESTION: Mr. O'Neill, wouldn't you say that OMB itself represented that in-between level? Isn't that, in fact, what OMB is?

MR. O'NEILL: Ideally it does represent that level, but I think that it is a very delicate flower. As I reflect on the change in the institution of the presidency, but more particularly on the institution of the Office of Management and Budget, I'm concerned about that layer. Going back to 1974, if I may remind you, as a consequence of the so-called Nixon impoundment program in 1973, Congress passed the 1974 Budget Control and Impoundment Act. One of the things that was included in that Act was a provision requiring, from that point forward, Senate confirmation of the director of OMB, which I think is all right, but also the deputy director of OMB, which I don't think is all right.

The reason I don't think it is all right is this. When you go back into the history of the institution of the presidency and the institution of the Bureau of the Budget, as it was created by President Roosevelt, what you find is a kind of institutional memory of the presidency. Until the 1974 Budget Control and Impoundment Act, there was, at the upper reaches of the institution, a layer of career civil servants that represented the finest in terms of the institutional memory of the presidency. As a consequence of a requirement for Senate confirmation, two layers down in the organization, the third layer, and I think now even to an extent the fourth layer of the institution, has become nonpermanent. That is to say it revolves. Not only does it revolve with administrations, but it revolves with directors. As an example, when Jim Miller became director in the Reagan administration, you may have noticed in your newspapers that he brought in a whole new group of people to serve with him as general counsel and an associate director to oversee the major functional parts of OMB. I think that practice is dangerous to the idea of continuity in the institutional presidency.

Now that isn't to say that I think there ought to be a permanent government in the sense that a president can't change the people in the OMB. But I worry that, as several of the upper layers of that former institutional memory become more transient, an important presidential resource will be lost.

As a consequence of this change in the structure, the people in OMB are no longer being asked to do the kinds of analysis they were before. In a way, it is a paradoxical thing that to the extent a person is very strong analytically, like David Stockman obviously is and was, the less likely they are to ask their staff to do the analysis. Instead, my sense of it is that it was more common in his time to ask the staff to provide supporting material for decisions he had already reached. To my mind, that's not the proper way to run the organization. You have to discount that as advice from a distance of ten years.

QUESTION: When you were in the Ford administration, did President Ford bring about much of a change in the leadership of OMB? He did bring in a new deputy. I've forgotten about the rest of them.

MR. O'NEILL: He brought in Jim Lynn as director, but before that he recommended my confirmation by the Senate as deputy director. That perhaps is an interesting footnote. The then deputy director was Fred Malek who had been there about a year and a half but had indicated his intent to leave. I believe it is true that President Nixon, before his resignation, was about to recommend my appointment and confirmation as deputy director. When I first went there I was a career official and only became a political appointee at the behest of George Schultz in 1971 after I had worked with him for about a year. I had, at that point, been at the top of the career service for, I guess, three years and George said, "I would like you to be an assistant director," and so I got that position. And then President Ford appointed me deputy. I don't know whether you would say that's a change of the top level or not. I didn't feel that I was different than I had been for the eight years I had served before he asked me to be deputy, but he did bring in Jim Lynn as the director of OMB. I would say that aside from Fred Malek there was relatively modest movement in the other key people in the OMB through the rest of the Ford administration. Bill Greener, who had been with Jim, came from the Department of Housing and Urban Development. There were a couple of others later on, not at that time but later on in 1976. They were there for a year or so. But there were no changes in the division structure of OMB through that time.

QUESTION: Is one way to show how far it has gone to say that the top fifteen positions in OMB are now politicized?

MR. O'NEILL: I think that's pretty fair. Perhaps another way to say it is that so far as I know there is no one in the top positions of OMB who has come from the career service. If you go back and think about Sam Hughes, Sam Cohen and Roger Jones and the other people who were part of that institutional presidency, they all came from the career service. They all came with ten or fifteen years worth of experience in doing something else before they got to that point. They weren't layered on as apprentices.

QUESTION: I finished a book recently that required me to interview a lot of people at OMB and I can confirm that their nostalgia for the Gerald Ford presidency is tremendous. I interviewed the senior civil servants—Dale McComber, Pete Modlin, and a number of other people—and very clearly the delight they took in working for Gerald Ford came through because of the feeling they could sit down with him as a co-worker. He was first among equals; he was the President, but he treated them as fellow professionals and they said they delighted in discussing the budget with him because of his grasp, and also the fact that he was willing to let them go to the barons of Congress and try to explain impossible deals and ask that they be cut even as he was warning OMB that the deal would not fly. They appreciated that enormously.

Of all the people I interviewed I think Jim Lynn was probably the single most valuable source of information I had. He offered two concepts which I hear reflected in your remarks. He said, "There are two great failings in government: one is, we don't take advantage of our analytical resource, the people we have who are strong in a particular area, and secondly, we don't explain problems to the public at the level at which they actually have to be solved." But there is a lot of good feeling about those days among the people who are still at OMB and a real sense of respect for President Ford.

QUESTION: Did Nixon and Johnson have this same respect, do you think, for the career service?

MR. O'NEILL: Let me answer you in this way. President Johnson, as you know, had been in and around government for a long time and he had people that he knew in departments and agencies because of his experience on the Hill. It wasn't unusual for him to pick up the phone and call a GS15 in the Labor Department and say, "Tell me about this" or "Get me this fact." But I think he didn't have as much use for the analytic process. He was interested in using analysis if it supported a deal that he wanted to make. I don't mean that in a pejorative way, but his idea of governance was markedly different than President Ford's.

Maybe the best way to communicate President Nixon's approach is the way it is reflected in a transcript that we did back in 1977. He was constantly calling for a "Brandeis brief." The term Brandeis brief was shorthand for a brilliantly argued document that illuminated all the important recesses of any important issue crisply—no wasted words, to the point—and then with all the recommendations of key advisers listed with any conditioning remarks they wanted to add to the decision memos. I guess I can tell you that in the time he was there I never recall having a discussion with him on a detailed, analytical piece of government business. Part of the reason for that, I think, is that he got most of what he felt he needed from the written documentation.

I think this is a point worth making in differentiating between the Nixon and Ford presidencies, with the former using the documentation approach with a requirement for excellence in a written document that went to the President. I think if you look in the archives when they are available on the Nixon presidency, you will be amazed at the quality of the documentation that went to the President. It was extraordinarily carefully done because I think all of the participants in the process understood those documents were probably going to control the decision. In other words, whatever President Nixon decided probably flowed out of that so-called Brandeis brief. It led to extraordinary care in their preparation, the explanations of arguments, and in the crispness of presentation.

My own perception is that after President Ford became President, while a lot of the mechanisms for producing those documents remained in place, the quality of the papers deteriorated some, not because the people had changed but because people understood that what they put in writing might not be their last opportunity to influence the issue. The President would sit around the table and listen to arguments and draw people out and test the emotional depth of their position, adding this to whatever he was able to get out of the written documents.

I would say, although I was not as far up the line in the process in the Johnson days, that there was less organization to the Johnson process than there was to the Nixon process. It was less thorough-going and we tended to do more things late at night. We had to have a health message, for example. Jim Gaither, who was then in charge of health programs working for Joe Califano, would get a bunch of us together and we would create a health program, or maybe ten health programs, to go into a presidential message.

It was different in the Nixon presidency. I remember—I think it was in February of 1971—President Nixon sent a health message to the Congress laying out all of the dimensions of what he thought the nation ought to be doing with regard to financing health, doing research, construction of facilities, preparation of professionals to deliver health care and all the rest. It was a combination of months of pulling together thoughts and ideas and refining them. It wasn't something that was done over a weekend by a group of smart people who needed to get a message done. It was a laborious detailed process.

So I think there was a marked difference between the

presidencies and how they approached issues and problems, especially when they were controlling the pace.

QUESTION: In the example you gave where President Ford was so thoroughly prepared on the budget and gave such an excellent presentation of it, was it completely under his or his staff's control about when he would give it, whether it would be embargoed or not, or the circumstances? Were there some in the staff who didn't have complete confidence in President Ford's ability to get his messages across in view of the remarks that Johnson had made, such as that he didn't wear a helmet when he played football?

MR. O'NEILL: I suspect there was, Ralph. There were some staffers who thought they were smarter than the President and that he couldn't hold his own in an open forum. Honestly, I do think there was some of that and it causes me to remember another issue of that time.

You may remember that Jim Schlesinger resigned as secretary of defense in October of 1975. In a way it was related to this very issue. We were in the process of preparing the President's budget and legislative program, importantly including his ideas as to what programs should be for defense in his budget which would go to the Congress in January. He got a letter from Jim spelling out what Jim thought were the consequences of living with the amount of funding that the President had tentatively decided should be the amount for the defense activities in his upcoming budget. I think the major reason for Jim Schlesinger's departure was President Ford's own deep understanding of the defense program, of defense activities and his sense of unhappiness that Jim chose to represent the consequences in a way one might represent them in a public forum where you were being the devil's advocate rather than in a sense of a confidential memorandum to one of the best informed people in the world on the subject. I frankly think Jim seriously underestimated the President's own understanding of those issues which was much greater than his own. It had a fair amount to do with the fact that we had a new secretary of defense and a president with experience in defense.

But it is true that there were many who then and who still today do not understand the depth of understanding

President Ford had of what the government was all about
and what the issues of the day were all about.

QUESTION: With regard to this dichotomy between
understanding and political communication, what are your
reflections on what the results of the 1976 election might
have turned on and how it might have come out differently?

MR. O'NEILL: The important thing is that the economy had
been through the wringer beginning in late 1974. Things
were improving markedly as we went through 1976 beginning
in about May of 1976 and carried forward interestingly
enough in 1977 so that President Carter got the benefit of a
much improving economic situation with major reductions in
unemployment and major retrenchment in the rate of
inflation. I think the economy had something to do with it.
But clearly the pardon was an issue that was very difficult
to overcome because there was such a strong feeling among
important constituents that President Nixon shouldn't have
been pardoned. To his credit, I think President Ford made
a decision about which he has commented in his own
memoirs, saying that it was his sense that the country was
not going to do well if it had to continue to focus on the
Watergate affair and all the events associated with that. I
think even if he had it to do over again, he still would
pardon President Nixon because he thought it was the right
thing to do.

Now the other thing that might have made a difference
in the 1976 election would have been if the other candidate
for the nomination had spent some time in the southern
states. Even then I suspect President Ford would have been
elected in his own right and probably we would have had
different nominees in 1980 than those that we did.

QUESTION: So the candidate who held out from his own
strategic viewpoint did the shrewd thing.

MR. O'NEILL: From his viewpoint I think he did the
shrewd thing, yes.

QUESTION: You make a good case as did those who
preceded you here, that Ford was a much better president
than is commonly perceived. I personally want a president
who graduated from the University of Michigan to go down

in history with a much better reputation. The perception
today by most people though still centers around hitting
people in the head with golf balls and falling down airplane
steps. Yet today's President, whether you support him or
not, is rather removed from these things. Hardly a week
goes by that somebody isn't correcting all his misstatements.
Today we think that's charming and actually enhances his
reputation. What has happened that Ford is still ridiculed
for these stupid little things that had nothing to do with
the kind of presidency he ran? Yet today the whole value
system seems to have changed.

MR. O'NEILL: I'm not so sure it is the whole value system.
Let me set a scene for you which you may not remember.
In 1976 at the Republican Convention in Kansas City, after
all of the vote counting, President Ford gave his acceptance
speech. You probably don't remember, but aside from his
thoughts after being sworn in and a speech that he did at
the Old North Church in Boston in 1976 as part of the
bicentennial, probably his third finest public appearance was
the acceptance speech that he gave to the nominating
convention in Kansas City in 1976. He worked at it very
hard. He knew it was important; he knew there was a
major television audience and he really worked hard for it
not only to be a thoughtful speech but a well-delivered
speech. He did very well.
     But then, because of the charity of his spirit, he
invited the defeated candidate, Ronald Reagan, to come
down and share the spotlight with him. Ronald Reagan
came down to the platform and the President invited him to
speak, and he did for about fifteen minutes, apparently
without notes or previous preparation. I can say to you as
a partisan, one who felt very strongly about which of the
two should be President of the United States, I was moved
by what Ronald Reagan had to say. That's not quite right.
I was moved not so much by what he said as by how he
said it. That man has an unbelievable ability to evoke
positive emotions and other kinds of emotion. He really can
move people. Thank God he's not a demagogue. But I
guess the sum of that is to say that I'm not sure our values
have changed. I suspect if President Carter were still
President and he created factual errors or made factual
misstatement or didn't know the U.S. resolution was 242

instead of 422, that he would be beat up in the media every day. It's a very curious thing.

I don't know of any other living politician who is able to get away with such misstatements, but our current President has that ability to move people and I think maybe to communicate a sense of value that people can associate with that covers all sins. It doesn't matter. It's a very curious thing.

NARRATOR: To come back to President Ford for a moment. We all heard Tom Brokaw interviewing him and remember that his coach was quoted as saying that one of the main things he remembered about Reagan, as a football player, was that he talked a lot. Most of us, if we've done anything in athletics, have been able to trade on it for thirty or forty years. Yet here was a man who was virtually an all-American and who probably is the greatest athlete we've ever had in the White House, who never seemed to trade on that strength. How does one account for that? How do we explain that the genuine thing, the real thing, somehow didn't attract public recognition?

MR. O'NEILL: I think we like to focus on the negative. President Ford was a very good skier, but you may remember that we don't see any pictures of him charging down the slopes at age sixty-five. Many of us are not even trying any more. But what you see is President Ford falling over in the snow. You don't see President Ford the near-scratch golfer, who can play with the professionals with ease. What you see are pictures of someone getting hit in the noggin with a ball. The professionals do it too but you never see pictures of them; you see President Ford. And you see Bob Hope, his dear friend, making fun of his friend Gerald Ford hitting people in the head with golf balls. I don't know why it is.

It may not be true, but I think in a way it makes your point very well. President Nixon is not a graceful person; he's not an athlete as President Ford is. At least the inside story was that when President Nixon went some place for an appearance and he had to go up a staircase, the advance people would count how many stairs and it would be on his briefing card so he could count as he went up. That may overdo it a little bit, but President Ford would bound up the stairs three at a time. Yet we have this impression, brought to us by television, of this person who can't get out of his own way. It's a very curious thing. And most importantly, I think, it causes a question about the competence of a person's ability to deal with the major issues of our time. That's a very damaging thing.

QUESTION: But isn't this a reflection of the power of television as much as any question of people's values? It's the choice of TV producers and other kinds of media to present that side.

MR. O'NEILL: Oh, I think so, but I don't know how we deal with it unless we isolate presidents even more than we do now so that they are not ever exposed to anything but what they want to focus on.

I remember that Ron Nessen was so aggravated by this problem of the media picking up things and making a lot out of them that at one point he wouldn't allow the photographers to get a clear shot at the President getting on the helicopter because he was big and he was forever bumping his head getting in the helicopter. I don't think, at least in my construct of what our democracy ought to be like, that we shouldn't be able to see pictures of our president bumping his head. But it shouldn't influence what we think about his ability to govern. Yet it does. I just leave it with you as a paradox, but as a very important paradox, as to how we can elect someone who has a good value system but works through the analytic layer and then can communicate it to us in some symbols. It is frightening to think of what a demagogue could do the way the media now communicates things.

NARRATOR: All of us wish the International Paper Company well in the days and weeks and months ahead. If, however, for any reason there is an open space in the career of its current president, one of the things we might dream of would be that the Miller Center academical village might provide a residency for him, for a shorter or longer period, to continue to think thoughtfully and significantly on the central issues of governance that he has raised today. We are delighted, Paul, that you joined us today and look forward to future visits.

III.

FORD
AND THE
ECONOMY

FORD AND THE FEDERAL RESERVE

ARTHUR F. BURNS

NARRATOR: Ambassador Burns was born in Stanislaw, Austria. He was educated from the bachelor's through the Ph.D. degree at one institution, Columbia University. Throughout, one notes a recurrent pattern in his academic career. At Rutgers, he began as an instructor and ended as a full professor of economics. He was first a visiting professor at Columbia and then John Bates Clark Professor. He was initially a research associate at the National Bureau and ultimately chairman of the Bureau. That was one stage in his life when I had a very modest contact with Ambassador Burns. The Rockefeller Foundation gave support to the National Bureau of Economic Research, largely because of the immense confidence they had in Professor Burns and in the work that he and others were doing there. Many would say the golden age of the National Bureau was when Arthur Burns was chairman. In the Eisenhower administration, Ambassador Burns served as chairman of the Council of Economic Advisers from 1953 to 1956. From 1969 to 1970 he was counselor to President Nixon. From 1970 to 1978 he was chairman of the Board of Governors of the Federal Reserve System. Only recently, he returned to Washington from his position as ambassador to the Federal Republic of Germany in the Reagan administration.

Among many other awards, he is the recipient of the Alexander Hamilton Award from the Department of the Treasury and the Jefferson Award from the Institute of Public Service. Next to Father Hesburgh, he must have the

largest number of honorary degrees of any living American.
I counted thirty before I stopped counting. In every way
it's a great honor to have Arthur Burns with us. We
thought we would conduct our session essentially on a
question and answer basis.

QUESTION: What is your opinion of the conflict that has
arisen between Martin Feldstein, chairman of the Reagan
Council of Economic Advisers and President Reagan?

AMBASSADOR BURNS: Feldstein is one of the ablest
economists in the country. His advice to the President on
economic issues was consistently sound, but he made the
fatal mistake of pursuing a quasi-independent role. If you
are the President's adviser you can't quarrel, or even appear
to be quarreling with the President in public. You can
quarrel and fight, yes, but you must do it privately.

QUESTION: A subject that has been discussed and debated
over the years is the relationship between the chairman of
the Federal Reserve Board of Governors and the President.
I wonder if you could describe your relationship during
those years, and the extent to which the President may
have wished or tried to influence the action that was taken
by the Federal Reserve.

AMBASSADOR BURNS: As chairman of the Federal Reserve,
I had the opportunity to work with President Nixon,
President Ford and President Carter. I also had the
opportunity to observe the relationship between the
President and the chairman of the Council of Economic
Advisers. Confining my remarks for the moment to these
three Presidents with whom I worked as chairman of the
Federal Reserve Board, I would say that, from the viewpoint
of the Federal Reserve, Mr. Nixon's record was by far the
worst. Mr. Ford's record was by far the best. Mr. Nixon
tried to interfere with the Federal Reserve both in ways
that were fair and in ways that, by almost any standard,
were unfair.

Mr. Ford, on the other hand, was truly angelic. I met
with President Ford frequently, alone in the privacy of his
office. He never inquired about what the Federal Reserve
was doing. He never even remotely intimated what the
Federal Reserve should be doing. The closest he ever came

to it was during a conversation which began on his part with the statement, "Arthur, I'm going to ask you a banking question and the question may be improper. If it is please attribute it to my ignorance, my innocence, and don't hold it against me. Just ignore it. Don't answer it if it's even remotely improper." I said, "Well, I'd like to hear your question, Mr. President." Around that time a series of articles had appeared in the *Washington Post* on problems in the banking world. These articles gave some emphasis to problem banks. They were somewhat sensational articles. The *New York Times* couldn't be far behind and began publishing articles of a similar nature. Mr. Ford said, "I've been reading articles about problem banks. Is this something that I should be interested in?" That's as close as he ever came to asking a question that the Federal Reserve was at all involved in.

President Ford's record, to repeat, was perfect. Mr. Carter had a good record but not a perfect one. Mr. Eisenhower had a good record, but again, not perfect.

I recall President Ford announcing one day that he was coming over to the Fed. Some of my colleagues were disturbed. I wasn't disturbed, but I was curious. Why would he want to visit the Federal Reserve? I began making some discreet inquiries and the only item of information that I thought might be useful was that it was his birthday. I had some fun introducing him to the Fed staff, telling him the awful thoughts that had crossed my mind about his purpose in coming to the Fed, and how I dismissed one awful thought after another, finally deciding that he couldn't think of a better place to celebrate his birthday. Actually, he came there to tell us what he thought of the Federal Reserve and how he valued the Federal Reserve's independence. Every president I've known has made remarks to that effect. Gerald Ford believed it and practiced it. It's almost hard to believe that a president could act so judiciously and show such great self-restraint about matters that were obviously significant to him.

QUESTION: One of the things that's come up in visits of other members of the Ford administration has been what the sports writers call, "disarray in the team." The one weakness that we seem to sense is that the Ford loyalists—the people who had been with him in the Congress and in

Michigan—saw themselves, and were perceived as being in opposition to what they refer to as the "Praetorian Guard," the group who were carry-overs from the Nixon administration. We've heard a lot about that, and our visitor yesterday, Hedley Donovan, said that President Ford's one weakness was that he didn't knock heads together. I wondered whether that was the other side of this great strength that you have seen in his restraint on the question of the independence of the Federal Reserve?

AMBASSADOR BURNS: I don't think it's true that he did not knock heads together. He listened to a great many and listened carefully. I think those whom he inherited from the Nixon administration, the people that he brought in and occasional visitors, all had their say and all had his ear. I give President Ford very high marks as President.

QUESTION: I was wondering if perhaps the explanation of Ford's very unique relationship with the Federal Reserve might stem in part from his congressional background. Unlike Nixon, who believed that he had a right to give orders to anybody including the chairman of an independent agency like the Federal Reserve, Ford was a man who believed in compromise and listening and working out arrangements. So, while he valued the independence of the Fed, he may also have been the kind of person who was interested in behind the scenes compromise, behind the scenes advising. While he supported strongly, the legal independence of the Federal Reserve, what he was interested in was a close and informal working relationship that may very well have been unique in the history of the Fed. I was wondering if you might subscribe to that?

AMBASSADOR BURNS: I was informally a member of President Ford's economic team. If there was a name for it, I don't recall. I attended meetings, expressed my views, but, perhaps a little unfairly, it was a one way street. I did not indicate to any of the presidents I worked with, or their secretaries, what the Federal Reserve was all about and what it was planning. In fact, I would inform the Treasury, the White House and the Council of Economic Advisers about two to five minutes before the press was informed. My intentions were never disclosed. The reason for reticence was that I feared leaks and their effect on financial markets. Thus I learned what the administration was doing and gave my advice, but I never disclosed what the Federal Reserve planned to do except in the most general terms. We aim at stability. We aim at full employment. We aim to drive out the monster of inflation. I did not disclose to anyone in the administration or to anyone else how we would proceed and what actions we might take. This, of course, was resented by some who might perhaps criticize me for conducting the Federal Reserve System as I did. But if I were doing it again, I would do it the same way. Right or wrong, it's my way. But I am profoundly convinced it's the right way: the Fed must not play favorites or run the risk of rocking markets.

FORD AND THE ECONOMY:
NATIONAL AND INTERNATIONAL

KENNETH RUSH

NARRATOR: Kenneth Rush has served as secretary of state ad interim, deputy secretary of state, deputy secretary of defense, ambassador to Germany, and ambassador to France. He was our principal negotiator in the Berlin negotiations, and the quadripartite negotiations in Berlin. He has been chairman of the Atlantic Council for the past eight years. He graduated from the University of Tennessee and the Yale Law School and taught at Duke University Law School. He has been active in a number of presidential commissions dealing with both economic and foreign policy matters. It is a great pleasure to welcome him to the Miller Center.

AMBASSADOR RUSH: Thank you very much, Ken. My acquaintance with President Nixon was of course far more extensive and far deeper than my acquaintance with President Ford. At the end of President Nixon's tenure, I was counsellor to the President for Economic Policy. I was also a member of the cabinet and of the National Security Council and was the coordinator of domestic and international economic policy. As the president's principal spokesman on economic affairs, I was supposed to keep peace and order in Washington, which of course is an impossible task. I continued in this post when Ford became president.

Since Ford had become vice president I had periodically briefed him on the economic picture. We played golf occasionally; he loved golf, and I did too. I had known

141

him when he was minority leader in the House. One reason
he was chosen by Nixon was that the confirmation process
would not be as long and difficult as it would have been for
someone who was not a member of Congress. Remember
what Nelson Rockefeller went through in the Senate
confirmation process when President Ford named him as vice
president.

After the resignation of President Nixon, President
Ford took control at once. He had had no executive
experience, although he had been in the Congress and been
a politician most of his adult life. I was very impressed by
his openness and his willingness to learn. For example, my
approach with President Nixon had been that I would meet
with the members of the economic team, Bill Simon,
secretary of the treasury, Alan Greenspan and before that
Herb Stein, chairman of the Council of Economic Advisers,
and Roy Ash, the head of OMB, sometimes joined by Arthur
Burns, chairman of the Federal Reserve. We would thrash
things out and reach a consensus, then go in and present it
to the President and get his views or decision. Usually, the
discussion with Nixon didn't last all that long. In addition,
I insisted that no one of the economic leaders could get to
the President directly without my being there because it is
impossible to coordinate things if people are running around
your back to see the president. I continued this policy
when Ford came in.

President Ford, however, liked to hear all the
arguments, so we spent large amounts of time hearing the
whole discussion all over again. I think that was due in
part to the fact that President Ford didn't know the
background the way President Nixon did; he liked, therefore,
to get all the different points of view directly.

President Ford was much more informal than President
Nixon had been. At White House dinners, for example, we
would usually meet with President and Mrs. Nixon and
whoever the honored guests might be upstairs in the Nixons'
private sitting room. Then we'd go down to the formal
dinner. By way of contrast, Ford started out with a dinner
for Nelson Rockefeller up on the second floor. It was the
first time we'd ever done that. Then we had a dance and
the entire evening was festive and informal. President
Nixon would usually leave shortly after the dinner.
President Ford and Mrs. Ford, both of whom liked to dance,
would stay until one or one thirty in the morning. They

might be the last ones to leave. We didn't have to follow protocol; we could go home without waiting for them to leave. President Ford loved life; he loved the job. He fitted in very well.

There were four really big issues that were immediately and urgently confronting him when he became President: One of them was organizing the White House. The second issue was deciding whether or not everyone who had held a top position on the White House staff under Nixon should be replaced. The third was a question of whether or not President Nixon should be pardoned. The fourth issue was that the economy was increasingly worrisome. Of course I was deeply involved in that.

On the organization of the White House, I felt that Ford should not retain any top Nixon personnel. So, shortly after President Ford came in, I went to see him and told him I wanted to leave. He asked me what I wanted to do, and told me that he would like me to remain in his administration. I told him that if he wanted me to stay with him, I didn't want to be in Washington, that I would like to be ambassador to France. He said, "Oh, fine, that would be wonderful." So I was appointed ambassador to France. He wanted me to stay on for three months, however, as economic counsellor, primarily because he was going to have an economic summit. He wanted me to be chairman of the Congressional-Presidential Steering Committee for the summit and then continue until he organized his own economic staff.

The big focus of attention, however, was directed toward Al Haig. Al had been chief of staff, of course, for President Nixon. He had done a magnificent job and was now continuing on during the transition. He had handled the transition wonderfully well and Ford liked him.

Ford's right-hand man and really his chief of staff when he was vice president was Bob Hartmann. Bob, for whatever reasons one may attribute to him, whether his convictions or his desire for power, was very anxious to get everyone associated with Nixon out of the White House. While Ford kept telling me how much he admired Al Haig, Bob Hartmann was feeding the press all kinds of bad stuff about Haig that I really couldn't understand. It was obvious that Al should not stay on too long. I discussed it with President Ford. He thought about making Al chairman of the Joint Chiefs. I and others told him we thought that

was very unwise because then Al would have to go before
the Senate for confirmation by the Senate. Then we'd be
back into the whole Watergate thing all over again. The
politically motivated senators would inquire about everything
that Al had ever done in the White House. Then President
Ford himself came up with the idea of making him SACEUR
(Supreme Allied Commander of Europe). He performed there
in a magnificent way.

On the other hand, the dominant man in the Nixon
administration on foreign policy, the most brilliant and the
most controversial man in the Cabinet was Henry Kissinger.
Even Bob Hartmann didn't think Ford should remove Henry
because Henry was the only one in the administration who
had a lot of support in the press. He had considerable
support from the eastern liberal establishment which was
otherwise not very friendly toward the Ford administration.
There were other people in the Cabinet who were outstanding. Jim Schlesinger was secretary of defense; Bill
Simon was secretary of the treasury. President Ford kept
them, which I think was wise. As far as the White House
was concerned, however, I felt it was best that we have
pretty much of a clean sweep. Anne Armstrong, who is
tops, was made ambassador to the United Kingdom. In
essence, President Ford adopted a policy of putting his own
people in the White House and keeping a lot of the
excellent Nixon people in the Cabinet and other areas of
government.

With regard to the pardon, President Ford felt that
unless he gave President Nixon the pardon his whole
administration would be crippled by a hangover of
Watergate. There would be continued reinvestigation of
President Nixon, continued playing up of Watergate in the
media. The emotional feeling against President Nixon in the
press, in the eastern establishment, and the more liberal
foreign policy establishment was very intense; they weren't
going to let Watergate die.

In fact, I was to go on television on "Meet the Press"
the day the pardon came out. When I arrived for this
presentation on the economy, there were people from the
New York Times and other journalists there. They were
like a group of jackals who had just seen the rabbit plucked
out of their mouths. They were literally livid; they were
absolutely furious over the pardon. But President Ford felt
that if he were going to start the country on a new course

and try to erase the differences and decrease the destructive emotionalism, the pardon was absolutely essential. I thoroughly agreed with him.

With regard to the economy, we had a very serious problem. You can't settle economic difficulties by sleight of hand or by voodoo economics or anything else. Ford decided to start off with an economic summit where we could bring together the top economists in the country. He hoped to have a discussion and work out something of a consensus on policy among the leading economists of the country. To show the kind of man Ford is, one man who had great personal publicity as a so-called economist, and who knew President Ford, found out about the Summit and asked Ford to be invited. Ford agreed. As soon as we heard of this, Alan Greenspan, Bill Simon and Arthur Burns came to me very upset, saying that this particular economist looked on the Summit as a political rather than a purely economic, nonpartisan thing and his presence would hurt the credibility and stature of the Summit. They wanted me to assume the very unpleasant task of going to President Ford and asking him if he would reverse himself after he had promised the man he could come. I did that. Knowing I wasn't going to continue in Washington anyway, I wasn't worried about being fired; so it didn't take too much courage. President Ford listened to me as I told him how the others felt and then he said, "All right, go ahead and withdraw the invitation." He really did adopt an approach that he would do what was good for the country irrespective of its effect on his being elected in 1976; he was going to be a good President. He was dedicated to doing a good job.

President Ford developed a good rapport with President Giscard d'Estaing which helped me a great deal when I was in France. President Ford continued to have excellent relationships with him and also with Helmut Schmidt, who is one of the great statesman of our day. As a matter of fact, Schmidt was so indiscreet as to come out very strongly in favor of Ford for president, something a foreign head of government doesn't normally do. This did not improve his standing with Carter when Carter won. In any event President Ford got along well with the other heads of State and he conducted himself well. A lot of people tended to deprecate Ford, but I have a very high admiration for him.

When I came back to tell him goodbye in January, 1977, after he had been defeated, he told me that when he became President he had been concerned about taking on the presidency. Of course no one is trained for that office, but he had had very little training for it. He wondered whether he was up to the job. He felt that he was not equipped to do an outstanding job as President and now just when he felt that way he had been defeated. He is not a vindictive man at all. As you know, in 1976, Reagan ran for the Republican nomination for President and then when he lost did not give enthusiastic support to President Ford's campaign. There were a lot of people in the Ford camp who felt that Reagan may have been an important factor in Ford's defeat. Yet Ford has substantial admiration for Reagan. Reagan is a great President and Ford has supported him pretty much down the line. Politicians in fact are not likely to be the most favored candidates to go through the pearly gates. One of their distinctive traits is vindictiveness against people who oppose them, but Ford is not that way. I deeply regret that he wasn't elected President again in 1976. If he had been it would have been a much better world, I think, than we have had.

Since he left the presidency we've stayed in touch. I asked him to be on the board of the Atlantic Council, which he agreed to do. He held a conference on the Congress, the President, and Foreign Policy at the Ford Library. This was a study which Ed Muskie and I co-chaired, sponsored by the Atlantic Council in association with the Association of Former Members of Congress. Ford, also a former member of Congress, agreed to kick it off. He wants to turn his library into a living thing, to have discussions and seminars there, to contribute primarily to foreign policy but also to economic policy and to study presidencies. The first meeting held there was this one on the Congress, the President and Foreign Policy. It was very interesting and constructive. We got almost all the ex-secretaries of state and the ex-assistants to the President for national security policy there. Ken Thompson was the rapporteur for the study. I hope all of you have read his report. I urge you to do so because Ken did a great job.

QUESTION: Ambassador Rush, would you comment on the First Ladies, both Mrs. Ford and Mrs. Nixon? As you said, the press was so ugly to Mr. Nixon and I have read how ugly it was to Mrs. Nixon.

AMBASSADOR RUSH: The wife of a full-time politician usually has almost no family life, as you know. Politicians are running for office all the time; they are out campaigning for fellow politicians; they are out in the evening. It's a tough life and the wife has a very tough time. President Nixon has a great respect for his wife, as I know. I think she is very unhappy about the way she and her husband were treated in the press. She went through a terrible time and her health has suffered. But as far as I know, the Nixons have always had a very fine relationship. It was not, however, one of those relationships of interdependence where they went home every night, ate across the table from each other, and discussed their mutual problems.

Mrs. Ford, as you know, had an alcohol problem which she now has completely overcome. She is a very charming person. I never knew of this problem until she announced it herself. I'm not intimate with either of the Fords. I've had dinner much more often with President Nixon in a small group than I have with President Ford. But I would say that for political families, as husband and wife, they certainly seem to have as good a relationship as one could expect. To be the wife of a politician who is running for office all the time is not a recipe for a close marriage. It just isn't.

QUESTION: Ambassador Rush, this morning you commented that one of the weaknesses of President Nixon was his refusal to face up to firing people. But Ford did fire James Schlesinger. We thought the reason was the conflict with Kissinger. Would you elaborate on that, is that true?

AMBASSADOR RUSH: I'd like to comment. What I meant about President Nixon was not that he wouldn't fire people but that he didn't want to do it personally. He fired a lot of people. Just as he never asked me to serve in a position until he had somebody ask me first so I wouldn't feel that I had to serve or turn down the President, he never, that I know of, fired anyone directly until he had to fire Haldeman and Erlichman because Bill Rogers wouldn't do it. He really just hated to hurt people.

Now on Jim Schlesinger: Jim is a very able man. However, his strong point is not diplomacy. He antagonized President Nixon to a point that Nixon would have fired him if it hadn't been for Watergate. For example, I was sitting at a Cabinet meeting just before President Nixon was going over to see Brezhnev. There was a great controversy about just what we should do on the pending SALT II discussions. Jim got up in the Cabinet meeting with a lot of charts and the like and sort of lectured the President and the rest of us. He told the President, "With your great diplomatic skills you can put this over. You can put this over very easily." President Nixon was furious at him. Pretty soon President Ford developed the same attitude toward Jim.

Jim did not always espouse the policy of the President. For example, Jim came to France and I asked him to stay with me at the Residence. He was seeing the top people of France, such as the defense minister. His approach on many matters of defense was not President Ford's approach. It is true that Henry Kissinger didn't get along with Schlesinger, but he hadn't gotten along with any of the secretaries of defense anyway so that didn't make any difference. It wasn't a vendetta of Henry Kissinger's. It was more, I think, Jim's inability to sell himself to the presidents. Carter fired him too, you know, as secretary of Energy.

QUESTION: How would you compare Ford's and Nixon's grasp of foreign policy questions such as U.S.-Soviet relations, European integration, and other issues?

AMBASSADOR RUSH: There was no comparison. President Nixon knows foreign policy probably better than anyone in the country, and that doesn't exclude Henry Kissinger who is a master in this whole area. President Nixon's judgment was, I think, far better than Henry's, although Henry is a brilliant and a very able person.

President Ford had had very little experience in foreign policy. Kissinger had become such a folk hero to the press and the opinion makers that President Ford, if he wanted to, which he didn't, was not in a position to fire him. It would undermine his administration very seriously, so Ford didn't have the ability to control Kissinger the way presidents want to control their secretaries of state. On the other hand, Henry was loyal to him and they are fond of each other. They worked well in tandem. In contrast to President Nixon and Henry, where before Watergate you had more of a relationship of master and employee, a partnership developed between Ford and Kissinger.

President Nixon dominated foreign policy making completely, President Ford did not. But as someone in charge of foreign policy, President Nixon was so far ahead of any other President that I know of that there is no comparison.

QUESTION: There has been conflict over the years between secretaries of state and national security advisers, depending on who is in the two offices. Do you have any comments or thoughts about whether we have a good workable system there now or whether it should be changed in some way?

AMBASSADOR RUSH: There are two basic concepts of what the assistant to the president for National Security Affairs should do. One concept is that he will coordinate for the president: present the differing views so the president can decide. The other is that he will dominate foreign policy through the president. Brzezinski under Carter and Kissinger under Nixon wanted to dominate foreign policy through the president. In contrast, Brent Scowcroft, Bud McFarlane and Bill Clark have tried to present the differing views without trying to be the preeminent person next to the president in foreign policy. There is no doubt at all that George Shultz is the one that President Reagan looks to most of all on foreign policy. So much of foreign policy is tied up in defense and national security that you do have serious conflicts between Defense and State, however.

I don't quarrel with these different points of view. What I do quarrel with is the attempt to eliminate a State or Defense input to the President. He should really know the whole story and make a decision. I think that the approach of both Kissinger and Brzezinski was that "The view I just expressed is the right one."

QUESTION: I'd like to know how President Ford personally evaluated the European allies, NATO, and perhaps France in particular, as in some way necessary to the conduct of American foreign policy. In other words, what importance did he attach to a working relationship in foreign policy with France, West Germany, the UK?

AMBASSADOR RUSH: President Ford and of course Henry Kissinger, realized that the NATO alliance and our alliance with Japan are the foundation of any sound foreign policy. They also realized that if we are going to be able to keep our allies strongly behind us, they have to be consulted in advance of any dramatic steps such as the opening to China, or the Year of Europe, or the oil conference. But those principles have to give way sometimes to practicality. If Japan and Germany in particular, which is a sieve as far as leaking is concerned, had been told about the proposed opening to China, it would have immediately come back here and become a great domestic issue. We never would have been able to go anywhere. You are faced with a problem of desiring consultation but realizing that the other governments leak just as much as we do. When a President doesn't even consult his secretary of state on some things, it's a little hard to go out and consult the president of France and the chancellor of Germany. It's a dilemma all the time.

QUESTION: I'm sure that's true and I think it is true for other governments as well. I was wondering whether he thought that it was important to the United States to retain the working cooperation of countries like Germany and France. Or whether as some people have alleged, he didn't really think these countries mattered very much.

AMBASSADOR RUSH: First of all, actions are the best proof. During the reelection campaign of 1976, Helmut Schmidt, came out strongly for Ford. He wouldn't have done so if he'd felt that Ford was not in favor of cooperating fully with Germany. Giscard d'Estaing was very strongly in favor of Ford and his reelection. The same thing was true of the U.K. and of our other allies.

   Al Haig did a great job as SACEUR in helping to solidify the support of the administration in the defense field. Henry Kissinger had the high regard of our allies. President Ford cooperated very fully, I thought, with the allies in trying to solve economic problems, security affairs, and monetary issues.

   I remember when the U.S. dollar was down to 3.9 francs to the dollar. President Giscard d'Estaing would call me in periodically to say we were destroying France and

Europe with this cheap dollar. The dollar is now up to 10 francs to the dollar and the French say that we are destroying their economic structure with our strong dollar. We are going to be criticized no matter what we do because there are pluses and minuses to any policy.

In terms of strengthening NATO, our allies cooperated pretty well during the Ford administration. We backed NATO strongly. Vietnam was removed as a serious irritant to the allies. We were progressing on the SALT II talks. The thing that worried the allies most was the fact that our defense establishment was deteriorating rapidly and their security was also deteriorating as a part of the post-Vietnam War syndrome in the U.S. The defense budget was cut way back by the Congress every year. Our allies were very worried that under our system, even the President could not get the support needed for proper national security purposes.

I would say the allies thought Ford cooperated with them about as much as any of our recent presidents. The one they admired most was Nixon by far because they approved thoroughly of detente; they approved thoroughly of the opening to China; they approved thoroughly of his overall foreign policy considering it to be very enlightened and very beneficial to their own security.

You had a Ford-Kissinger foreign policy; you couldn't separate the two. Henry had a huge influence. While the accomplishments are not as great as Nixon's, the effort was very great in the Middle East particularly, and elsewhere. The year of Europe was a very serious irritant and a rather foolish idea. We didn't even consult them in advance about it. Overall, however, I think the relations with our allies under Ford were good.

QUESTION: Could you throw any light on the so-called lapse in the Carter-Ford foreign policy debate when President Ford seemed to suggest that the Soviet Union had no dominance whatsoever in Eastern Europe?

AMBASSADOR RUSH: That was very sad. He does stumble, like all of us. What he was trying to say, I think, and didn't was that the Soviet Union could not crush the spirit of the Polish people. They could never really conquer the Polish people, but what he actually said was that the Soviet Union didn't dominate Poland. That's a very different thing, and you can't correct it once you are on television. When you are on nationwide television and running for president you're stuck.

NARRATOR: Somebody said Kissinger had briefed him and that that had added to the confusion.

AMBASSADOR RUSH: I think actually that that was just one of those things where he didn't say what he meant to say and it was too bad.

QUESTION: Here are two Presidents who have both arrived at the presidency from Congress. Once they reached this lofty position where most members of Congress want to be someday, what was their attitude towards Congress? Did they have different ways of dealing with the members?

AMBASSADOR RUSH: As you know, Johnson came from the Congress; Kennedy came from the Congress; Truman came from the Congress. All of them, once they were President, felt that the Congress was in their way. Your perspective changes as you shift your vantage point. Johnson had been a most successful majority leader. Yet his relations with Congress became deplorable. They were terrible because of Vietnam and various other things. President Nixon never had a close relationship with the Congress. He had been in public life too long—he had been away from Congress since he was elected vice president in 1952. He was only in the Senate for two years and in the House for four years, so he was not truly a creature of the Senate and the House. Carter knew nothing of the Congress, of course, but all of them managed to have great difficulties with the Congress. I think it is inherent in our system of government. The President is thwarted by the Congress and the Congress is dominated by regional concerns and special interest groups.

QUESTION: What about the legislative staff?

AMBASSADOR RUSH: I think one of the real problems of our society today is the fact that the Congress is no longer just a Congress, it's a bureaucracy. They have thirty-two thousand employees in the Congress. That bureaucracy is constantly fighting with the bureaucracy in the executive departments. Each one is trying to say that the other is wrong, is not cooperating, is misleading. They do work together at times.

QUESTION: Ambassador Rush, is it possible in looking back that Secretary of State Dulles and Secretary of State Kissinger may have weakened the presidency because they appeared to stand out above the presidency?

AMBASSADOR RUSH: I think Eisenhower with his great prestige was able to handle Dulles very effectively. He liked Dulles. They were very close. Dulles carried out Eisenhower's foreign policy. When I say that I don't mean that Dulles didn't help develop that foreign policy, but Eisenhower initiated and approved it. In the case of Kissinger, President Nixon dominated Henry completely until the Watergate thing came along. In the case of President Ford, he had not had great experience in foreign affairs; Henry played a much bigger role than he would have with another newly elected President.

The question is whether or not the foreign policy is a good one. If it is a good one, a good secretary of state can help bolster the prestige of the president. If it is a bad one, a good secretary of state can't save the president.

QUESTION: One of the criticisms that some people have made is that Nixon always tried to please people. In private discussions, he would tell individuals what they wanted to hear. Ford's weakness was that he couldn't knock heads together. It is argued that there were inherent weaknesses in each administration for those reasons. Is there any truth in that criticism?

AMBASSADOR RUSH: I don't think so. President Nixon certainly didn't hesitate to differ with people or to overrule them, but he tried to do it diplomatically. He was much more prone to do that than he was to take them on concerning personal matters. President Ford showed a lot of courage, I thought, in sticking to what he wanted to do.

NARRATOR: How would you compare the Ford or Nixon White House with the Reagan White House in terms of its organization and the quality of its personnel?

AMBASSADOR RUSH: I never served in the Reagan White House, and I only served a few months in the Ford White House. But I would say that you have many things in common between the Nixon White House, the Ford White House, and the Reagan White House. One is that there is always controversy going on within the ranks and that several people are trying to undercut the others for the president's attention. You do not have a homogeneous group but a diverse group. The intrigue in the White House will compare in intensity with any place that I know of. I think that was true under all three of the administrations, but I think Reagan is exercising more of an iron hand.

QUESTION: Mr. Ambassador, we have some tendency to think of Presidents Ford and Truman as accidental presidents who were thrust into the office without much preparation. Yet both of them in their very different ways made good. Do you think there are useful parallels between them, especially with regard to the learning process by which an uninitiated fellow learns to take over?

AMBASSADOR RUSH: When McKinley died, Theodore Roosevelt came in and Roosevelt did a fine job. When Harding died, Calvin Coolidge did a good job. When Franklin D. Roosevelt died, he was already so physically weakened that he was not very effective; Truman took over and did a surprisingly fine job. After Kennedy died, Lyndon Johnson did an in-between job. Ford did a very fine job, I think. Maybe the answer to our problem is to have presidents kick off sometime and have vice presidents take over! Overall I would say that Ford and Truman had a lot in common: they both were very likeable people; they both were close to the people. I think Truman was more decisive than Ford, and much more jealous of his control over his Cabinet. I think both of them were effective Presidents. They chose pretty good people. Each of them had some bad eggs, but so did all other presidents.

QUESTION: Ambassador Rush, in trying to understand the differences in the way presidents manage the Executive branch, I've been intrigued with how they handle criticism. The criticism has been leveled against the Nixon White House that President Nixon was too insulated and couldn't take criticism very well, or at least he failed to get outside views. John Erlichman has said that he found that it was most effective to write Nixon a short note, because he could take criticism in a note rather than in person. On the other hand, Dick Cheney has said that President Ford was more open to hearing, "Mr. President, I don't think this idea is such a hot one." Can you comment on their different styles?

AMBASSADOR RUSH: Yes, I would agree with that. One had to be a lot more careful with President Nixon. He liked to hear different points of view. But on this economist incident I mentioned, I went to President Ford and in essence told him he had made a mistake in inviting that person. I don't think I would have done that with President Nixon. I might have let the invitation stand. Or I might have tried to adopt President Nixon's approach and try to get somebody else to carry the ball!

QUESTION: Many observers talk about the difficulty that a president has in getting his directives carried out. Is there any truth in the fact that a lot of the people who carry out the orders of the president are protected by the Civil Service and cannot be fired easily? Is that the roadblock?

AMBASSADOR RUSH: The president is the equivalent of both the Queen of England and the British prime minister combined where the inordinate demands on his time are concerned. He is both Head of State and Head of Government. He has to see many people; he has to run the government and get it coordinated. Even if people try to carry out a presidential directive you have to make changes here and there. By the time the President sees the result of his decision, it may not look like the decision he made, so he gets suspicious. Sometimes he makes a quick decision that you have to protect him against. For example, when I was deputy secretary of defense, Gordon Rule, a troublemaker, was in the Defense Department. Gordon testified before the Senate that Eisenhower would have turned over in his grave if he knew what Nixon was doing in certain areas of defense. I got home early that night and, at about eleven o'clock, got a call from President Nixon, who was deeply annoyed. He said, "I want you to fire that man tomorrow. What do you think?" and I said, "Oh, I think he is a bad egg; this never should have happened. I'll see that he is taken care of." Of course what I did then was shunt Gordon Rule aside into another job without firing him, because if we had fired him it would have taken years of bureaucratic hearings. If I had fired him, the press would have been full of accusations that Nixon was trying to suppress people from talking, even in testimony before Congress. You've got to protect the President against things like that.

On the other hand, when we had the massive surprise invasion of North Vietnam into the South in April 1972, President Nixon called me over. He was furious because he felt he had been deceived. It was the only time I saw him so angry. He thought he had been deceived by the Defense Department—not by me—but by Mel Laird and others; that they knew that the invasion was coming, but hadn't told him and had not made proper preparations to meet it.

You have this sort of thing all the way through. In a government like ours where, the minute you make a decision, particularly in defense, you have everybody who doesn't like it trying to undercut it and get away from it. You do have a feeling of frustration and inability to trust your subordinates to carry it out. Every president has it, but I think President Nixon was perhaps more suspicious and more secretive than most.

NARRATOR: May we ask one last question that we've always asked earlier guests? Did you change your mind with either of these Presidents about their quality as leader from your early association to the concluding stages of your relationship with them? How do you think history will judge the two Presidents?

AMBASSADOR RUSH: I changed my mind very dramatically, but all for the better as far as these Presidents were concerned. I knew Nixon when he was in law school. When he was President I felt that he had grown dramatically; his concept of foreign policy, particularly, and his overall concepts of government in general, were broad-based and sound. He continued to grow in the office. I think he'll go down in history as one of our greatest Presidents.

I think Ford also grew tremendously in the presidency. I think he did a fine job. In my opinion, he is not going to rate as a great president, but he will rate as a good

president.   He'll   certainly   rate   well   ahead   of   many   other
presidents.

NARRATOR: I know I speak for all of you in thanking
Kenneth Rush for the way in which, through his good humor
and informed thinking, he has lit up the room.   We hope he
will come back and become increasingly a part of the Miller
Center family.   Thank you very much.

DOMESTIC ISSUES AND THE BUDGET

JAMES M. CANNON

NARRATOR: Not only does James Cannon bring to a discussion of the Ford presidency knowledge of the domestic council, but also a well-grounded knowledge and philosophy of politics. He is currently a political consultant to Howard Baker. He is consultant to the Merrill Lynch private capital group and vice chairman of the Republican Majority Fund. He was a member of the White House transition team from February to April of 1987. I think one can see in these examples the major directions of his political interest and contributions.

Following military service and graduation from the University of Alabama in 1939 with a Bachelor of Science degree in business administration, he wrote for the *Gloversville Leader Republican* and then the Potsdam, New York, *Herald Recorder*. He went on to the *Baltimore Sun* first as a reporter, then assistant city editor, foreign correspondent and war correspondent in Korea. He joined the staff of *Time* magazine as a writer and then editor of its business and financial news. He was chief political writer and national affairs editor of *Newsweek* magazine from 1956 to 1959, and then became vice president of *Newsweek, Inc.* He served from 1969 to 1974 as special assistant to the Governor of New York, Nelson Rockefeller, maintaining his contacts and activities in Washington. From 1974-75, he was assistant to the chairman of the Commission on Critical Choices, a bipartisan group of forty-two, who looked at all aspects of the national problem under the chairmanship of Nelson Rockefeller. From 1975-77, he served as assistant to President Ford, not only as presidential assistant but also executive director of the Domestic Council. That group was made up of a staff of some fifty economists, lawyers, MBAs and business analysts who did such things as prepare alternatives for major policy decisions, examine national policy issues, and plans for the administration of the choices.

From 1977-85, Mr. Cannon was chief of staff for the majority leader of the United States Senate, Howard Baker. Out of this rich background in American politics, he speaks not only with authority on the Ford administration but a lot of knowledge and background of politics in general.

MR. CANNON: Thank you, Ken. What I want to do first, is talk about the man himself. As it happens, last week I was in Palm Springs to see President Ford on another matter, so I had a chance to confirm in a very positive way my own recollections about him, and reassert my friendship and respect for him. He is now ten years out of office, and it is interesting to me that he is as alert as ever to what is going on in the affairs of the nation, and he is as dedicated as ever to the well being of the country.

My impression of President Ford from the first time I ever met him was that I have never met a man so easy to like. He is good-natured, diligent, serious, confident and decisive. I think the media never did justice to President Ford. I know that individual members of the press liked him immensely. But some reporters wrote story after story suggesting that he was dull, kind of bumbling physically, and lacking in charisma. It was then, and it still is, a false picture. In the oval office, where we knew him best, President Ford was personable, sure and steady. He was always briefed, always did his homework, and he was always on top of the job. After Watergate, and after President Nixon's resignation, President Ford wanted to display a sure and steady hand. Those were his words describing what he wanted to do as President, and I think he did.

I arrived there in December, 1974, on the day that Vice President Rockefeller was confirmed as vice president, and I saw him from that day in December until the end of his term. The number one characteristic I felt about him, the quality that was always present, was confidence. He was fully confident of what he had to do, and what he needed to do. He worked quietly and patiently at the daily presidential tasks with a kind of genial intensity, and from a personal background of solid, if old-fashioned, American values. He knew who he was, and he was very comfortable with who he was. There was not a trace of insecurity about him. He knew what he knew, and he was not embarrassed about what he didn't know. He did not ever hesitate to ask questions. In a conversation with Brent Scowcroft one day, he suddenly asked him, "What does UNESCO do?" When the explanation ended, the President said, "Well, thanks, Brent. I was wondering about it the other day, and I thought I would ask you." For me that reflects his certainty and his comfort with who he was.

I brought along with me another little small example of something that he did. This is a memorandum that he wrote me in May, 1976. It says, in his handwriting, "Jim Cannon, can I have a chart by months (1975 through May 1976) showing by lines corn, wheat, and soybean prices, and then indicate the date of the embargo, and the date it was lifted?" Then he drew a little chart: price on the vertical side, months on the other side, and drew a squiggly little line with a couple of cross bars to indicate to me where he wanted the date of the embargo and the date it was lifted. And on the side of the memo he wrote, "I'm a lousy artist." This was a comfortable man. He was genuine, unaffected, authentic and curious. Those are all words that would describe him to me.

I suppose it took me no more than a week or so, after he appointed me as his domestic policy adviser to conclude that Jerry Ford had in full measure the three qualities that every president needs most: (1) he knew how the federal government works; (2) he had common sense, an abundance of common sense; and (3) maybe the most important of all, he had the guts to say yes and to say no, and he never second-guessed himself on the major decisions.

The first point, how the government works: he probably knew more about how the federal government on the day he took office, he was better prepared in terms of being ready to take over the presidency, than any other person of modern times with the possible exception of Lyndon Johnson. Let me explain why. The country still does not understand why Jerry Ford was well prepared, but it is worth going into. The essence of it is that President Ford spent twelve years full-time inside the little known power center of federal decision-making, the House

Appropriations Committee. Not many people pay much attention to it. Appropriations sounds like a dull subject, and to a lot of people it is. But the raw power of the House Appropriations Committee can be traced directly back 200 years to Madison and the other draftsmen of the Constitution, and their fierce determination to end the autocratic practice of taxation without representation. Article One, Section Seven of the Constitution reads: " All bills for raising revenue shall originate in the House of Representatives." From that constitutional mandate there evolved the tradition that only the House, which can initiate a tax, can initiate a bill to spend that tax. You get some argument about this from the Senate sometimes, but in a general sense that is the way it has worked for most of our history. The House initiates the spending and the Senate functions as a court of appeals on spending. Sometime in the 1800s, the House delegated the first decisions on what the federal government shall spend, to its Appropriations Committee, which has traditionally been a select group of people and omnipotent authority, a deliberative group of people who decide how every single dollar of the federal money could be spent.

President Ford, then Jerry Ford, was elected first to the Congress in 1948. He served one term. In Ford's second term, a crusty old conservative from upstate New York named John Tabor had taken a liking to him, and got him appointed to the House Appropriations Committee. Two years later, in 1952 when President Eisenhower was first elected and brought in a Democratic House and Senate with him, and the Republicans won control of the Congress, Ford became chairman of the defense appropriations subcommittee, and later he served on the foreign aid and intelligence subcommittees. The way the system works in the House Appropriations Committee, those subcommittees make the decisions on how money is to be spent, and their decisions are rarely overturned. Again, it sounds dull and it is dull, but Ford served on that committee for over twelve years, until he became minority leader, and even after that he paid close attention to the people on the committee, to its work, to its chairman, and all that they did.

This work generally is endless, unpublicized, unreported, and generally unappreciated. If you are on that committee, you spend every morning and every afternoon listening to what I think of as the factory managers of the vast federal operation that we call the American government. These factory managers come in every day trying to prove their need for more money, always more money. By talking endlessly to these people and by listening to their proposals, Ford learned the essence of the American federal government system: who spends how much, for what and why, and how effectively is it used.

Ford's training on this committee extended from the end of Truman's years through all of Eisenhower's years of Peace and Prosperity, through Kennedy's New Frontier, to the vast expansion of the government when Lyndon Johnson created the Great Society, and through Richard Nixon's first term. So when he took the oath of office on August 9, 1974, President Ford had a more realistic grasp of what the government can and cannot accomplish than anyone since and anyone before him with the possible exception of Lyndon Johnson.

In January of 1976 President Ford personally briefed the press on live television on the budget he had just sent to the Congress. I remember very well that TV anchormen, such as John Chancellor, were astonished that he did it with such knowledge and skill. But those of us who worked with him in the White House on preparing that budget were not surprised at all because we had gone through with him a long process of deliberation on the budget, what would be spent and by which department. In that process most of the items are worked out between the Office of Management and Budget (OMB) director and the Cabinet officer, but the Cabinet officer has a right of appeal. So he can come to the president if he feels he has a strong case. There may be one in four who come in and want to see the president about a particular item and say, "Mr. President, we really need more for this." So they appeal their case.

Case after case after case, President Ford knew more about that budget in that department than its Cabinet officer did and it was not happenstance because he had been there at the origin of those programs. He knew who had invented those programs, who had supported the member, the constituency behind him, and what was wrong with the program. He still does, as a matter of fact.

It was fascinating to me in Palm Springs last Friday, ten years after he was out of office, that he was talking about what might be done about the deficit reduction. He started talking about their last continuing resolution. For

some years now Congress has not been able to pass
appropriations bills. They just simply can't get it done. This
is partly the reason we have the deficit. So the President
started talking about the so-called continuing resolution,
which is the catch-all that is a substitute for the
appropriation process. He picked it up, it was on his desk,
he had been reading this thousand page document and he
said to me, "I wonder how many members who vote on this
know what is in it." You can be sure that he is still
interested and he is still engaged.

Now with all of this that we knew about him, why was
it that he was not reelected in 1976, or rather elected in
1976? There are several answers, but my own answers are
these: (1) We who worked for him were not able in the
campaign of 1976 to convince enough of the electorate of
his abilities and his qualities of leadership. That was our
fault. And since he had not run for public office or any
public office except his House seat, he had not developed
the political skills of communication, television performance,
and symbolism that are now essential if you want to be
elected President of the United States.

Ken, in the papers you sent me you asked when did I
first get to know Jerry Ford. I first got to know him in
1971 when he was House Minority Leader and I was then
working for Governor Rockefeller as his assistant for a lot
of things, particularly relating to Congress and the Nixon
administration. We were working on revenue sharing. I
went to see then Minority Leader Ford about this proposal
that we in New York were very interested in. My initial
impression was then that Congressman Ford was rather a
quiet man, easy to talk with, ready to listen and—important
to any leader of the House or Senate, and important to any
president—he knew how to count votes. That is the essence
of legislative leadership in our system and Minority Leader
Ford certainly had it.

This revenue sharing program was designed as a model
of how the federal system should work with the Feds
sharing the taxpayer's dollar which Washington is very good
at collecting, and which local governments are better at
delivering, especially local services to the communities such
as police, fires, public education, streets and public health.
The idea was the Feds would collect the money and share
part with local government. It was a good program,
efficient and effective. It is over now. I think it ran for

fourteen years. But President Ford was essential to its passage when he was in the House. He personally delivered more than half the votes in the House of Representatives.

I observed him again after Governor Rockefeller started his commission on critical choices. He came to meetings, was very studious, spoke little and listened a lot. It was clear to me that he was there to learn, to broaden his perspective, and listen to the outside experts, academics and businessmen that Rockefeller had assembled and to consider the future of the U.S. in the world. No participant was more diligent than Ford. We thought, when Ford was appointed vice president by President Nixon, he might drop out. Governor Rockefeller and I talked to him about this, and we said that we would understand if he felt he couldn't continue. He said, no, he wanted to continue, that he had learned a lot and wanted to continue learning. He had begun studies outside of Congress and he wanted to finish them.

When Ford became President and asked Rockefeller to be his vice president, I went down to Washington to help Governor Rockefeller get confirmed. When he was confirmed, President Ford asked the new Vice President Rockefeller to take responsibility for domestic policies. Vice President Rockefeller responded that if he was expected to do that he wanted to have his own person on the job. So I was appointed over the objection of Don Rumsfeld who was chief of staff. It was soon obvious to me, as it had been to Rumsfeld, what the problem was. Structurally, Rumsfeld understood that a person in the job of presidential adviser could not work for the vice president; he had to work for the president himself.

The first issue that prompted me to confront this reality was the creation of a science adviser to the president. It came very soon after I was appointed. President Ford had asked Vice President Rockefeller for a recommendation on whether he should have a science adviser. In his typical fashion, Rockefeller assembled at his own estate in Westchester County, New York, a large group of scientists, government experts and others to study this matter. He finished his study, and brought in a recommendation and—because he had been accustomed to running a state himself—he expected to have it accepted. But it was not. Instead, Rumsfeld and the President wanted it staffed out in the regular way. That is, they sent it to the President's principal assistants and to appropriate members of the House and Senate to get their views. Rumsfeld handed it to me and said that this was what the President wanted done, and then it was up to me to tell the Vice President, who had been my boss, that my new boss, the President, wanted me to analyze and pass judgment on the Vice President's proposal. Rockefeller did not accept that happily. Somehow, I felt that I was walking on a high wire between the twin towers of the World Trade Center in New York.

The experience taught me a lot about the President. This was my first major task for the President, so I went in to see him and said, "Is there any special information you would like to have? What would you like me to deliver on this?" He said, "Well, one thing. I would like to know what each of the previous science advisers to the president actually did." To me, this was exactly the right question, but I had not thought of it, and it told me a lot about the way Jerry Ford's mind worked, with precision and directness and clarity. So as it happened, I thought, "I can best do this myself." I had been a reporter. I found all of the living former science advisers to the president, and talked to them personally, because I wanted to get their views as to what they had accomplished. I also commissioned an outside consultant, who was a very good scientist himself, to take all the data that was available and evaluate what each of the outside science advisers had done. It was an education to me. I can't remember the names of all the science advisers, but I remember that Eisenhower's adviser, James Killian, felt that he had helped President Eisenhower calm the country after the Russians sent up the first Sputnik. He felt that was his major contribution in his regime as the science adviser. I remember talking to Jerry Wiesner, who was Kennedy's science adviser, and he said, "Well, it was a very interesting experience." He went in to see President Kennedy from time to time with various proposals, ideas, things he wanted to pursue, and Kennedy was always very respectful. But Professor Wiesner said that invariably the conversation ended up with Kennedy saying, "Jerry, now I know we've talked about this before, but tell me again: how does a radio really work?"

At any rate, when we finished the report, we recommended that there be a science adviser, close to the Rockefeller recommendation, but somewhat different, and

President Ford said, "I want this done through Congress, because if it is done through Congress, Congress will have a stake in it, and they will feel that it is as important to them as it is to future presidents. The record of the science adviser to the president was very much a mixed record, because if you remember Johnson's adviser said the wrong thing about Vietnam, and Johnson fired him. Nixon's science adviser (Richard Garwin) was not whole-heartedly supportive of everything he did, so he never spoke to him again. So we got a science adviser in the legislation. That was my baptism working for President Ford.

One thing that Rockefeller did take a great interest in was the quality of the Domestic Council staff. I had inherited all that Nixon had left us, and a few were very good, but many I had to change. Rockefeller made me a great gift of three outstanding people: Dick Dunham as my deputy, Art Quern to work on health, education, and welfare problems, and Dick Parsons to work with the Justice Department and be my counsel, which, given the fact that my predecessor, John Ehrlichman, had gone to jail, was something that I wanted to avoid. With those three, all who had worked in high capacities in New York state, and several others that I kept on, I set out to put together the best staff in the White House. That was the first thing Rockefeller and I decided that we wanted to do: create the best quality staff. Kissinger at that time had the best staff in the White House. We said that we were going to make ours better, and I think we did. In fact, four of the some twenty professionals that I had at that time are now presidents of corporations and three are partners in major law firms. The thing we had then, and if we didn't get it at the outset we trained these people for it, was judgment. Technical expertise is important, but even more important is judgment. You must have good judgment to work in the White House to advise the president. It is a rare quality for every president, and a rare quality in Washington, but it is essential.

How did we work? The Domestic Council organization was quite simple. We assigned one highly qualified person to each appropriate Cabinet officer except for the State Department. We did not have a full time person in the State Department. For example, a young woman lawyer named Judy Hode worked with Secretary William Coleman in the Transportation Department. It was her responsibility to know in advance everything that was about to happen, everything that might conceivably involve the White House, to let me know about it, to prepare a report on it, to prepare a briefing paper for the President when necessary, and to get Secretary Coleman in to see the President if necessary. We worked on problems related to it but we did not try to intervene with the department. If it was within the department's scope, fine; they went ahead and did it. Where we got involved, and where the President would get involved was where it related to more than one department, and many issues do.

Much of our day-to-day work was taken up with putting out fires, daily crises. There have been questions as to whether Rockefeller lost interest in the Domestic Council. The fact is that he did not ever express much interest in these daily crises. He told me when I tried to take the papers over to show him, "Look, I'm not interested in those things. What I want to do is look at the broad matters, the positive decisions that we want to make in the future." Since the budget crunch at that time was so pressing that President Ford had decided that there would be no new initiatives, domestic or otherwise, it made it very difficult for Rockefeller, who was interested in new programs, to be very effective. But we did work together with him on it. He was not interested in the day-to-day problems that were more than 75 percent of our work. We did try to anticipate a problem before it got to the President's desk but, with the range of issues, we could not often do it. The fact is that if a problem is soluble, it is solved. If it's not soluble, it ends up on the President's desk. Every insoluble problem in the world ends up on the White House doorstep.

Let me give you some examples of the variety of things we had to discuss and deal with in Domestic Council. One of them, believe it or not, was coyotes. We spent more time on coyotes than we did on almost anything else. I chuckle too, but coyotes are a very real problem for a lot of people. Many ranchers in the West have a major capital investment tied up in their sheep. On the Indian reservations in particular, all that an American Indian may own is thirty sheep, and if the coyotes get them, his capital is gone and there is no compensation anywhere. The Agriculture Department and the Interior Department in a general sense wanted to protect the sheepmen. On the other side were the environmentalists. The poison that had to be used to deal with the coyote pups in their den was a kind of poison that killed golden eagles. The golden eagles would find a dead coyote and eat the dead coyote and die. It was depleting the golden eagle population in the West. So, it was a tense, controversial situation. Members of Congress would have the most vehement meetings over this issue. Some of these Texas and western congressmen could not understand why they couldn't use this poison to kill these coyotes. EPA was just as adamant that we had to protect the golden eagles. I remember vividly one of these sessions, which must have had thirty-five members of the House and Senate arguing vociferously about the issue. This session had to be interrupted while the President went to the NSC crisis room to make some decisions about the evacuation of the last Americans from the rooftop of the embassy in Saigon. It was interesting that President Ford could leave this intense discussion about coyotes and go down to the crisis room where these matters are considered and deal with them, and come back to the coyote session without losing a step. I was impressed by this.

Among other issues, the supersonic *Concorde* coming into Dulles and JFK airports raised great noise questions with a strong overtone of protectionism by Americans who had not built an American supersonic plane. That involved Transportation, Justice, State, the Special Trade Representatives and others. That's a typical case that Bill Coleman dealt with and did very well. Airport noise was more than the *Concorde*. People around the country were looking for federal legislation to do something about airport noise. President Ford decided by executive order to require that all new planes built after 1976 would have the quiet engines that most new planes now have, and he gave the airlines five years to, as the bureaucrats put it, retrofit all the old planes, with new engines that were quieter and more fuel efficient. He decreed this by executive order, but next year the Congress overturned it.

American Indian claims, were made on the basis of a quite valid treaty. It appeared that the Indians owned almost half of the property of the state of Maine, including a lot of very well developed properties in cities and their surroundings. We never solved that. It was solved in part two years later by President Carter when a compromise was reached.

We had to deal with statehood for Puerto Rico. This was a very complicated matter. Interior, Justice, Treasury, National Security, Defense, State, and especially the FBI, all had a stake in this and President Ford said that he wanted it to be dealt with. Should it continue to be a Commonwealth or should it have the right to become a state? President Ford told me, "Let's keep this confidential, and I want you to staff it out, but I've always favored statehood, and see if it makes any sense." Because discussions of this issue of Puerto Rico usually led to violence, we kept it tight within the White House until just before the decision had to be made. It was one of those unusual cases where we kept something in the White House before it leaked.

Education, I believe it's Title Nine, was a big question. The Congress had passed a law which seemed to say in effect that any college which took federal funds would be required to treat men and women equally. Some coaches thought this meant that a woman student, at the University of Virginia, say, could ask to be on the football team and try out for the team. This upset some of President Ford's old football friends at Michigan beyond belief, and he sat there bemused while they worried. Congress had left this so open that it could be interpreted either way. President Ford found a way that it could be resolved so that the University of Michigan football team didn't have to accept women players.

Secretary Matthews wanted to make strong efforts for all the handicapped people in the country. The sloping sidewalks you see at every intersection in Washington and throughout the rest of the country were part of the result of that.

The swine flu epidemic was an extraordinary issue and a highly risky one. President Ford had to make a decision on the basis of imperfect knowledge, as presidents often do, but he made the right one. It was not popular, but he did go forth with the idea that everyone had to have an inoculation against Swine Flu, and at least it was not as bad as it might have been. But we never knew, as with so many things that happen, whether it was the best thing or not.

We tried and tried to do something about food stamps. Our purpose was to make certain that all those who deserved them had them, and those who did not deserve them did not. One of the striking things to me about this—I had worked as a journalist—was that we had great difficulty finding out how well they did work. I wanted to send a team out around the country to select places and to find out how they worked. But Congress made it clear that they would consider this an intervention that they could not accept. It would be usurpation of their authority to oversee programs, and they stopped us from doing it.

These are a few of the many things that came to us which we couldn't avoid. In addition, we undertook some initiatives which were difficult in light of the fact that the budget permitted us to have no new programs. But one of the best studies we did was on the whole question of illegal drugs. We had started with President Ford's encouragement the first government-wide examination of the problem with recommendations that have not worked as well as they might have, but are still more or less there today. They propose that you deal with the foreign producers, catching them at the borders. We helped get some marvelous new machines that would mechanically sniff the person coming in say, to Miami. He would walk up to the desk, and the desk was built so that he would have to lift his arms and open his coat. The little nozzles were right here where he stood, and they would draw in enough molecules of the air around his body that could be tested instantly, and a red light would come on if he had evidence of drugs on him. They then brought him over to the side and searched him. In the drug program we also tried to provide some better information to state and local governments who had the problem of law enforcement.

Another initiative of the Ford administration was deregulation. We began the process of deregulation which, for better or worse, still goes on today in everything from transportation to airlines to business deregulation. As part of the program, President Ford asked Governor Rockefeller to conduct some Domestic Council hearings around the country. President Ford felt that Congress always took the credit for all the hearings, and got their point of view across, and he did not. So he asked Rockefeller to conduct, I believe it was six, major town meetings around the country, region by region. We invited the leaders of the community and people of all walks of life in to talk about what the problems were, what they felt the federal government could do better and what they should stop doing to people. They were partially effective, but unfortunately were all designed for the full-term that President Ford hoped to have that never came.

Before we go to questions, let me just give you my part of the letter of resignation that I wrote to him just before he left office. Even though you know that you are going to be out of office on January 20th, it is traditional that you resign to the President you served before you go out. So let me read a few paragraphs which express my feeling about him then and I can tell you that I reaffirm them today. This is what I wrote the President on January 15th:

> I came here in December of 1974 at a critical time of the history of our country to work with the vice president and you, and through you for the country. There was a job to be done, and you succeeded. You expressed this success with eloquence and directness last night when you said, "Today we have a more perfect union than when my stewardship began."
>
> Mr. President, we do have a more perfect union, and it is due in great measure to your leadership. Any one of three accomplishments—restoration of the integrity of the President, ending a war, ending a recession—would insure your place in history. You accomplished all, and historians will record your achievements as a great chapter of American history.

I felt that way then, and I still do. Thank you.

QUESTION: One of the questions that will continue to haunt Mr. Ford, and will bother future historians, is why he pardoned President Nixon.

MR. CANNON: I was not there at that time. This was before Rockefeller's confirmation. It was literally a few days after he appointed Rockefeller. Because I know President Ford, I accept his explanation totally. I think that, and I know from Jack March and Bob Hartmann and others who were working with him at the time, that every day he spent hours trying to decide what should be done about various aspects of the Nixon papers, the Nixon documents, the trial, how to proceed with it, and so on. I believe he felt that it was consuming his time, which it was. He had other vast problems to address, such as the economy, which was getting worse and worse. He felt that it was going to be distracting to the country for a long time to come, perhaps years, and he felt that the only solution was to end it swiftly. He knew that he would pay a terrible political price for it, but he felt that was the best decision for the country, and I think that's why he did it. In retrospect, I agree with it but in retrospect it cost him a full term of his own but he felt that it was the right thing to do. People will debate it a long time, but I accept President Ford's explanations because I know him to be an honest man, and I do not believe that he would do anything other than be honest about it. I think that Al Haig made a tremendous mistake in trying to discuss it with him, but it was done. Al Haig came over and talked to him about the possibility that Nixon might resign implying that he might need to be pardoned, and that was a mistake on Haig's part. You could argue it was a mistake on Ford's part to listen, but he got out of it as fast as he could and never spoke of it to Al Haig again.

QUESTION: In 1980 at the Republican convention, Ford had to face a tremendous decision. He could have been Reagan's vice president. He elected not to. From your knowledge of Ford, would you care to speculate what our country might have been like if he had agreed?

MR. CANNON: I knew something about the deliberations. We would have had the possibility that, because Ford was so familiar with the way the government worked, it would be beneficial to the country. On the other hand, I know that a vice president can't really do anything substantive of great consequence. If Ford as vice president had tried to get Reagan as President to do something, the conservatives such as Paul Laxalt and Ed Meese would have objected. There would have been a tremendous internal collision on the issue and might have stopped the effectiveness of a vice presidency in its tracks.

The vice presidency is an interesting question in itself. My conclusion from what I have seen of Bush, Mondale, Rockefeller, Ford as vice president to Nixon and Hubert Humphrey, is that there is nothing substantive that they can do. They can stand and wait. There is not a lot more that they can do. Each president says, I'm going to make this vice presidency important but, constitutionally, there is nothing they can do. They can't make any decisions, and probably shouldn't while they are vice president.

QUESTION: I interpret you to say that his relationship with Mr. Rockefeller was fairly good, and that he was trying to get Mr. Rockefeller to take over some responsibilities. Was the relationship between them good?

MR. CANNON: It started out as very good, but it deteriorated. It started out because Rockefeller was so deeply loyal to the country that he wanted to do everything he could to help the President. He did not want to be offered the job, frankly, but there was no way he could not accept it. He had never wanted to be vice president of anything, he used to say, and he had been offered the vice presidency before. He was offered it in 1960 by Nixon, and in 1968, Hubert Humphrey sent a message to him that he might want to join on the Democratic side as vice president. But he never wanted to be vice president. Now he had to be, so he was very intent on doing his best. But the vice president cannot have any power, he cannot express any power. My own experience with Rockefeller on this matter was that there was no way he could decide domestic policy. It had to be done by the President. He could make a recommendation, and his recommendation might weigh more than, say, Bill Seidman on an economic matter, or Frank Zarb on an energy matter, but it could not prevail. In fact, he did personally persuade President Ford to commit to a major energy program over the objections of most of the President's other advisers. It did not get very far. The Congress wouldn't accept it. There was no way it could, and once it became known that it was Rockefeller's idea, it attracted opposition that it might not have otherwise attracted. In late 1975 when President Ford's political advisers told him that if he were going to win the nomination he would have to get Rockefeller off the ticket, President Ford did ask him to give him a letter taking himself off the ticket, which Rockefeller did. It was a traumatic experience for President Ford and for Vice President Rockefeller, but it was done and the relationship worsened after that. Nevertheless, Rockefeller was still totally loyal to him throughout the balance of his term and in fact, along about April of 1976, when Ford, having won New Hampshire over Reagan, then lost North Carolina and Texas, his nomination was in peril. Rogers Morton, who was then Ford's campaign manager, came to me and said, "Look we've got to have help here. How do we get Rockefeller to bring us New York?" I said, "Rodge, there is just one way to do that. The President has to ask him." So Rodge took that back to President Ford, who in turn did ask Rockefeller, who in turn did deliver not only New York's delegates, almost all of them, but with the assistance of Hugh Scott, most of Pennsylvania. From that point on, Ford was never behind in the delegate count. I think without that he might not have succeeded in the nomination.

QUESTION: What was the underlying reason for a less than enthusiastic support from Reagan for the Republican party in 1976?

MR. CANNON: They thought Reagan ought to win. They thought it was his turn. The John Sears, the Ed Meeses, and the conservatives around the country who were supporting Reagan felt that they deserved the nomination more than President Ford did. If you could go back and look at the farewell that then Governor Reagan and Mrs. Reagan gave at the convention in Kansas City when they had been defeated and were going home, you get the drift that they lost and were not going to play. Ford tried to reach out to them and in fact, I think a large part of the reason that Bob Dole was chosen on the ticket with Ford was because this was a recommendation of Ronald Reagan.

NARRATOR: We've asked other speakers if they could single out one or two major strengths of their president, and one or two weaknesses. On the weakness side, Ford's failure to knock heads and his difficulty in dealing with contention within the ranks has been mentioned. Was that a weakness, or were there other weaknesses?

MR. CANNON: I think he was better at it than most. Howard Baker is just as bad, and President Reagan is worse. They got elected because everybody liked them. They do not like conflict within their own family, and have a very tough time dealing with it. To make the point, typically when I and some other senior staffer in Senator Baker's office got into a spirited difference about something in front of him, he would leave the room and say, "Well, boys, I'm not going to listen to any more of this," and just go out. They don't like to hear controversy. Ford didn't like it either. He wanted people that could differ with him, but he did not want these differences to appear to be personal. Ford's best way of dealing with an issue was to have us put it on paper, send him a document or briefing paper summarizing the issue with a brief background of who stood where, and we put a tab on everybody's view. He would read that the night before, and then he would come in the next day and say, "Okay, Jim Lynn, I see you recommended this. Tell me this. Answer these two questions about it." He would go around the table, and then he would say, "Well, does anybody else have anything?" He would call on people, he would listen to people. But he told me then, and he has told me many times since, that he prefers the combination of a good memorandum and a firm discussion, a civil and correct discussion. He treats it more as if he were a judge. He listens to one argument and the other argument, then he retires into his office and makes a decision on it. I remember one discussion, I guess it was before the 1976 State of the Union address, when we couldn't agree and were all sitting around. Ford was getting visibly angry about this. At one point, he pounded that table with a big fist and that table jumped about a foot. He had a temper, and he could display it, but he didn't hold any animosity. That was a weakness. He didn't like to deal with conflicts among subordinates, and it is a weakness of almost all politicians, for the reason I mentioned, that they want everyone to like them. They want a comfortable, happy situation. They are in the business of pleasing people, and when there are obviously strong differences, it perplexes them.

NARRATOR: Cannon is a famous political name, as all of you know. Speaker Cannon, now Jim Cannon. It is a tradition that those of us who studied political science have heard about as fledglings. The tradition hasn't suffered at all today. Secretary Marsh was right when he said, "If you can get Jim Cannon, you will get a dimension you haven't covered on the Ford presidency." So, thank you very much.

IV.

FORD,
THE MEDIA
AND
THE PUBLIC

THE FORD PRESIDENCY
AND THE PRESS

RON NESSEN

NARRATOR: Ron Nessen was enormously helpful at the time of the Presidential Press Conference Commission at the Miller Center and participated actively in discussions of that group. So in a sense, he is coming back to us at a crucial time because in the Ford presidential portrait we have not covered the press in the way that we had hoped to. He is a person whose early career revolved around areas neighboring the capitol. He was born in Washington and is a graduate of American University. He served as a news announcer for the Martinsburg, West Virginia radio station, and later the Arlington station. He became a writer for the *Rockville Sentinel Maryland* newspaper. He worked with the UPI in Washington as an editor and for NBC as a radio and TV correspondent. He became press secretary to Gerald Ford in 1974 and served until 1977. He is the author of a number of books, including *It Sure Looks Different From the Inside*, and two novels, *The Hour* and *The First Lady*. He has won two of the most distinguished awards that journalism has to offer, one of them being the George Foster Peabody Memorial Award and the other the George Polk Award. He is currently vice president for news at the Mutual Broadcasting System.

MR. NESSEN: I'm honored to have been asked to take part in this on-going program. I am a supporter of and believer in what the Miller Center does. As an undergraduate I was a history major, so I believe in the need to preserve history and get the facts straight, so we can study the presidency in the future.

One of the questions I was asked to deal with is how I got involved in the Ford White House after actually spending my life to that point as a journalist. I guess it was all in the timing. I was a correspondent for NBC news for a long time, and I was home asleep one morning in 1973, when the phone rang very early. It seems that the early edition of the *Wall Street Journal* had come out, and there was a story saying that Spiro Agnew, who was the vice president then, was being investigated for taking bribes. It happened that I lived only three blocks from Spiro Agnew, and naturally I was awakened and asked to go to his house and wait outside to ask him about this investigation. I spent the whole summer of 1973 covering the story of Agnew, the investigation, and his eventual resignation. Jerry Ford, who was then a congressman from Michigan, was appointed by Nixon to replace Agnew as vice president. NBC, with a certain lack of imagination, decided that since I had covered the old vice president, I ought to cover the new vice president. And I did.

Ford was vice president from October of 1973 until August of 1974, and he traveled a great deal. He campaigned for Republican candidates for the congressional election of 1974, by traveling in a little two-engine Convair. Only five or six of us reporters went with him and, in those circumstances, got to know him as a person.

After he became President, NBC assigned me to cover the White House, and Ford appointed a journalist whom he had known for a long time, Jerry terHorst, to be his press secretary. Jerry resigned after 28 days to protest the pardon of Nixon, and I was chosen as the second and final Ford press secretary.

When I went to see him to talk about the appointment, I asked him the following question: I have been in Washington for a long time, and I have seen a lot of press secretaries come and go—all the way back to Eisenhower—and there are really two kinds of press secretaries. There are those who get their information first hand by attending the meetings, listening to the discussions and the decisions, and they know what's going on and can supply first-hand information to the press. Then there are those press secretaries who are not in all the meetings, and they get their information second-hand. They have to go to some other member of the staff, or to the president, and say, "I have been asked, how shall I answer?" I told him that that was a good way to get into trouble, and I only wanted to get my information first hand, and he said that was really what he also wanted. Looking back on it, that's the way it worked out. I did attend all the meetings. I had some difficulty in getting information about foreign policy developments because Kissinger liked to be his own press secretary. He believed that information is power, so he wanted to hold on to that information and use it for his own purposes, and for the purposes of advancing America's interests. But, generally it worked out as I had agreed with Ford.

Just to show you how it can sometimes not work out if the press secretary doesn't get first hand information, I will use the example of Larry Speakes, the second Reagan press secretary. It was dramatically demonstrated at the time of the Grenada invasion, when CBS' Bill Plante asked Larry the day before the invasion about rumors that the United States was planning to invade Grenada. Larry went to a member of the National Security Council, reported this rumor, and asked what he should say. The National Security Council member told him, "That's preposterous. Knock it down hard."

If you've been in Washington a while, you develop an ear for those code words. "Preposterous" doesn't mean anything, and "knock it down hard" is a strategy for dealing with the question, not an answer to the question. But, nevertheless, Larry went out and said, "No, we're not planning any invasion of Grenada." And the next day we invaded Grenada. This demonstrated the classic dilemma of any White House press secretary, which is that Larry was perceived either as knowing the truth but lying about it, or not knowing the truth. Therefore, how can one pay any attention to the guy if he doesn't know what's going on?

A final word about my coming to the White House and joining the press office. People always say, "Why did you do it?" Sometimes looking back, I wonder myself why I did it, but as the newspaper people here know, after you've been a journalist for a long time, which essentially means standing on the sidelines watching other people do things, you get the itch to get into the game at least once and see how it feels to be doing something instead of observing other people. I also feel that citizens have an obligation at some point in their lives to do some kind of public service at some level. I had the itch to participate, and I did. Somebody gave me a little framed quotation by Churchill that I hung in my office at the White House. He was a journalist, too, before going into government. After doing so he said, "It's better to be making the news than taking it. It is better to be an actor than a critic." So, for once in my life I decided to try it.

When I got to the press office at the White House, it was a very large operation. There were 54 people. It included the people who helped out with the daily briefings and the people who made the traveling arrangements for reporters when the President traveled. We prepared a daily news summary for the President and his staff of what newspapers and magazines all over the country were saying. Usually when they couldn't figure out where to send a letter or a phone call, it came to the press office. I think it has grown even larger. After all, this was more than ten years ago. When I got there, I was surprised at how large it was, because when I was a White House correspondent for NBC covering the Lyndon Johnson administration, the whole press office was five people: Pierre Salinger, Bill Moyers, and three secretaries. That was the entire press office. And when I got there, there were 49 more people than there had been during the Johnson administration.

When I joined the Ford administration it was a very difficult time, I think, as far as the relationship between the White House and the press. It was after Watergate and after Vietnam. There was a tremendous amount of cynicism and distrust by reporters toward the President and toward members of the White House staff. Theodore White had written his book on Watergate called *Breach of Faith*, and that really summarizes what had happened. The Nixon-Watergate episode shattered a fundamental faith that the American people had always had in their president and in the White House. You could believe that the town councilman or the state representative might be a crook, but you could never believe that these things could happen at the presidential level, but they did and it shattered people's faith and affected the press. In addition, there was a lot of frustration on the part of the reporters who covered the White House every day. They had been right there, thirty feet from the Oval Office, and they never got a whiff of Watergate. These two guys who had never gone in the White House gate, Woodward and Bernstein, broke the story. So there was a tremendous amount of frustration built up in the press corps, and that was the atmosphere when Ford took over.

Ford had been a member of Congress for 25 years, and he had a lot of friends who were reporters. He had them to his house, he went to their house, and he still did that, incidentally, after he became president. He understood reporters and what they did for a living. He respected what they did. He was a genial person, not hostile. He didn't have a list of enemy reporters. I think he was open and honest, and civil in his dealing with reporters, and that did a lot to heal the relations between the White House and the press. You can really quantify that. He had 29 news conferences during the 2 1/2 years of his presidency. That is about one a month, not a bad record. He had 200 individual interviews with reporters, face-to-face, one-on-one interviews—200 in 2 1/2 years. One of the best things he did concerned an organization in Washington called the Gridiron Club, which is an organization of the senior people in the media. Until 1975 it was an all male organization. Each year they have an annual dinner to which the president, the Cabinet, and all the other top government officials are invited. In 1975, Jerry Ford refused to go until the Gridiron Club admitted women. I think that was quite an accomplishment.

There were other innovations. He agreed to have follow-up questions at his news conferences. Until then, reporters got up, asked their questions, the president could filibuster, ignore them, answer a different question, not answer the question, laugh them off, whatever. We let reporters stand up again and say, "Now, wait a second, you didn't answer my question" and ask a follow-up, and I think that was an excellent innovation, and it has been utilized since then by his successors.

Another innovation was the out-of-town news conference where local reporters could ask questions along with the White House press corps. I think that has proven to be quite helpful. One of the things about Ford was that when you came to him and said, "Here is an idea of how to improve relations with the press," he always had the same answer, which was: "Let's try it." So when we talked

about the follow-up question, he said, "Let's try it." And
the same thing with the out-of-town news conferences. He
had John Hersey, the writer, come and spend an entire week
on the Oval Office, from the minute he arrived until the
minute he went home. The result was the book, *A Day in
the Life of the President.* John Hersey had been a
classmate of his at Yale, and although Hersey disagreed with
his politics strongly, we agreed to do this, again a gesture
of openness toward the press.

One of the first things I asked Ford was how much
time did he want to devote every week to dealings with the
press. He said about two hours. So we used the two hours
every week sometimes divided up between interviews, news
conferences, other press activities, and out of town
conferences. Sometimes he would do interviews over the
telephone and so forth.

I'll tell you a little anecdote about those interviews.
Ford and I had a little routine worked up where usually on
the President's schedule there would be 30 minutes allotted
to say, Lou Cannon of the *Washington Post* who would come
in and interview the President for 30 minutes. After about
25 minutes, I would cut in and say, "That's it. We've run
out of time, let's wrap it up." And the President would say,
"Oh no, I"m really enjoying this. Let's let it go on for
another five minutes." So, he would get credit for being a
good guy!

I think that the notion of hostility between the White
House and the press corps is somewhat exaggerated, despite
Sam Donaldson. I just recently returned from Tokyo, the
site of the economic summit, and I produced and managed
the coverage of the summit for the Mutual Broadcasting
System, where I work now, and it reminded me of the fact
that a certain hostility and the element of an adversarial
relationship prevail. But the relation is about 80%
cooperative. The White House makes all the travel plans,
sets up the press room, the telephones, and the teletype
machines that provide all the information. It is basically a
cooperative enterprise with some elements of hostility. The
White House often is accused of manipulating or managing
the news. I never found that we were very successful at
doing that. Don Rumsfeld used to read these stories in the
paper in which they would spin out these elaborate
conspiracies that we were involved in, and he would always
say, "We're not smart enough to do that." Usually what

happens is that when you try to do something like that, the story always comes out in the paper, and it says something like, "In an obvious PR move today, concocted by his communications specialists, the President . . ." and by the time you get down to whatever it was he did, it is pretty well discounted, and you don't get any benefit out of it.

I think the most difficult times for the Ford White House in dealing with the press occurred during various crises of one kind or another. I got a quick lesson in that, after I had been at the White House for exactly one week. I came to work on a Friday. The following Friday, I was out having dinner, and I got paged. The White House doctor was on the phone. Dr. Lukash told me that Mrs. Ford was going to go into the hospital the next day for her cancer operation. And so that was a real quick lesson in dealing with the press during a time of crisis.

I think probably the worst problem we had started during the second presidential debate with Jimmy Carter when President Ford kind of freed Poland. This was a difficult time. This debate was held at the Fine Arts Center in San Francisco, and I and other staff members watched it from a little room off the stage, with some reporters. We heard him say in answer to a question that the Soviet Union did not dominate Poland or Eastern Europe and realized it was a mistake. I don't think we realized how serious a mistake it was. Incidentally, neither did some of the reporters who watched it with us. Later, we always had a late night press briefing after these debates to give comments to the morning news shows and the early afternoon newspapers. Brent Scowcroft was going to be the chief briefer, and before we went in, he called the staff together and said, "Look, let's understand before we go in and talk to reporters that the President made a mistake. He said the wrong thing about Poland." At that point, someone should have gone to the phone, called the President, and said, "You made a mistake, and we are going to correct it, and it will be what we call a one news cycle story." We knew that the morning papers would report that Ford said this silly thing about Poland, but since it would be corrected later, it would go away. None of us made that phone call, and I don't really know why we didn't. We went into the briefing and tried to explain what the President meant to say. By the next day the political people in Washington were burning up the phone lines saying the President had to correct this mistake because it was harming the campaign. Several staff members did go to the President and recommend that he either issue a correction in writing or go before the press and acknowledge he had made a mistake and said the wrong thing. A lot of public figures just don't like to stand up and acknowledge error, and he didn't want to. So it dragged on for about a week.

We in the media subject public figures to a ritual, which is that if the public figure makes a mistake, or what we perceive of as a mistake, we keep that story on the front page and on the evening news until they go through the public ritual of acknowledging or confessing error. Jimmy Carter had to go through the same thing that year with his "lust in your heart" interview with *Playboy* magazine. Ford had to go through the ritual of standing up and publicly acknowledging error, but this thing had dragged on for a week, and it was harmful. The harm was not that anybody thought he was announcing some new policy on Eastern Europe, but it was harmful because it reinforced his bumbler image by making people thing not only that he was a physical bumbler, but that he also couldn't think on his feet.

The bumbler image was the single worst problem any of us faced in dealing with the press during the Ford administration. It probably all began when Lyndon Johnson said, "Jerry Ford can't walk and chew gum at the same time." The actual language he used was, of course, a little tougher than that. And then in Salzburg (Ford was there to have a meeting with Sadat) he got off the plane, tripped, and fell the last few steps off the plane. There were hundreds of cameras there. We never talked very much about that episode, but what happened was that the night before, Ford was in Madrid as part of this tour, and the Spanish, in setting up the quarters that he was going to live in, had given him a little narrow short bed. Ford is 6'2", a husky man, and when the advance team went over, they said, "Well, that's unsuitable. He needs a real full size bed." For some reason the Spanish were stubborn. They argued and haggled, and finally they brought in a second bed and put it next to the first one, but they were two different heights. This is a true story. Of course, Ford didn't sleep very well that night. He flew to Austria the next day, had stiff knees, it was raining, and he got off the plane and tripped and fell.

He always took it in pretty good spirit. I saw him bitter about that coverage only once. He was in Vail on one of the Christmas trips to Vail. He is for his age and for any age a very good skier. But like all skiers, he falls occasionally. He certainly falls much less than I do. But anyhow, there were pictures of him falling every night in the news. I went over to his house for New Year's Eve that year, and he was very bitter. He said, "You know, all those reporters who are reporting how clumsy I am on the ski slopes get most of their exercise sitting on bar stools." That is very uncharacteristic of him. But it really did get to him that one time.

I remember an article that was published at that time (I think in *The New Republic*) called "The Flowering of Contempt" about how, as a result of Watergate and Vietnam, we had grown contemptuous of our leaders, and were therefore contemptuous in the way we covered them in the media. Ford was the first victim of that attitude. I remember after Carter replaced Ford in January of 1977, about a week or so into his administration, there was a picture on the front page of every paper in the country of Carter slipping on the ice just outside the Oval Office in the Rose Garden, and I thought, "Here we go again."

It is true that ridicule is a damaging weapon, and of course Ford was ridiculed by Johnny Carson in his monologue every night, and by Chevy Chase on Saturday Night Live. It is harmful to a public figure to be the subject of ridicule. Americans don't want a clown for president. We tried a lot of things to reverse this image, and I must say that looking back on it, they seem laughable to me now. We thought that it was important to place Ford in situations where he did look presidential, and to keep him out of situations where there was the likelihood of him not looking presidential. Every year the turkey growers of America come and give the White House a turkey just before Thanksgiving, and we wouldn't allow any pictures of him with this turkey. Another time he gave a speech at Disneyland, and they had these little characters running around dressed up like Mickey Mouse, and we had the Secret Service practically tackle this little character to keep him out of any pictures with Ford.

Another thing we tried to do was to co-opt Saturday Night Live. This show was the source of a great deal of ridicule with Chevy Chase doing his imitation. Ford appeared at a dinner in early 1976, which was a White House Correspondents Association dinner, and Chevy Chase was the entertainment. He did his whole Jerry Ford number with Ford sitting really close to him. But we had rehearsed for it, and Ford got up, did his own number, and he absolutely topped Chevy Chase and put him down. We thought the next step was to try to go on Saturday Night Live. I went on as the guest host, and Ford went on via video tape to show that this White House didn't take itself so seriously as others had, and that we could laugh at ourselves and, if we could take part in the fun, how could the ridicule be damaging? I think in hindsight it did not work out that way, especially if you read some of the things that have been said later in interviews by Chevy Chase and other cast members. The motive was not entirely good clean fun in our traditional way of making fun of our leaders. There was a political motivation, and I don't think it worked out the way we had thought it would to show ourselves as being able to take part in the fun.

I do think that the bumbler image was one factor in the outcome of the 1976 election. I don't think Americans want a clown or someone who has mental abilities they doubt as president. There were many other factors, such as the pardon, being another Republican president, being someone who had been in Washington for 25 years and still there at a time when Americans were clearly thinking that what they needed was someone who had not been involved in Washington over a long period of time. The economy, although recovering from a deep recession, was not really healthy then. Eugene McCarthy ran that year (a lot of people don't remember this) on the liberal party ticket, and the Supreme Court in New York State ruled that his name could not appear on the ballot. Had his name been on the ballot in New York state, Ford might have taken New York from Carter and turned the election around.

One of my frustrations as the press secretary, and I think something that I've learned about my own profession and I've tried to practice since I've gone back into journalism, was to see some of the serious matters that we dealt with in the White House handled in a somewhat trivial or simplistic way. Again there are lots of stories and anecdotes. To illustrate, Ford gave a major energy speech in January of 1975. It was the most comprehensive energy program of any American president—with thirty-one separate parts. He gave this as a fireside chat in the library of the White House and afterward we brought reporters in to ask questions. On this complicated, complex subject they could only think of two questions. One reporter wanted to know why he gave the speech from the library, and Helen Thomas wanted to know how he liked using the teleprompter. There wasn't enough expertise on this complex subject to even ask the right questions.

Another time Ford went to give a major farm speech at Iowa State University. In beginning the speech, he made a slip of the tongue, as he sometimes did, and said how glad he was to be at Ohio State. He quickly corrected it, but that night on the evening news, it was the meaningless, trivial slip of the tongue that was shown and not anything about the farm policy. Those were some of the frustrations I felt as press secretary.

One time Ford went to China, and the staff and I were put up in a guest house in Peking. The phone in my room rang at three o'clock in the morning and the call was from the *Detroit Free Press*. They had heard that at the banquet the Chinese had given for Ford that night, the Chinese army band had somehow played the Michigan State fight song instead of the victory march of the University of Michigan, which is where the President went to school. They wanted to know how the Chinese got the wrong sheet music, and asked me to wake the President up and get his reaction. That is a true story and again it shows some of the frustration I felt with seeing serious issues trivialized or ignored.

Honestly speaking, we brought a lot of our troubles on ourselves in the Ford White House primarily because of constant feuding and public fighting among members of the White House staff. The primary reason for this was the manner in which Ford came to the White House. He came practically overnight. Most candidates get to the White House after a long period of campaigning in which they get to know staff members, and staff members learn to work together. The good ones are put in the proper slots, and the bad ones are dumped overboard. But Ford didn't have that opportunity. He came literally overnight upon the resignation of Nixon. And his staff was always a very mixed group that had not worked together before. There were a lot of leftover people from the Nixon administration, and he brought in some people from his congressional staff. I think you've had Bob Hartmann speak at the Miller Center already. He brought some people from his vice presidential staff, including Jack Marsh, a native Virginian who was very competent. He brought some old friends from Grand Rapids such as Phil Buchen and some people from the outside who had never worked for him before—Don Rumsfeld and myself, for example. So there was no single overriding loyalty to Ford, and we had never all worked together. I think we finally got our act together toward the end of the 1976 campaign, but it was too late by then.

I hate to say this, but I think whenever staff feuding happens, and it is not uncommon in White Houses, it is the president's fault. The only person who can stop that kind of public fighting among the staff is the president. It makes him look bad, and it makes him look like he is not in control of his own staff. People tend to claim credit for what goes right and to blame the president for what goes wrong when it should be just the opposite. Ford was too nice a guy to crack heads and stop this fighting, and I think he was harmed by the appearance of not being in control of his staff.

Many memorable episodes of dealing with the press come to mind. There was the *Mayaguez* episode in which an American merchant ship sailing in the Gulf of Siam was captured by Cambodian gunboats and held for two or three days. Ford ordered a military attack, and all the crew members were freed unharmed. Unfortunately, about forty-one Marines and others were killed in the process, and I don't think we did a very good job of explaining why that had to be done. Also the Pentagon delayed and delayed and delayed in announcing the final casualty figures, which made it appear as if something was being hidden. I know to this day Ford feels that he did exactly the right thing and used exactly the right amount of force that was necessary to assert the right of Americans to sail on the high seas without being captured. This was over ten years ago and, in light of what we see now with terrorism and hijacking, it certainly was the right lesson to assert.

The end of the Vietnam War occurred during the Ford administration. I had a particularly emotional reaction to that. I had spent a good deal of my career as an NBC correspondent in Vietnam, five tours in fact. I was wounded there; I had a lot of friends there still, and as the thing wound down I felt very strongly and emotionally torn by some of the things that were going on. Ford went to Palm Springs for the Easter of 1975. He and his family traditionally took two vacations a year together. They always spent Easter at Palm Springs and Christmas at Vail. So he went to Palm Springs, and every night on the television there would be contrasting pictures of Jerry Ford playing golf and of the South Vietnam army being routed, of evacuation planes trying to get away, of soldiers knocking women and children off the planes, of people hanging on to the skids, and many horrible scenes as the war wound down. And of course the President and I were bombarded with questions from the press about how insensitive could he be, playing golf while Vietnam falls. Not that there was anything he could have done, but it certainly didn't look good.

Finally, on April 28, 1975, when it appeared that Saigon was about to be captured by the North Vietnamese, Ford ordered the evacuation of all the remaining Americans and whatever friendly South Vietnamese could be taken out. The evacuation lasted for longer than had been anticipated, for over twenty-four hours until the helicopter pilots were becoming so fatigued that the end of the evacuation was ordered. Then we announced that all the Americans were out of Vietnam. That was a mistake because all the Americans were not out of Vietnam, we discovered to our horror. Fifty or so Marines had been left in the embassy compound while the helicopter pilots flew out and delivered their refugees to aircraft carriers off shore and would then come back to get them. So we had to decide what to do about having erroneously announced that all the Americans had been evacuated.

There were various views about what to do, one of which was to do nothing. "The evacuation is going to be really over in another two hours anyhow, so just don't say anything." Don Rumsfeld, to his eternal credit, said that this war has been marked by so many lies, let's not end with one. So we told the truth. I went back to the briefing room and said, "I've made a mistake, the evacuation isn't over, there are fifty or so Marines left. They will be out in a couple of hours, and then the evacuation will really be over."

After the evacuation, there was an unpleasant mood in America of rejecting any help for the refugees. There were pickets and signs posted outside some of the refugee camps saying, "Gooks Go Home." "No gooks allowed to use this beach," and so forth. Congress rejected any aid for the refugees, and I remember I was the one who took the piece of wire service copy into the Oval Office to show to Ford when the House of Representatives voted down the aid. He was normally a very mild-mannered man, but he was angry and turned his attention to personally trying to turn around public opinion and congressional opinion on the refugees. He visited a refugee camp in Arkansas, and he did in fact turn public opinion around and persuaded the public and Congress that we had an obligation to support these people. I think it was probably the finest example of moral leadership by Ford during his administration.

Then we come to the 1976 election. I almost got the election coverage off on the wrong foot because of some dealings with the press, actually with Lowell Thomas, the great old newscaster. (When I was a little boy I used to listen to Lowell Thomas reporting from Lhasa, Tibet, on the roof of the world, and I think that's what persuaded me to be a broadcaster. I didn't know exactly what he did, but whatever it was, I knew that's what I wanted to be.) Lowell Thomas lived a very long life and was the person who publicized *Lawrence of Arabia*, and he had always kept up his interest in the Middle East. He asked whether he could come to visit Ford and talk about some of the things he was hearing about the Middle East and pass on some intelligence that he had. He came in, and they talked about that, but they also talked about skiing, because Lowell Thomas was a great skier late into his eighties. He asked Ford if he was going to ski in New Hampshire, and Ford said, "Nah. I skied up there when I was at Yale, and its too icy and too uncertain." So, I heard that, and a couple of days later, an AP reporter asked me whether Ford was going to ski in New Hampshire during the primaries, and I always liked to make sure that I was accurately reflecting the President's views, and I thought, "Well, I really know what he thinks about New Hampshire." So without thinking I said, "Nah, he's not going to ski in New Hampshire. It's too icy up there." Well, skiing is the number one industry in New Hampshire, and every newspaper in the state had these headlines about the White House criticizing New

Hampshire's skiing. I thought, "Oh, if I cost him the New Hampshire primary because of that stupid statement . . ." I was really worried. Fortunately, he won the New Hampshire primary, and then he won the Illinois primary and then he won the Florida primary.

Here's a man who had never run for national office, had never gotten a single vote in any national election. He had only run from the sixth congressional district of Michigan. And he had won three primaries: one in the north, one in the mid-west, and one in the south. At that point I think he should have said, "Okay, that's it. I've shown that I'm popular with the public. I can get elected. This is too busy a time for me to be out campaigning. What the country needs is leadership in the White House. You are going to elect me because of my accomplishments as President, not because of my abilities as a campaigner." He should have quit campaigning in the primaries, but he didn't. His primary race with Reagan went on and Reagan had lost all the primaries. He came to North Carolina, was running out of money, and decided to make one last effort to win a primary. He bought television time and won the North Carolina primary. That turned it in to a tight race. Reagan won a lot of the primaries that year, and the nomination wasn't really decided until the Republican convention in Kansas City.

I think it would be valuable to set the historic record straight on this question of why Ford didn't offer the vice presidential nomination in 1976 to Reagan because Reagan has muddied the waters on this issue. Reagan has said publicly that if Ford had offered him the vice presidency, he would have taken it, and Ford would have won. Well, the facts are these. Prior to the night of the nomination, Dick Cheney, who was Ford's chief of staff then, and John Sears, who was Reagan's leading adviser, got together to plan what to do after the nomination was decided. At this point it wasn't clear who was going to win. What they decided was that the winner would go to the loser's hotel for a peace meeting. The Reagan people insisted on one condition, and that was that Ford would not offer Reagan the vice presidential nomination. Cheney said, "Okay, it's a deal. We will not offer him the vice presidential nomination if that's what you insist on." So that's really what happened. Reagan has rewritten history since then, but that is really what happened. He said he didn't want it. He made Ford promise not to offer it to him, and Ford took him at his word and didn't.

The four finalists for the vice presidential nomination were Bob Dole, who was the eventual choice, Bill Ruckelshaus, Howard Baker, and Anne Armstrong. Anne Armstrong was then the U.S. ambassador to Great Britain. She had been a counselor in the White House to both Nixon and Ford. Bob Teeter, who was Ford's pollster, found that Dole lost Ford the fewest votes, and often that is the way the vice presidential candidate is selected. There was a positive aspect to it which was that there were some polls showing that the Republicans were in a little trouble in their traditional strong states in the farm belt, and that Dole, who was from Kansas, might help there. So Dole was the choice. I think, in my own opinion, a better choice would have been either Anne Armstrong or Nelson Rockefeller. Rockefeller had been Ford's vice president and had been dumped because of a perceived need to appease conservative southerners, where Reagan had a strong appeal. But having won the nomination, it seems to me that Ford could have gone back to Rockefeller, and I think that would have helped in the general election, particularly in New York, which was decided by such a small number of votes.

Looking back on the coverage of that election by the press, and having myself been involved in so many elections—as a reporter in 1964 I was assigned to the Johnson campaign; in 1968 I covered first of all George Wallace and ended up with Nixon; and in 1972 I covered the Sergeant Shriver campaign, the vice presidential candidate for the Democrats; of course, in 1976 I was on the Ford staff; and in 1984 I supervised the election coverage for Mutual—it seems to me that after every one of these elections we in the news business make the same complaints about our own coverage. And of course the politicians make the same complaints too, but we generally agree on what we do wrong. We complain about shallow reporting, and we complain about attributing political motivations to everything: the candidate did this or said this or made that decision in order to attract that block of convention delegates or that group of voters, as if candidates have no convictions. We overemphasize mistakes and trivia. We don't cover the issues as well as we should. Instead, we concentrate on the horse race aspects of the campaign—the hoopla, the parades, supposed behind the scenes maneuvering, the polls, and so forth. We attribute a great deal of advantage to the incumbency, when, in fact, the incumbent often loses because he is tied to his official acts while in office whereas the challenger doesn't have to take responsibility for any official acts. Johnson, Carter and Ford were all incumbents, and all were not reelected because they carried around this heavy load of responsibility for what they had done while in office. There is no benefit of incumbency by any means. The final complaint is that particularly in the case of television, complex issues are sacrificed for one minute of dramatic pictures or some correspondent standing in front of the camera telling you what it really means rather than what the candidate said.

Two professors at Syracuse, Patterson and McClure, have written a book on the coverage of the 1972 and 1976 presidential campaigns, and they found that the voters learned more about where candidates stood on the issues from paid political commercials than they did from the nightly news coverage by the networks, which is really a putdown for the networks. It's one of the reasons why I am a strong supporter of presidential debates. I think it is much better to choose a president based on hearing him at length, talking in his own words about what he stands for and what he would do if he becomes president, rather than relying on a little 15 second snippet on the nightly news which often doesn't concentrate on the issues but only on some trivial matters.

It is a mystery to many people why Ford, the incumbent president, would agree to debate Jimmy Carter in 1976. The traditional political wisdom is that the president, or whoever the incumbent is, is better known, has a built-in forum due to his public office, and has an image of leadership and being in command and that by giving all this TV exposure to his challenger, he only raises the challenger up to his level. I think that is generally true, but I think in 1976 things were entirely different. Ford was very far behind in the public opinion polls. In fact, the calculation that was made by the Ford administration was that by the late summer of 1976, Ford had to convert 125,000 people a day. Between September 1 and election day, 125,000 people a day had to be shifted from their support of Carter to support of Ford. The only way you could reach that many people was on television. Yet the new election law had gone into effect (as a reaction to Watergate), and the

amount of money candidates could spend on television was
very limited. There weren't enough funds to buy television
time to reach that many people. So, what was needed was
a lot of free television time. That's why Ford agreed to
the debates with Jimmy Carter that year.

The outcome of the election was that Ford lost by a
narrow margin. He constantly closed that gap, and he did
pick up the 125,000 people a day he needed. A lot of
people have said that if the campaign had only gone on a
few more days, he would have caught Carter. Actually, our
polls, although it is difficult to fine tune them quite this
much, show that Ford probably was ahead on the Sunday
before the election and tailed off enough on Monday and
Tuesday to lose the election by a very narrow margin. It
was heartbreaking for Ford. I'm sure you saw some of the
television pictures. He looked crushed. He is really one of
life's consistent winners. That partly accounts for his
personality. He had succeeded at everything he tried. He
had been a high school football hero; he had a good
academic record; he had a good navy record. He got to go
to the Yale Law School when he didn't think he was going
to be able to go. He was elected the first time he ever
ran. He never lost an election for Congress (thirteen times
straight), and he became vice president and president. He
didn't really count on the presidency. He didn't lust after
it. This was the first time he had lost anything; he was
crushed by it. I think perhaps the most poignant thing
written after the election was by David Broder in the
Washington Post who said, "Many people voted for Carter
because they thought they would get the qualities they
already had, but didn't appreciate in Gerald Ford."

Finally, before questions I would like to review what I
think are the accomplishments of the Ford administration.
He generally gets credit for returning honesty and civility
and common sense to the White House, but I think there
were more specific accomplishments. He did lead the
country out of the deepest recession since the 1930s in a
way that did not re-ignite inflation. He did preside over
the end of the Vietnam War. He did turn public opinion
around on the refugees. By his own conduct and approach
he made sure there wasn't this period of recrimination, of
"who lost Vietnam," and given the divisiveness of that war
and the divisions it had caused in our country, it is amazing
that we didn't go through that terrible period of who lost

Vietnam. He did assert with the *Mayaguez* incident, that we would, despite having retreated from Vietnam and Cambodia, defend our interests and the rights of our citizens in the world. He did restore trust after Watergate. Another accomplishment of Ford was the high quality of his appointments. For example, compare Ed Levi, the attorney general, with some of the people who have had that position. Carla Hills as the housing secretary, was an outstanding woman of accomplishment and a native Virginian. John Paul Stevens on the Supreme Court is a man who is going to leave his mark on the Supreme Court for generations to come. Good appointments were an accomplishment of the Ford administration.

During the Ford administration the CIA was found to have been guilty of past abuses, and yet Ford was able to preside over the reform of the CIA without wrecking the intelligence services that we need. He at least began a public discussion and concentration on some serious issues which we have now gone on to deal with. One was energy. Another was the size and taxing power of the federal government. He got a public debate going on that issue, and of the need to restore our country's defenses after a period of decline. Those were some of the outstanding accomplishments of the Ford administration.

Before concluding, let me say that when I was poking through a lot of old notes to get ready for this, I came across a letter written about a week before the end of the Ford administration. Larry O'Rourke, who was then the White House correspondent for the *Philadelphia Bulletin* and the president of the White House Correspondents Association, sent a letter to Ford that said: "As president of the White House Correspondents Association, I want to express to you as you leave office the gratitude of the working reporters at the White House. You have provided opportunities for reporters to meet with you, and members of your staff in an open and honest manner. In turn, there has been a rebuilding of the healthy tension that must exist between the government and the press in a free society for the benefit of the country." I think that is as good a legacy of the Ford administration as any I can think of.

NARRATOR: Some people identify themselves by understatement. When Mr. Nessen described his Mutual Radio Broadcast relationship he said that he worked for them.   He happens to be the vice president of that company.   That may tell you something about our speaker. Who would like to ask the first question?

QUESTION: First of all, I would like to know what you said to the 3:00 a.m. caller in China.   You said you had spent a lifetime of observing, you took this period as a doer, and now you've returned to observing.   How would you assess that period as a doer?   Was it a satisfactory period in your life?

MR. NESSEN: Well, it was a difficult period.   I found out pretty quickly that it was more fun to ask the questions than to answer them.   I learned something about myself as everybody does from a difficult situation, and I think I emerged as a better journalist.   That's the best part of it. Everybody who has had an experience in the government and gone back to journalism, whether it is Moyers, or Chancellor or Carl Rowan or any of us, learns something that makes him a better journalist.

    In my case, I think the main lesson is reflected in the title of my book, *It Sure Looks Different From the Inside*. It's far more complex than it appears from the outside.   I can remember as an NBC correspondent standing on the lawn of the White House with my microphone saying the President decided to do this today and I would give a reason or two of why he had made a decision.   I know now from attending those meetings that there are probably a dozen reasons for any decision.   And there are probably a dozen reasons on the other side why he shouldn't do it which he rejected.   So I've tried since then, both as a journalist myself and now that I am running a news operation, to get my own people and myself to reflect that kind of complexity.   The public needs to understand that kind of complexity in order to understand these issues and to make and form decisions about these issues.   That was a great lesson for me from going through that experience on the inside.

QUESTION: Almost universally the people who have talked to us about the Ford administration have emphasized what a decent man he was and what a nice guy.   On the other hand, there has been some feeling that this was probably his biggest fault, and that a president has to be utterly ruthless and unprincipled in order to succeed. Would you feel that that was his greatest fault?

MR. NESSEN: I don't think it was his greatest fault. I think it certainly was the fault that kept him from getting his staff settled down and stop fighting in public with each other. There is an expression in Washington that says to manage the White House as a president you either have to be ruthless or you have to have a ruthless and unprincipled person as your chief of staff. Unfortunately Ford was neither such person nor did he have a scoundrel as his chief of staff because certainly Dick Cheney was not that kind of person. In that sense I think it was a problem of not being tough enough. But I don't think it was his major fault.

I can't think of what I would list as a major fault. One of the things that we in the press do that sometimes disturbs me is that we suggest that one president after another is not smart enough to be president. You hear that question raised about Reagan; you certainly heard it raised about Ford; you heard it raised about Carter in a different way, in that he had an engineer's mentality and not a broad enough scope to be president. I disagree with that. I don't know what the qualifications in terms of intelligence are to be president. In Ford's case, he had been a member of Congress for 25 years. Most of that time he had been on the appropriations committee, and he immersed himself in the budget. He knew what all those lines meant. His view was that the best way to learn about an organization, whatever it is, is to master the budget. I believe that. I think that's true. He brought that kind of intelligence to the White House. It wasn't a creative kind of intelligence, but it was a kind of intelligence that he felt was useful and helpful in doing that job. I happen to agree with that.

I think his not being tough enough certainly didn't apply across the board. It did apply in not disciplining his staff, but at other times I think he showed a great deal of toughness. He made tough decisions. He made the pardon decision practically by himself. He felt that it was right, and he toughed it out. When he fired Schlesinger and Colby and a bunch of others, he made that decision basically on his own. I saw him a lot of times making strategy for how to deal with Congress and how to push certain legislation, and it was a really tough-minded kind of strategy. So I don't think that was his major fault.

QUESTION: My question is why was it always anti? I followed this very carefully because I was campaigning in Michigan soon afterwards for Ford, and it seems to me it was all anti, all the bumbling, all the things you brought out, and none of the things that were so positive about him, including the budget, which you just mentioned.

MR. NESSEN: Well, you should, because I feel it was partly a failure of mine, and I want to say that in my answer. I think there are two reasons. One, some of the things I mentioned—the contemptuous attitude toward our presidents, the breach of trust that Teddy White talked about—was partly due to the times. It was the period after Watergate and Vietnam and we had a pretty low opinion of our leaders. The White House press corps was frustrated and never wanted to be taken advantage of again, never be trusting again, never be taken in again. So there was that kind of cynicism that colored all the reporting. That's one side of it. Secondly, we can't expect reporters to come and say, "Tell me something good about the Ford administration." We, and particularly myself, should have been clever enough to figure out how to tell the positive things the Ford administration did, despite the mood of the time. To come back to my view about the debates, I think debates were great because there you have somebody standing up and telling, in their own words, what it is they have done and what it is they propose to do as leaders of their country. I watched the one that was held at William and Mary, the last debate. Roger Mudd came on and said, "That was the dullest 90 minutes in television history." I don't believe that two men who want to be your leader telling you what they will do for you and what they have done can be considered dull television or dull anything. The answer is (a) it was partly the temper of the times, (b) we didn't do a good enough job in telling his story to the reporters.

QUESTION: I'd like to go back to something you said early on in your talk about the role of the press secretary. Should he be in on all the discussions and therefore not be in a position to look dumb, or should he not? I suspect most of us know that President Kennedy said to Pierre Salinger during the Cuban missile crisis, that he didn't want his press secretary to be in the position of lying to the press. Therefore, he didn't cut him in. I think this is a fundamental question, and I'd like you to elaborate on the trade-off there.

MR. NESSEN: You are right, it is an excellent question. It is a fundamental one and I have a very strong opinion on it because I've known all these guys back to and following Pierre. I don't believe in that philosophy, although I know that is a philosophy many follow. Don't tell the press secretary, and then he won't be in the position of lying. On the other hand, I'll tell you the truth, in my opinion Larry Speakes didn't lie. He didn't know. So you put him in that position, and he lies inadvertently. My view is that the press secretary needs to know everything, and then he can decide how to answer questions. That's a whole separate matter. But he ought to have the information.

There are only three legitimate ways to answer a question if you are the press secretary, and about 90% of the time, you'll get a question and you give the answer. You know the answer and you give the answer. Sometimes you will have to say, "I don't know the answer, but I'll get it for you," and you do and you give it. A small percentage of the time you know the answer but you can't give it. So what do you do then? Well, you ought to do some variation of "I don't have anything to say about that; I don't have anything to tell you; or I can't give you anything on that." It's not lying, but you are just not telling the guy. Sometime you may be able to tell him an hour later, or 15 minutes later, or tomorrow, but you are not lying.

Now, I know sometimes that is difficult to do. Jody Powell got a question one night from an old friend of his, Jack Nelson of the *Los Angeles Times*. He asked, "Are you planning to go and try to rescue the American hostages in Iran?" Jody, who knew that we were, looked him straight in the eye and said, "No, we're not." Jack wrote that we were not, and then within a day or so the rescue operation occurred. Jody will tell you to this day, "I lied. I knowingly lied. I'm glad I lied. It was the only thing to do, and I would lie again under the same circumstances." Well, I was never put in that position. That was his approach. I find it a little bit hard to disagree with him, but I do think its better if you can, to protect your own credibility and the credibility of the White House, just say, "I don't have anything to give you, or I don't have anything to say about that." It's a little code. People's ears will perk up. They'll know that you've got something to say, and if they keep after you, you will be able to do it later maybe, but you don't lie.

COMMENT: That would have been a clear signal, if he had evaded it.

MR. NESSEN: Jack has been around Washington long enough to hear that signal, so maybe that explains Jody's approach to the question, and he defends it. I can see his point of view. I'm glad I was never put in that position, but that's the way he approached it. I would try to approach it without actually lying, I think.

COMMENT: There have been an awful lot of secretaries who have resigned. I'm talking about press secretaries at any governmental level, not necessarily the president's, because they have not been kept informed. They have been put aside so they won't accidentally or otherwise divulge information, and it is a tough way to operate as a press secretary. You've got to know what is going on.

MR. NESSEN: It is. It's like Larry Speakes and Grenada. He was put in an embarrassing situation. Nobody thinks he lied. Everybody knows he didn't know what was going on. And then, it's damaging to the person he is working for, in addition to his own credibility and sensibility, because he just loses value when nobody thinks he knows anything. So when you have something important to say, people sort of discount it and wonder whether you really know what you are talking about. It is important to keep up the credibility.

QUESTION: Couldn't the press secretary's position be complicated by the fact that he may suspect that the reporter knows something more than general knowledge?

MR. NESSEN: That's a technique that we use in the media. You do know something, but you pretend to know less than you know and you say, "Could you help me to understand this?" So one technique is to pretend to know less than you really know. Another technique is to pretend that you know more than you really know. You go to the press secretary and say, "You know, I was talking to the congressional liaison guy, and he was telling me about this . . . and your strategy for pushing the tax bill; could you tell me more about that," as if you know a lot. So there are various techniques. You have to be wary. We are a wily bunch in the press.

QUESTION: Mr. Nessen, presently we have Larry Speakes who seems to be abrasive almost in the Ziegler mold and Bernard Kalb in the State Department who also tends to be that way. Do we run the risk of having several voices speak on similar press issues?

MR. NESSEN: In my time in Washington, most of the information function had been pulled into the White House. I think that began during Eisenhower, and it certainly got its impetus during Kennedy, where the White House wanted to announce all the good news. Although the State Department made a bit of a comeback during the Iranian hostage crisis when Hodding Carter was the spokesman, in this case there was just the opposite effect. The White House wanted to get that hostage crisis out of the White House and have somebody else talk about it, so they gave it over to Hodding at the State Department.

The trend has definitely been for the White House to be more and more the center of press statements and that function has followed the general flow of decision-making to the White House. The White House makes decisions that used to be made by Cabinet members at the Cabinet level. When the decisions moved to the White House, the public information policy that goes with them moved to the White House. I am a big advocate of moving it back out of the White House, and for that to happen the President has to put more trust and faith in his Cabinet members. In the case of Ford, he did tell his Cabinet members to make the tough decisions themselves. For example, Bill Coleman had a couple of tough decisions to make, and Ford told him to make them himself and not to buck them to the White House if he could help it. The same thing with Carla Hills. Much of the information function has flowed to the White House in the past twenty or thirty years just because so much of the decision-making has moved to the White House.

In the case of personalities, Bernie Kalb, Larry Speakes and Bob Sims at the Pentagon are all different personalities.

I can understand a little bit if there is a tone of irritability or arrogance or something like that. God knows I displayed that enough in my time. It sort of goes with the job, I think.

NARRATOR: Would you want to say anything about the recent polls on the pardon?

MR. NESSEN: That was interesting to me. I think it was just the past week or so that there was a poll released saying that a majority of Americans now believe that the pardon was justified. That was a long time coming. Ford never had any second thoughts about the pardon at all. He and Mrs. Ford will both tell you that it probably had an effect on the election in 1976. A lot of people never forgave him for pardoning Nixon. But there are a lot of people in their teens and early twenties who don't have a clear memory of Watergate at all. It's not such a vivid memory to them as it is to us. I think that with the passage of time, the strong emotions generated by that period have been softened. But Ford never had any second thoughts about it. He felt that there were some very important foreign policy, energy and economic issues facing the country, and that if he didn't get attention and energy focused on those issues and if attention continued to be totally on Watergate and its aftermath and the likely trial of Nixon and so forth, the country was going to be in even bigger trouble. So the only way to get this out of the headlines was to pardon Nixon. He believed that then and he believes it now, and I guess what these polls show is that, after a decade of reflection, a lot of people share that view.

QUESTION: What was the response to terHorst after the pardon? Did his resignation have any effect on the relationship between the Fords and terHorst, and you and terHorst?

MR. NESSEN: Jerry was a reporter in Washington for a Detroit newspaper. I had known him as a colleague. Afterwards, of course, he went to the White House. He covered Ford's first congressional election back in 1947, so his friendship with Ford went back a long way. I was a White House correspondent during the first month of the

Ford administration for NBC, so I knew Jerry in that relationship.

There is some question still as to why Jerry resigned. I think the most popular view is that he resigned to protest the pardon. There is some feeling in Washington that Jerry found that he really didn't like that job very much, that it was a lot of work and tension, and that he looked for the first reasonably good opportunity to leave. I don't know. That is a question you need to ask him.

However, Jerry and I have two different views of the job. We have been on various programs and talked about it a lot. I get a lot of questions, and got a lot of questions then, about "Did you agree with X decision, did you agree with the *Mayaguez*, did you agree with the pardon, did you agree with the energy bill, did you agree with the choice of Bob Dole?" or whatever. Who cares? The press secretary is not a political official. He is not an elected official. He really serves the president and basically is a technician, and I don't think that my personal views matter one bit. Who cares? The job, as I saw it and still see it, is to accurately reflect the president's views. You are the surrogate, the spokesman, literally the stand in for the president. His days are too busy to spend a lot of time with the press, so you spend a lot of time with the press for him. When I was asked a question, I always tried to answer it as I thought Ford would answer if he were there himself. And that is why it was important to attend those meetings so you would be up to date on what he thought about various issues and personalities, and also to spend a lot of personal time with him. I would go up and have a drink with him in the evening, or have dinner with him, or fly with him on the plane just to make sure that I really understood what he was thinking. And every once in a while at a news conference, the reporters would want to make sure that I knew what I was talking about, so they would say, "Mr. President, Ron told us today that you believe so and so. Is that how you really feel?" I would hold my breath, waiting for him to disown me but he never did, except about skiing in New Hampshire.

So, terHorst and I had two different views of the job. I believe if you explained why the president made a decision, what his reasons were, then you had done the job. Nobody cares whether you agree or disagree. But terHorst felt that if he couldn't agree with a decision like that, he

had to resign. I must say that I was never put in a
position where I had moral qualms about announcing and
explaining Ford's reasons for doing something. At the end
of the Vietnam war, I held my breath because I think if
Ford had decided on another policy, to get reinvolved or to
bomb or something like that, I might have had a real moral
dilemma, but I never did. So, terHorst and I disagree on
what the role of the press secretary should be.

QUESTION: Did President Ford or any other president you
know of ever consult or ask for the opinion of the press
secretary on any particular issue?

MR. NESSEN: Well, yes, I think a lot, depending on what
the relationship is. It's a very personal relationship. I
think it's different from the relationship with any other
member of the staff because the press secretary is in effect
his surrogate, his public spokesman, because he doesn't have
time to be out there that much every day. So it is a
different relationship. It's a closer, more personal
relationship. Jody Powell had a very close personal
relationship with Carter. When he said the President thinks
or feels you knew that it was an accurate reflection.
Believe it or not, Ziegler very accurately reflected Nixon's
views. You knew that when he said that Nixon felt
something about this, he was accurately reflecting the
President's views. In the last days of Watergate, when
Nixon was totally invisible, never came out in public, there
used to be feeling in the White House press corps that
Nixon's mood could be determined by observing Ziegler's
mood. They were that close. There is sometimes a close
relationship. For others, it is different. I don't think
Speakes has that relationship with Reagan.

Regarding advice and advisers, every president
organizes his White House staff differently. In the case of
Ford, he had nine senior advisers. Each adviser had sort of
a dual role. Each ran his own department. I ran the press
office, somebody else ran the National Security Council, the
OMB, the Congressional Liaison Office, etc. From an
administrative point of view, each ran an office, and then
the nine together made up a senior advisory council. We
had a senior staff meeting every morning, and we would be
called upon for advice about our own area. We talked about
issues such as how will this play in the press, when should

we announce this or should we hold a news conference this week. But we would also be asked broader questions that were outside our immediate area of expertise. Every White House is different. The president organizes his White House as seems to suit his own particular view of what he wants and needs.

QUESTION: What was the effect of the pardon?

MR. NESSEN: Well, I wasn't in the White House at the time of the pardon. I was a reporter for NBC. TerHorst was the press secretary, and so obviously I wasn't asked for advice. I guess Jerry wasn't either. That was part of his complaint.

Ford has a little bit of a record, if you look over his record, of making these really big important, monumental decisions very much alone. I gather that the pardon was one of the decisions he made alone, although he got advice from Phil Buchen and probably some others. It was a decision that he basically made alone.

NARRATOR: You gave us a little more on the selection of the vice president than any of the previous people. The one thing you didn't comment on, and a couple have done so, is Ford's attitude toward Reagan. One person said that Ford rather graciously expressed it by saying he couldn't understand or didn't always understand Reagan, but he thought that basically Ford disliked and resented Reagan.

MR. NESSEN: I think he did, certainly at that time. I think some of that or most of that has faded now. But after all, here's an incumbent president who's doing a pretty good job in a difficult time, and another Republican challenges him for the nomination. It's a tough, strong challenge, and looking back on it, of all the factors that did Ford in, it was probably the most serious factor because he ended up looking like just another hack politician running for office, rather than staying in the Oval Office and looking and being presidential. Maybe that was the best way to turn the bumbler image around, to work every day in the Oval Office making the right decisions instead of being out there on the campaign trail looking like just another guy running after the office. So you can't exactly blame Reagan for that. It was Ford's decision to keep campaigning.   Instead of quitting after those first three primaries, he kept after them.   I do think he was unhappy that Reagan challenged him.   I think the other factor that made him unhappy was that Reagan really didn't help in the election of 1976.   Reagan, at that point and whatever his attitude now, didn't have any particular strong interest in building or helping the Republican party.   He was primarily interested in getting Ronald Reagan elected as president, and was not a particularly loyal or dedicated Republican. So when he lost the nomination to Ford, he more or less walked away.   And if you look at how that election came out, how close it was, and the fact that Jimmy Carter, being from Georgia, really took most of the southern states (all the southern states except Virginia), Reagan could have really helped.   Reagan was popular in South Carolina, Mississippi, Louisiana, and other states in the South.   So had Reagan campaigned hard for Ford, the outcome of the election might have been different.   Those were the factors that made Ford somewhat resentful of Reagan.

NARRATOR: I should have said in introducing Ron Nessen, that when we did our exercise on the presidential press conference, one thing that was notable was the respect in which he was held by the other people who were involved, other former press secretaries and newsmen.   That goes back to several things: one, the 1962-72 period when he covered the vice president and the White House as NBC reporter; then, his press secretary's job; and finally, the kind of honest and straightforward but clarifying discourse which he seems to engage in everywhere, and which he certainly has engaged in this morning.   We are terribly grateful to him.

PRESIDENT FORD AND THE MEDIA

JERALD F. TERHORST

NARRATOR: Jerry terHorst was President Ford's first press secretary and is director of public affairs at Ford Motor Company. He has had a distinguished career in the journalism field. He was born in Grand Rapids and is a graduate of the University of Michigan. He began his newspaper career in college and as a reporter in Grand Rapids, Michigan, with the Grand Rapids Press. He moved on to write for the *Detroit News*, first on state and political affairs, then as a Washington correspondent and eventually as director of the Washington Bureau. He has written two books: *Gerald Ford and the Future of the Presidency*, and *The Flying White House: The Story of Air Force One*.

Of all the people in the Miller Center oral history on the Ford presidency, Jerry terHorst may be the first who is not certain that the pardon was the best thing that could have been done. In that respect and on other matters as well, we have much to share with Jerry terHorst.

MR. TERHORST: Thank you, Ken. I often say that I have one Ford in my past and another one in my present and future. I couldn't resist saying that—although there is obviously no connection between the two Fords.

I would like to conversationally make some very brief opening remarks and then solicit your questions.

I probably knew Jerry Ford longer than anybody who came to work for him in the White House with the exception of Philip Buchen. After World War II when I was a struggling young cub reporter fresh out of the Marine Corps, Jerry Ford was a struggling young attorney right out of the Navy. His stepfather was chairman of the Kent County Republican Committee, which is the home seat of the county for Grand Rapids. Young Jerry Ford became very active in Navy affairs. The Navy League there, which during the war was largely a group of Navy wives, became heavily populated with ex-Navy men after the war. Jerry was very active in that group, particularly in the attempt to create low cost homes for returning veterans with four percent Veterans Administration loans. In those days, a two-bedroom home with an attached garage sold for about seventy-five hundred or eight thousand dollars. But it did require some zoning changes in the city ordinances. As a result he was frequently at City Hall, and, as a result, I often found him on my beat as a reporter.

In 1947 he decided to run for Congress against a Republican incumbent. In that era, the Fifth District of Michigan was as much a one party district as the deepest southern Democratic district could ever have been. If you intended to get elected you had to win the primary; if you won the primary you were a shoo-in in the fall. The Democrats put up nominal candidates but it was usually just a gesture because a Republican was guaranteed to hold that seat. Jerry decided to run against the incumbent because the incumbent had infuriated Senator Arthur Vandenberg. The incumbent was a chap named Bartel Jonkman, a Dutch name pronounced in Grand Rapids as Yonkman. In Congress he was known as Jonk Man or other derivations—not all of them printable. He was a very, very conservative isolationist congressman of the old school. Vandenberg, who was the leader of the Michigan delegation, had swung over to internationalism in support of many things that Franklin Roosevelt and Harry Truman stood for. He found the incumbent congressman to be somewhat of a political embarrassment, since Vandenberg also came from Grand Rapids. His own congressman spent more time attacking the senior senator than he did other things in Congress.

They persuaded Jerry Ford to run in the primary and lo and behold, he was successful. I covered that first campaign and I got to know him rather well. He was about thirty-six when he was elected. Eventually, I also found myself in Washington as a journalist for the largest paper in

Michigan, so Mr. Ford was constantly on my beat as a reporter. As he gradually moved up in the House of Representatives to become minority leader, he became increasingly a larger part of my national, political beat.

When it appeared toward the end of the Nixon presidency that Ford was about to become president, Philip Buchen and some of Ford's other good friends created a clandestine team to prepare him and the country for that day: if he had to step into the White House on short notice, at least somebody would have thought about the first, second and third things that a new president ought to do.

Ford himself did not know at the outset that this was going on. It was called the "Ford Foundation," a euphemistic excuse. It met in the home of Bill Whyte, the chief lobbyist for U.S. Steel, and Jerry Ford's good golfing friend. The members of that group were Philip Buchen; Senator Bob Griffin of Michigan, a long time friend and the Republican minority leader in the Senate; Clay Whitehead, who was the director of the Office of Domestic Communications Policy under President Nixon; former Representative John Marsh of Virginia, who had been Vice President Ford's military liaison and was a long time congressional friend; and two or three other close associates. That group did the basic planning.

It became apparent to me what this group had in mind when Philip Buchen called me a day and a half before President Nixon announced his resignation. Mr. Ford wanted to talk to me about being his press secretary. He had determined in advance that Ronald Ziegler would not suit him as his spokesman after the Nixon presidency, and Ford wanted someone new. I made arrangements with my Detroit paper to get a thirty day leave of absence, with the understanding that if Mr. Ford liked the cut of my jib and if I could stand the pace of the job, that we might continue the relationship.

At the outset, people wanted to know how Ford got started. It was relatively comfortable and easy for him, which shocks most people. But, after all, he had been minority leader of the House; he was very familiar with the workings of Congress after more than 25 years there. He was comfortable with the Democratic leaders. He had worked very closely with them when he served on the select intelligence committee and he was the ranking member on

the Appropriations Committee. Mr. Ford was well respected
as a man whose word was his bond. That is still one of the
great virtues of any top member of Congress.

Ford always had a very interesting relationship with
the press. He genuinely liked reporters. He didn't always
understand where they were coming from and often did not
agree with what they wrote—including myself—but he never
lost his interest in what they were doing. He liked them as
people because he sensed that they shared his interests and
curiosity in the workings of government and who did what
to whom, etc.

This trait helped him when he became president. As a
press secretary, it was therefore rather easy for me to
begin building a solid foundation for the new president with
the press. It was primarily because of Ford's genuine
rapport with and liking for members of the press; and
secondly, because he was obviously such a contrast to what
had gone before. Reporters, without being prompted, wrote
about such things as "a breath of fresh air." There was a
good feeling, a good ambience in those early days. Ford
thrived on that and it stood him in good stead. It also
stood the country in good stead because we were all
genuinely anxious for a breath of fresh air in the White
House and somebody who would throw open the windows for
a change.

I proceeded on that basis for thirty days. I probably
hold the Guinness Book of Records for the shortest term as
press secretary. I was his first appointment and,
unfortunately, the first to leave after the pardoning of Mr.
Nixon.

A good many things happened in those first thirty
days. Obviously, he picked Nelson Rockefeller as vice
president. That was a very interesting process. He also
made a major policy change from the Nixon presidency on
the question of amnesty for the young men who had gone
either to Canada or Sweden or evaded the draft in other
more discreet forms. He announced the amnesty policy in a
speech to the Veterans of Foreign Wars in Chicago. It was
a great disappointment to them because they expected more
of the no amnesty policy that Richard Nixon had imposed.

Ford held his first news conference as president in the
East Room. That had been a customary place for President
Johnson, who held the first news conferences in the East
Room of the White House (John Kennedy held them in the

State Department Auditorium). Lyndon Johnson wanted to make a change, so he decided to hold them in the White House in the East Room; Richard Nixon continued that. It was a very comfortable place to do it and it was handy. You didn't have to go any place to hold a news conference. But on the east wall of the East Room, there is a rather large open space between two windows which would be filled with blue drapes, both for sound effect and as a suitable background for cameras. The president would stand with his back to the wall and address the group facing the rest of the White House.

I decided to change that, partly because I wanted— whenever possible—to establish a difference between the Ford presidency and the Nixon presidency, and partly because I wanted to build on Ford's promise of an open presidency. So we put the podium right in the middle of the doorway, behind which the long great hall that runs through the White House on the first floor. It created a sense of space and openness. We no longer had the president talking with his back against a wall of dark blue draperies. The symbolism was right, and the cameras loved it. Actually we could get twelve more seats in the room than in the old arrangement, which was another advantage. It worked. Ford liked it, the sound effect was great, and the picture was superb. Others seemed to think so too, because President Reagan holds his news conferences there now.

Sometimes things reach the public through the White House by means other than public advertisements or press releases. It is nice to see, every now and then, that you've made a small contribution of lasting benefit. My contribution to American history was to rearrange the way presidents hold news conferences. With that I'd like to see if I can answer some of your questions.

QUESTION: Your resignation, sir, was a protest against Ford's pardoning of Nixon, was it not? And if that's the case how were the personal relations between the two of you? You'd grown up together, as it were, and been close friends.

MR. TERHORST: Well, let me answer the first one. You put it exactly right and I thank you because so many people, particularly in my profession, tend to look for a more tactical reason. I did indeed resign in protest to the pardon. I really felt it was wrong to establish two standards of justice in America: one for the ordinary people who were facing the courts and prison sentences, and another for our leaders. If the President was powerful enough and well known enough, he could get off scot-free. In fact so scot-free, he was pardoned before he had even been accused of anything by the courts. The pardon extended both forward and back, a bit of *ex post facto* work. But one thing bothered me as much as anything else about it. I was reared as a staunch Calvinist and had always been taught that before one is forgiven, one must at least express regret and ask for forgiveness. That had not been forthcoming from Mr. Nixon in San Clemente, so it seemed to me that the pardon was an obvious and untimely favor, and it came as a shock to the country. The president had not prepared the country for this and therefore the country was unable to do what Mr. Ford hoped—put Watergate behind it. In many ways, the pardon tore the scab off the Watergate wound just as it was beginning to heal.

The second question concerned the effect the pardon had on our personal relations. Obviously they were strained at the outset. Probably because Jerry Ford and I have known each other so long, it did not permanently mar our relationship. We have talked, and I have visited his places in Colorado and in California. When he comes to Washington I don't go out and seek his attention but he knows where he can reach me. When he does get in touch, we have a very pleasant conversation together and there is absolutely no hint of any ill will. I probably get along with him today as well as anyone who stayed throughout the Ford presidency.

NARRATOR: Were you consulted at all about the pardon?

MR. TERHORST: No, I was not consulted about the pardon and that is the reason that so many of my colleagues thought I left. But I was not upset over not having been appraised of what the president had in mind. To tell the truth, that strikes me as a rather shallow reason for leaving. I mean, there is nothing that requires the president to confide in anybody, least of all a press secretary. My big problem at that time with the holdover

Nixon staff was to educate them—to the fact that keeping me posted was not an act of loyalty to the president but it was a necessity if I was not to perform a disservice in briefing the press. But a good many of my colleagues in the press to this day believe that I left because I had not been cut into the loop and therefore my vanity was offended. That is not the case; I quit in great sorrow.

QUESTION: Who was the principal adviser to the President on this?

MR. TERHORST: Philip Buchen, who was his legal counsel, and Bob Hartmann, who was his speech writer and his chief of staff when he was vice president. The pardon was issued on September 9. About five days earlier, I later learned President Ford asked Philip Buchen to research the Constitution to ascertain precisely what his powers were under the pardon provision. How far could it be extended? Did one have to be formally accused in a court of law or be under criminal indictment? Could the president do this peremptorily? Did he have that kind of executive power?

Those questions involved a combination of constitutional and legal issues, so Buchen obtained assistance from some of his scholarly and legal friends. A good many of them thought the questions were part of a longer period of research and didn't have any idea that there was any immediacy to the answers.

Philip Buchen, Bob Hartmann, John Marsh, and Don Rumsfeld were all directly involved in that decision. Alexander Haig was close to that process, although he probably did not have any direct involvement in the group. At that time, there was considerable personal strain between Buchen and Al Haig, so Phil Buchen did not call him into consultation any more than was absolutely necessary.

Buchen, by the way, is the other person in the Ford White House whose friendship with Jerry Ford goes back as far as mine. Their friendship went back to Grand Rapids where he was Jerry Ford's early law partner.

NARRATOR: They were all from Michigan and presumably your friends as well. Was it a little surprising that they wouldn't talk to you? Were they holding it so close because of the sensitivity?

MR. TERHORST: Their explanation was that they were holding it close because the president asked them to hold it very close. Mr. Ford in his book is rather candid about it. He said the counsel he received was that there was a danger in telling the press secretary. If the press secretary knew and was asked questions in the newsroom by reporters, something might inadvertently slip, given my determination to be as open as possible. I thought that was a rather shallow estimate of my ability to keep confidences. For instance, I knew almost 48 hours in advance that Nelson Rockefeller was going to be vice president and I managed to keep that secret. I also knew about the new amnesty policy for over a week because I was part of the planning and managed to keep the lid on that. In fact, the leaking that occurred came out of the Pentagon, where James Schlesinger was defense secretary.

One time the President called Schlesinger in to the White House and dressed him down for allowing these leaks to come out of the legal counsel's office in the Pentagon. It wasn't clear yet what was going to happen but there was more coming out of the Pentagon than the President wanted. So he told Mr. Schlesinger—to turn Scotty Reston's phrase on its head—that "if there is any leaking to be done, the ship of state will leak at the top."

NARRATOR: Were you affected at all by what Bob Hartmann refers to as the "conflict between the Ford loyalists and the Praetorian guard?"

MR. TERHORST: I wasn't hurt by it but I was aware that it was going on and I had to be on my guard about it. I think that was one of the problems. If a vice president comes in on a short emergency, either through a catastrophe, an assassination, a sudden death, or an incapacitation of the president, he definitely inherits the staff. There is no new broom that can sweep everybody out and bring new people in and expect them to hit the ground running. It can't be done, whether it is in business, government or university life; human experience doesn't permit it.

So except for a handful of about six of us, everybody else was part of the Nixon White House staff. People said, "Why don't you get rid of the Nixon people?" They used to ask Jerry Ford this, but the plain fact was that there weren't many Republicans available for staff work who hadn't been Nixon people. Nixon had been president for six years. The Republican party basically had been a Nixon party since he was vice president, with the exception of the Rockefeller wing of the party or the so-called eastern establishment wing. Because of his long service in the party and as office holder, the Republican party held Richard Nixon in rather good stead. So it was natural to have them there.

Our problem with them was that they tended to view Mr. Ford's interests, candor, and openness as something they would have to live through for a while, but they wanted to get back to "normal" as quickly as possible. It was very comfortable in many ways for the White House to operate without having to go public very often. It was a lot easier to hold committee meetings without having to worry about making a report to the outside world. They hoped to return to those comfortable days. None of us Ford people were willing to have that happen, and we were determined it would not. So we had constantly to try to find out what they were up to and persuade them that this was not the proper way to go, and to let the President do it on his own if necessary. There was a constant tension between those who wanted to regard Mr. Ford as simply a caretaker and those who came in with Ford and were determined to let him be president.

QUESTION: Rockefeller certainly was not held in high esteem by many of Mr. Nixon's supporters. Can you tell us something about the process of his selection?

MR. TERHORST: Yes. It was a nice exercise in gamesmanship, both internally and externally. Everybody in the party, after Jerry Ford became president, naturally was very curious as to whom he would pick for vice president. There was so much pressure. Some of his closest allies—people like Melvin Laird and others—were hoping they might get the nod and exerted a great deal of pressure. In order to get out of it, Mr. Ford decided that he would hold a sort of beauty contest. He suggested having names submitted to the Republican leaders of the Senate and the House. "Anybody have a good idea for vice president? Just give your name to your congressman or senator and it will get up to me at the White House and we will whittle them down." Well, it was amazing; we had over one hundred and eighty names in a few days. We thought we might get 25 or 30 names and suddenly we had a real contest. Yet it all had to be done rather privately and secretly. It made a great game for the press and pleasantly occupied their attention for a time.

Ford had privately told us that he was going to look for several things in a vice president. He wanted somebody who could contribute to the administration, with a variety of experience and breadth of information that he, Ford, did not personally possess. He said, "I've been a creature of Congress all my life. I don't think I'm going to pick another member of Congress. I know that beat pretty well and I don't have to have somebody telling me how to get along with Congress." He talked about perhaps a big city mayor. At that time, the cities were in great turmoil. He himself had never served in a municipal office of any kind nor had he served as governor. So he also began to think that one of the state governors might be a logical choice to bring some breadth of experience into the administration. Those were the two guiding principles that he applied. Eventually he managed to co-opt Melvin Laird by making him a principal of the steering group that would help pick the right man, and he did the same with a number of other leaders in the Senate and in the House. It was August 19 when he announced his choice. He picked Nelson Rockefeller for that very reason. He said in effect, "I'm a Mid-Western conservative Republican and Rockefeller is an Eastern, liberal Republican; he is a governor and I've been a member of Congress; the Republican party is a big umbrella. I like the idea that he will bring some support into the party we haven't had politically under Richard Nixon." That was a nice mesh with Ford's idea of the kind of vice president he wanted.

I'll never forget the Saturday that Nelson Rockefeller came to the White House for a private session. Clearly, he was being watched by the press because they could see that he was on everybody's list as a potential candidate. He was naturally visible in his own right. So he had to discreetly extract himself from Albany and the state of New York, and get himself to Washington without being noticed. That was not an easy task for the governor of New York at any time, particularly a Rockefeller. At the same time he had to show up at the White House in a way that would be innocuous and not arouse the attention of my former colleagues in the White House newsroom. It was decided that Rockefeller would get to Washington on his own and if discovered there he would have to have some good excuse for being there. They would do it on a weekend after we had given the press a lid for the weekend and the president had said he was going to go golfing (which of course he did, but he delayed his golf game a bit). Rockefeller stayed at his own place out on Foxhall Road; we got him into the White House very early through the West Executive wing and brought him into the White House. There were only a handful of wire service reporters in the newsroom and they never even knew he was in the building. He met privately with Jerry Ford, and only about six members of the staff were even aware he was there. As far as we knew, few of the old Nixon guard knew he was there. It was mainly just the "Michigan mafia." They met for about 90 minutes, and then we were able to discreetly extract Nelson Rockefeller in the same way. He turned up later in the day in New York, visibly attending some meeting. It was a nice piece of undercover work.

NARRATOR: Was Ronald Reagan one of the 180 names with Gerald Ford, either then or in 1976?

MR. TERHORST: If he was one of the 180, I don't recall that he ever surfaced in the final selection process.

QUESTION: Did Rockefeller's international experience have anything to do with the selection?

MR. TERHORST: A great deal. Jerry Ford considered it one of Rockefeller's strong suits that he had been an experienced special ambassador for previous presidents, particularly in Latin America. That was a strong measure of his ability, as Ford saw it.

QUESTION: Do you know the reason that Rockefeller did not run with Gerald Ford in 1976?

MR. TERHORST: If Mr. Ford can be believed in his own book, and I think he can, he can't understand why he ever made the decision not to run with him. But by that time it was too late. Actually, it was rooted in the way presidents and vice presidents have coexisted for many, many years. Historically, it has always been a standoffish relationship. None of them have ever been really close to their president, perhaps until Walter Mondale came on the scene with Jimmy Carter. President Reagan has continued that with George Bush, and there are good and bad things to say about that relationship. One can witness what happened to Mr. Mondale and envision what might happen to George Bush. There is a problem of separating yourself suitably from the man who has said, "you are so important to my administration that I've got to cut you in on everything." But in those days there was a tendency not to do that.

While there was a great interest in making Rockefeller part of the Ford White House team, Rockefeller himself did not want to sit at Jerry Ford's elbow, and Jerry Ford did not think he needed Mr. Rockefeller that close, day in and day out. That atmosphere was also reinforced daily by the staffs of the two men. For those who were shaping policy for Jerry Ford, it took longer and was more difficult to cut the vice president staff in on everything. Publicly, Henry Kissinger was impressed with Rockefeller's international experience. Privately, Henry Kissinger wasn't going to share any more than he needed to with Rockefeller, his former boss. So the staffs held each other at arm's length. The decision finally was publicly noticed; the press spotted things that Rockefeller said which didn't sound like something Jerry Ford would have said in the same circumstance. The Ford White House would end up having to say, "Well, what we meant was this," and Rockefeller's staff would have to say, "Well, what the vice president meant was . . ." This was constantly going on in public.

A distance between the president and vice president is normal, but in this case a great deal of fighting was going on within the Republican party. There was a very strong feeling that Rockefeller had been a bad choice and that they were determined that a conservative should get the nomination or should be Jerry Ford's running mate in 1976. That feeling got to a point where Mr. Ford eventually yielded to it. He said that he would pick his own nominee for vice president at the convention.

One reason was that he was under tremendous pressure from the Reagan candidacy on the right. It is unusual for an incumbent president to have such strong opposition within his own party for the presidency. Perhaps it was because Jerry Ford had been appointed president—albeit ratified by Congress—but not elected by the public. In order to keep the lid on the party, Mr. Ford decided that he would have to dispense with naming Mr. Rockefeller. But as he suggested in his own book, perhaps he might have run better with Nelson Rockefeller on the ticket than he did with Robert Dole.

QUESTION: So it was his decision and not Rockefeller's?

MR. TERHORST: It was a combination of both their decisions at that point. At the time I happen to think Rockefeller was very happy not to be asked. The staffs had fallen into a great deal of strain at that point, and Rockefeller was getting a little turned off by the process. But if Ford had asked him to stay and run, Rockefeller might have changed his mind, but that never happened. As Ford has said in effect, "Perhaps it was one of the reasons I came within an ace of winning and didn't quite make it."

QUESTION: Do you think the pardon was a major factor in his candidacy for presidency or do you think Jimmy Carter had better publicity or do you think the Reagan opposition was the cause?

MR. TERHORST: I think there were a lot of factors at work there. Many of these reasons are equally valid. After all, the country had had eight years of a Republican president with Mr. Nixon and Mr. Ford, and things had not gone too well: we had the war in Vietnam with its inglorious ending; we had inflation that started to mount under Nixon but became a major public issue under Ford; we had the beginnings of a small recession; and we had Watergate. The country was really looking for a change, and that was the reason Jimmy Carter was elected. His "I'll never tell a lie" theme was like taking an eraser to the whole Watergate smear and wiping it off. The public was ready for that sort of Carter candidacy. The other choice was Jerry Ford, who had pardoned Nixon.

In his book, Jerry Ford says that, given the fact he only lost by two percent, the pardon probably had some effect, but he mentions other factors too. My own opinion is that the pardon had some effect. When something is lost that narrowly, it is hard to say that any single thing was the trigger, but the pardon did play a large role in a lot of people's minds, especially because the pardon made such big news at the time.

QUESTION: Did the reputation which Mr. Ford acquired of not being too bright have anything to do with it? Most people were certainly impressed with the breath of fresh air aspect, but there were also those nasty comments.

MR. TERHORST: I think it had a great deal of effect. It is such a hard thing to put your finger on except by way of a series of examples. Was this man awkward and disjointed? Not really. He was an all-American football player. He was the first president who publicly skied in front of cameras. I wouldn't do it in front of cameras; I wouldn't do it privately! Here was a man, in his early sixties, going down the slopes of Colorado. They had to train a squadron of Secret Service men to ski to stay with him, who were all in their twenties and thirties, some as young as his children.

Ford was a coordinated guy and always had been. But he had an unfortunate predilection to let funny things happen in public. Once he waved to the crowd before getting on the helicopter, turned, and the door was six inches lower than the top of his head. On another occasion, he was holding an umbrella in one hand and Betty Ford in the other on a rainy descent into Vienna. He slipped on the ramp out of the plane and fell on his knees. The umbrella went one way and a Secret Service man caught Mrs. Ford so she didn't fall. But he got up instantly and everything was fine—but he had fallen. His heel caught on the edge of the ramp. The series of little things just grew. Chevy Chase did a skit on NBC's "Saturday Night Live" of this humble president who couldn't get to the chair without falling. Ford himself tried to make light of it. Then, after a while, when Ron Nessen was press secretary, Ron tried hard to combat it openly. That didn't work either, and it just made more of an issue of it than it already was. But those things do tend to linger—and bother.

During the second week in the Ford presidency, he went up to Camp David for the first time as president. Susan Ford was still home and unmarried, and Steve, the youngest son was also there. On Monday morning when I came in the office for our first staff meeting at about 8:15, the president had a visible black eye. I said, "Mr.

President, what happened?" and he said, "Well, they have this trampoline out at Camp David and it was too cold to swim so Susan and I worked on the trampoline." Well, Susan was about nineteen then. They were trying to see who could jump the highest on the trampoline. But the next morning when he woke up, he had broken a small blood vessel in his eye with all this bouncing up and down. Dr. Lukash carefully applied some medicine. Mr. Ford put his glasses on and he didn't have any press contact that day. By the next morning it looked one hundred percent better. I thought to myself, "My goodness sakes! A man of that age, up there on the trampoline, competing with a nineteen-year-old girl!"

QUESTION: A good part of the answer to the previous question covers what I had in mind but I would like to pursue the alleged awkwardness one step further. These awkward physical instances seemed to have been a subject of great enjoyment in the press. Was an effort made to correlate the degree of lampooning with objective statements?

MR. TERHORST: There was a bit of both. Of course, the cartoonists and columnists, for the most part, were expressing opinion. Anyone is entitled to his opinion. But by and large, the press that were doing the page one stories on the Ford presidency were being as fair as they possibly could be. Occasionally there would be a page one story about Jerry Ford's problem with his coordination, but that was probably no worse than Jimmy Carter and the killer rabbit, and some of the others. But clearly, the columnists and the cartoonists did have a field day. It wasn't much different than Richard Nixon's very dark beard; Herb Block could never draw Richard Nixon without making him look as though he was a thug with that dark face and eyebrows. It isn't Nixon's fault that he inherited a very dark beard.

QUESTION: How much of a problem does the press secretary find in the fact that he must frequently be privy to information that he can't divulge? He is going to be asked questions and "no comment" is itself almost an answer. How much of a problem does that pose?

MR. TERHORST: That's probably the most difficult, constant problem a press secretary has. Quite often you are confronted with the necessity of finding new and novel ways to say "no comment." When you are on the record or in front of the camera, you aren't able to tug on the reporter's sleeve, and say, "Can I talk to you privately about this?" Obviously to be of service to the President, a press secretary should know almost everything about what is contemplated so that he doesn't misstate things, and yet at the same time, a good many of the things he knows are not ready for public announcement when the questions are first asked. This is particularly true in foreign policy, diplomatic appointments, and potential visits where a foreign leader's ego could be severely bruised by a preemptory remark, at the wrong time or place by the White House.

So you devise all kinds of little ways to try to get over that, such as, "that's not something I can talk about at this time," or "I'll see if I can get back to you on that," or if the questioning persists sometimes you end up having to say "I've said all I have to say on the subject. Does anybody else have other questions?" I hate the words "no comment," because it makes you very vulnerable. It looks almost like you do know but aren't prepared to confirm something. Instead you try to construct rhetorical dodges around things. If somebody says, "Is the president of France coming over or is he not?" You can't really say, "No, he is not," or "Yes, he is" even if you know he is coming in ten or twelve days. So you will say, "Well, when we have an announcement on that, we will let you know in good time." You keep doing this, hoping you will at least wear them down.

NARRATOR: Lincoln said that both sides appealed to Holy Scripture and said they spoke for God, and both couldn't be right but only God could know for sure which one of the two was right. We've had a number of people say that the pardon cleared the air, and freed President Ford for the many tasks that he had to do. He would have been swamped with inquiries if he had not issued the pardon, and it was in keeping with his healing message. You say that it tore the scab off and that it may have influenced the two percent vote that he lost. Are both true or which one is true and why?

MR. TERHORST: May I plead *nolo contendere* and throw myself on the mercy of the room?

No? Well, I think that the intent was clearly to heal. I do not think there was any private deal made with Richard Nixon that if he resigned, he would be given a pardon in thirty days. Jerry Ford is just not that kind of guy. He never could have pulled it off so cleverly because he is not a Machiavellian person. It would have offended him to think that he could be part of a deal-making process like that. Yet the perception of a deal will linger as long as people discuss the pardon issue. It is one of those things where the public perception is sometimes greater than the reality. God only knows whether I'm wrong saying there was no deal and those who say it was a deal, are right.

It did not heal as it was intended to do because it suggested to the country that Jerry Ford was not prepared to let justice run its course. It appeared as if he had this good friend who had been president, and for one reason or another he'd find some excuse to let the guy off the hook. Other people might have to go to jail or face fines or go to prison, but Richard Nixon wouldn't. He was the guy for whom all the others went to prison.

Ford ended up looking either not too bright in having done that or having taken bad advice to do it. People began to wonder if it really was such a nice, open, candid White House after all. People's estimation of how great a president Jerry Ford could be dropped considerably as a result of the pardon. In his autobiography, Ford admits that it was probably a factor in his defeat. There wasn't any other motive but the intent to heal and to get beyond Watergate so Jerry Ford's presidency could move on to other issues. There were plenty of other issues, yet I faced the same thing every day in the press room.

I called Leonard Jaworski and the attorney general one day to plead for the discovery of some legal way to get all the Watergate tapes out of the White House. They were still there, being held under custody by a court order. I thought it would help if we could get them out of the building to the General Services Administration or to the archives or any place but in this building where the president lives and works. The press explained that the Watergate tapes were still being held in the White House, and there was always the subliminal suggestion that maybe somebody was erasing again.

The problem hung over Ford's White House. In fact, in the first Ford press conference, of the 29 questions he was asked in 30 minutes, 11 of them had to do with Watergate. The very first question was: did he agree with the American Bar Association that the law should be administered fairly regardless of station, or did he think that President Nixon deserved a pardon like some of his people were saying in California? That first question was from Helen Thomas and we had ten more of them at his very first news conference.

QUESTION: The other day someone asked President Nixon what would he have done differently if he were back in the White House and he said he would burn the tapes. There is no remorse in that statement. I wonder if some of the things President Nixon has done since he left Washington have caused President Ford any second thoughts about pardoning him.

MR. TERHORST: I am not aware if they have. Every time Mr. Ford is asked about it his answer is consistent. Yes, he would pardon Nixon again for the same reasons that he gave the pardon then. I don't sense any change of heart on his part in that respect. When Mr. Ford made up his mind, he did it knowing he would be stuck with the decision and that it would become a piece of history. To my knowledge, he has had no private second thoughts, and he certainly hasn't expressed any public ones. I suppose burning the tapes would have solved a good deal of the problem.

QUESTION: Do you know if Mr. Ford was acquainted with the nuclear code? I've never been able to find out when Nixon actually gave him the code.

MR. TERHORST: Well, he never did get it from Nixon; he got it from James Schlesinger. The day before he resigned, Nixon talked to his staff at the White House and said, "I'm getting ready to resign but, of course, I'll be president right through to the end, and the black box will be with me," etc. That is not the exact quote but that's a paraphrase. In fact, the black box was never placed on Air Force One that took President Nixon away. The box stayed back at the White House with Jerry Ford. Jim Schlesinger's military attache at the White House was delegated to carry the box. He kept the box near Jerry Ford. It did not get on the plane with Richard Nixon even though he had more than an hour to go on his presidency. As a matter of fact, Schlesinger set in motion a sort of national security operation down in the Situation Room to anticipate any attempt by a president who momentarily lost his mind over the pressures of Watergate to do something drastic.

QUESTION: Yes, but the president also has something in his pocket. Did you get that card out of his pocket?

MR. TERHORST: I don't know if he had the card out of his pocket, but he would not have had access to the box, according to Jim Schlesinger.

QUESTION: Did you have an opportunity to try to dissuade the President on the pardon?

MR. TERHORST: No, I first learned about it at 6:30 on the Saturday night before the Sunday morning announcement. We were still at the White House holding a staff meeting and I learned about it then from the President. As press secretary, it was my duty to get the press back to the White House the next day, arrange for the announcement and get the cameras back, and do it in a way so that they would be on hand and yet not know in advance what was going to happen.

At that point it was clear that he had made up his mind. There were six people in the room. It was very clear that the die had been cast and that the group had decided, including the President. It was not imperative to tell me but it was my task to make the conference happen.

QUESTION: Do you think that the alternative of criminal trials would not have been very damaging to the country?

MR. TERHORST: Oh, it would have been, but perhaps it would not have gone that far. Of course, I was only a press secretary even then, but in my own mind, I hoped that at some point in the process of presidential education of the public, the public would become aware that an indictment would fall from the special prosecutor's office on the former president. That would raise all kinds of questions. Should the President stand trial? Is he well enough to stand trial? Remember, at that time he was very ill; he had phlebitis in his leg and was actually moved into a hospital. Does anybody want a former president to go to jail? Isn't that an unseemly and unsightly thing? To raise all those questions in the public's mind with some help from the White House, and particularly the President, would have brought the country around to face the facts. If Richard Nixon was indicted and the country faced the fact that it was going to have to put a former president on trial, then the country would have wanted to persuade Jerry Ford to try and avoid the necessity of having to put the country through this. And the administration could have done it in a way without showing any overt sympathy for Mr. Nixon. All the reasons could have been public issue reasons rather than personal health reasons.

At least that would have prepared the country for what Jerry Ford had in mind. It would have helped him a lot. Also, it would have given an opportunity to get those who were close to Richard Nixon, perhaps even Jerry Ford himself, to say to Mr. Nixon, "Well, Dick, I've got the legal power to do this; nobody questions it. If you want a pardon, I'd like you to stand up and publicly say that you would appreciate a pardon and you are sorry for what you have put the country through." There were so many ways that it could have been done to get away from creating the "if you know somebody you can get off" attitude. It wouldn't have cured it totally but it would have mitigated the circumstances and the hullabaloo that arose as a result of the pardon.

NARRATOR: So in summary, it is not the pardon as such but it is the timing, the style, and process that trouble you?

MR. TERHORST: And the fact as I mentioned, that before you can be forgiven you at least ought to say you are sorry. Most people find a way in their hearts to do that and don't say, "Well, I guess I should have burned the tapes." I wouldn't call that an apology. That was what the country was worried about.

QUESTION: Following up on your last remarks, once the process had gotten under way toward an indictment, would the American public have let it stop? It would have been harder to stop then, given our propensity for courtroom scenes on TV and our enjoyment of the Watergate hearings and all the rest of it.

MR. TERHORST: We've become television junkies, there is no doubt about that. You might be right.

QUESTION: What do you think of current efforts to rehabilitate Nixon's reputation?

MR. TERHORST: There are efforts being made to rehabilitate Nixon's reputation but the Nixon presidency will always be known as the era of Watergate to a lot of people. It also should be known, and will be known to more thoughtful people, as a presidency that accomplished some major changes in foreign policy. That can never be taken away from Nixon or Henry Kissinger. Both of them will also have their detractors forever. But the modern opening to China and to Moscow could not have happened under a Democratic president; the Republican right wing would have eaten them alive. It took a "Commie fighter" like Richard Nixon to pull it off. Those were very important accomplishments and the world is better for it.

NARRATOR: I think all of us would agree that we understand a side of the Ford presidency a little better than we did before. I hope all of you also sense the rockbound integrity that Jerry terHorst personifies. The last time he was here and gave a presentation in the Dome Room, somebody asked him about the Miller Center press conference, and he said he thought it caused more trouble than it did good. So if you want to hear somebody say it as he believes it wherever he finds himself, you ought to invite Jerry terHorst.

SPEECHES, HUMOR AND THE PUBLIC

ROBERT ORBEN

NARRATOR: Bob Orben has written that humor is one of the glories of human experience. It warms, amuses, instructs and opens emotional doors. Maybe that is one of the reasons we are very pleased that he would visit us. He was the director of President Ford's speech writing department. He is the editor of Orben's Current Comedy, a humor service for public speakers published in Wilmington, Delaware. He is a consultant, a speech writer, and adviser to entertainment personalities, political leaders, and business chief executives. He wrote scripts for the Jack Paar Show and for the Red Skelton Hour. He is the author of a number of works including the *Encyclopedia of One Liner Comedy*.

MR. ORBEN: There are 46 books altogether. Even I don't try to remember the titles.

NARRATOR: Anyway, he has done all of this. He is now a member of the group that for months, I have been told, was hush hush, nobody wanted to admit that it existed, but *Time* magazine evidently unveiled them in a recent issue. This is the group of presidential speech writers who had their first meeting last Friday at Bill Safire's home in Washington. So he is recognized not only by people who are desperate for something to say to women's clubs, but he is highly regarded by his own peers, namely, former speech writers. He was close to President Ford; he was his consultant and special assistant. He is one of the people who surely doesn't need any introduction because from now on it is going to become less heavy, less boring, and less pedantic than most discussions, especially the discussions of the converted speaking to the converted.

MR. ORBEN: One of the things you should be aware of is just as the shoemaker's children are poorly shod, you should never ask a speech writer to come with a prepared speech. They just don't do it. What I've done is put together what speech writers call some "talking points" and they will get me started. Then if at any time during what I'm saying or after you have questions, jump in and we'll tackle them on the spot. Of the twelve or thirteen specific questions that I received, I'm truly able to answer only a few of them because speech writers, in spite of their own desire to appear to themselves and the world very important, are merely spear carriers in the operation. Our whole responsibility is to put the president's words or client's words into a form that's appealing and recognizable to audiences. And so, overwhelmingly, we're not advisers, we're not movers and shakers, we're spear carriers. And please keep that in mind in light of whatever I say.

One of the questions I'm often asked is: "How does someone go from being a Hollywood television writer to writing speeches for the president of the United States?" That was always a much more intriguing question until a Hollywood television actor became president of the United States. So it isn't all that unusual any more.

But my story goes back to 1964. As Ken indicated, I had written at that time perhaps 25 or 30 books on the uses of humor by public speakers, performers, and political figures, in addition to writing for show business personalities. And so in 1964 I found myself with three major responsibilities: I was a writer on the Red Skelton Show, one of eight writers—I was the one who did the monologue on the show, the one that always ended with Gertrude and Heathcliff, the two seagulls, talking to each other; I was also at that point sending a page of material a day to Dick Gregory, the activist comedian; and I was sending a page of material a day to Senator Barry Goldwater, who was then running for President of the United States. People always ask me, are jokes interchangeable? Well, obviously not. Each time I sat down

to the typewriter I would have to put on my thinking cap
as one of the three personalities and write from that
viewpoint.

As you remember from reading the papers, Barry
Goldwater did not make it and I went on for four more
years as one of the writers on the Red Skelton Show. We
now fast-forward to 1968, another presidential year. I'll
attempt to give you a little background that you may or
may not be aware of relative to political personalities in
Washington. If you put together a job description for
presidents of the United States or a congressman or a
senator, you would put down a born leader, a great
communicator, a good legislator, and all those good things.
But you would also, in this day and age, have to put down
the capacity to be a good stand-up comedian because there
are at least a dozen events in Washington where the
president of the United States, if he is a savvy president of
the United States, will appear and do eight to ten minutes
of stand-up comedy *a la* Johnny Carson. One of the most
prestigious of these events is the Gridiron Dinner held in
March or April of each year. It gathers together six
hundred of the movers and shakers in this country: the top
CEOs (Chief Executive Officers) of large corporations, the
leading political figures, the Supreme Court justices, all in
all a very prestigious audience. Political fortunes have been
made and destroyed by good or inept performances.

At a recent event in Washington, I reminded Clark
Clifford, who wrote for Harry Truman, that we once shared
seats at a Gridiron Dinner. I had said to Clark Clifford at
that dinner, "You know, coming from Hollywood I'm rather
astonished how important people here in Washington feel
this Gridiron Dinner is." I said, "In Hollywood we have a
roast every other day and people really don't attribute that
much importance to them." And he said, "Well, the value of
the Gridiron Dinner is this: if any of the political figures
gave a serious speech, you would pretty much know where
they are coming from, what they would be saying. The
question is: how would these political figures conduct
themselves in a situation that's alien to them and what
could be more alien to a rock-solid political figure than
standing up and doing eight minutes of comedy? It's a very
intimidating bit of business." And so, Washington judges
the political figures on how well they react to this
emergency situation.

At any rate, back to 1968. The format of the Gridiron Dinner is that in addition to sketches they pick one leading Democrat and one leading Republican, and each is required to do eight to ten minutes of stand-up comedy. In 1968 the leading Democrat chosen was Vice President Hubert Humphrey, who was very adept at the uses of humor. The leading Republican was Congressman and Minority Leader of the House of Representatives, Gerald R. Ford. Congressman Ford gave many speeches but he really didn't use humor to any great extent and so it was felt that it might be profitable to get some professional help. I have to preface this by saying I'm not a note taker nor a diary keeper, so I may be wrong in the actual details of this. But as I understand it, Bob Hartmann, the chief of staff for Congressman Ford, came out of California to ask Senator George Murphy, the former movie star and then senator of California, for help. Senator George Murphy sent him to Red Skelton; Red Skelton sent him to the producer of the show; the producer of the show, Sy Berns, sent him to me as the monologue writer on the show, and the only card-carrying Republican on the writing staff, if not in all of Hollywood. So I wound up writing a good part of Congressman Ford's Gridiron Dinner speech. In a way I think Congressman Ford was stuck with me because Bob Hartmann came out of Hollywood with two names: one was Senator George Murphy to look up, and if that didn't work out, the other name was somebody who had been sending a lot of material to Barry Goldwater back in 1964, me. So one way or another they were stuck with me.

It proved to be a turning point speech in many ways for Congressman Ford in that Washingtonians had thought it was going to be a wipe-out in this battle of humor. Congressman Ford wasn't given much of a chance to excel over Vice President Humphrey and after it was over, it was generally considered that Ford had scored more points than Humphrey had. The thing that I remember most about the speech was the amazingly prophetic finish of Congressman Ford's Gridiron speech. To set the scene, it was March or April of 1968. The presidential campaign was heating up. Lyndon Johnson had already dropped out of the race so the nomination on both sides of the aisle was up for grabs. There were probably at least a dozen people in that audience who had their eye on the nomination. As Congressman Ford finished his speech, he looked over the group and acknowledged this situation—and then he turned to Hubert Humphrey, who was obviously the leading Democratic possibility, and solemnly assured the vice president that he, Jerry Ford, had absolutely no designs on the White House. He said, "I love the House of Representatives, despite the long irregular hours. Sometimes though, when it's late and I'm tired and hungry and taking that long drive back to Alexandria, Virginia, as I go past 1600 Pennsylvania Avenue I do seem to hear a little voice within me saying, 'If you lived here, you'd be home now.'" And just six years later he was.

When he became vice president in 1973, I was taken on as a consultant, and then about eight or nine days after he became President, I was called down to be a speech writer, and eventually wound up as director of the speech writing department.

The next question is, how are presidential speeches written? How were they written in the Ford administration? From the standpoint of personnel, we had six speech writers including myself, four researchers, three secretaries—a department of about thirteen people. We had, in retrospect, and in talking to other presidential speech writers, amazing access to the President. I took it for granted at the time since I had never worked face to face with a president before. I had done other high-level, political writing but never on staff. I just assumed this was the norm. On average we met twice a week for roughly one hour a meeting. One hour would be devoted to going over the schedule of events coming up in which the President would have to speak. Before I took over, Paul Theis, who was the executive editor and head of the speech writers, would bring in three options for every speech. These represented the speech writers' observations on what might be said in the speech. But it was always the President who made the key decisions. He either went with one of the options or told us "No, I don't want to do that. This is the area we should cover." So we left this one-hour session, knowing where we were going on every major speech. The exception was what Washington has characterized, I think unfairly, as "Rose Garden rubbish." Those are the speeches that are *pro forma* speeches that are sometimes done by a president where the speeches, to some extent, write themselves. But for the major speeches we always had presidential guidance.

Then, whoever was the head of the speech writers,
would assign the speech to one of the writers; the speech
would be written; it would go back and forth a few times,
usually between the writer and the editor or director of the
speech writers.   When the director signed off on it, it
would go to Bob Hartmann, who was counselor to the
President and responsible for the speech writers.   When Bob
signed off on it, it went to the President.

Sometime later in the week we would have a second
meeting with the President of about an hour and he would
go over these speeches with us.   (By "us" I mean it was
usually Bob Hartmann, the director, me, and whoever wrote
the speech.)   So the speech writer always had the option of
knowing what was right, what was wrong, and had a chance
to fight for his or her words, and that's an extreme rarity.
At any rate, the President went over every line of the
speech, and if he didn't like something it would be changed
on the spot, or if it called for a major rewrite, it would be
redone.   But essentially the President gave the speech that
he wanted to give.

There were usually one or more *ad lib* meetings with
the President that consisted of me and the President going
over the speech, usually on the plane going to an event.   It
was a combination of out-loud rehearsal and noodling, a fine
tuning of the speech, because you can have the greatest
words in type but there are some combinations of words and
syllables that mortal tongues were not meant to utter.   And
you only find this out when you say it out loud.   And so
we eliminated the tongue twisters and that sort of thing.

This was pretty much the procedure that we followed
up until the Bicentennial speeches and then Bob Hartmann
dropped a bombshell as far as I was concerned.   He said,
"We're going to multiple track on the Bicentennial
speeches."   There were six or seven of them and the
President placed great emphasis and importance on them.

I was appalled; I remember getting involved in an
argument.   I said, "As speech writers, we all like to think
of ourselves as creative people, writers.   You can't throw 42
pages into a pot and pick and choose and have any of us
happy."   Well, that debate was won.   It was won by Bob
Hartmann, as it always was, and we multiple tracked.   And
it proved to be a marvelous idea.   It was incredible.   I still
suggest it now for some corporate clients.   It rubs writers
the wrong way because when you hear a speech and you say

to yourself, "Hey, that sentence is mine," it's not the same as saying to yourself, "Hey, that speech is mine." Nevertheless, we took the best thinking of everybody and as a result the Bicentennial speeches were exceptionally good.

The way we did this was to call everybody into the room, everybody including some who normally were not involved in speech writing. We told them "This is the way the speech is going to go. We are going to start with this, we are going to make these specific points, and then proceed to the close." They followed this form and then we'd lay out all of these speeches side by side on a table not quite as big as this, but not much smaller, and with paste pot and scissors, we selected the best sections from each of them. It proved to be a very good idea. In fact, the acceptance speech of the nomination was put together in this form, and it got something like 65 rounds of applause because we had so many of good punchy lines that would activate and excite an audience.

As for access to the President, we never really appreciated how much access we had. Bob Hartmann, of course, was the counselor to the President—he always saw the President. I had what was known as door knock privilege where if I had to get in to the President with something, I could get in there between appointments to talk to him for a few minutes. This hasn't been the case in all administrations.

We also always had a speech writer on the plane with the President, or a speech writer going to any event with the President. In the early days usually that was me, whether I had written the speech or not, because of the rehearsal factor. But even later on it was usually the speech writer who had written the speech who was on the plane. The value of this was most dramatically demonstrated one time when we were coming back from Los Angeles to do a speech in Ohio. Just as I got on the plane I was talking to the advance man about some of the details of the event and I suddenly realized that we had been totally misinformed about the audience. I don't know how it happened but we thought the speech was for health care providers and actually the audience was representing organizations of health care recipients. The speech didn't make any sense for the group that we were heading for, and yet the President was going to give that speech in just four hours.

Now one of the nice things about Air Force One is that it's a flying office. We had copying machines and typewriters, and now I'm sure they have word processing machines, but we also had a phone system that maintained instant communication with Washington. So immediately I got on the phone and I explained the situation to my office—that it was the wrong speech, we can't use it. I said, "I'm going to do the start of the speech and the end of the speech, so and so is going to do the development of this thought and somebody else is going to do the development of that thought, and telex it back to me on the plane." Before we got off three hours later, the President had a speech that was brand new, that had been developed by his staff and coordinated by the speech writer on the plane. So it proved to be a lifesaver in that and other situations.

How much time did it take to write a speech? President Ford did twelve hundred speeches and prepared remarks in two and a half years. I think it is an all-time record. We did better than a speech a day. The average amount of time that we were given to write a speech was usually too little. We were understaffed for the amount of work that we had to do. Usually we got three to four days to write a speech and that proved to be an average. Major speeches, particularly the State of the Union, always began earlier. The State of the Union Address in any administration begins to be thought about in November and is worked on constantly until delivered.

In my own experience the closest I've ever come to writing before the time the speech had to be given was on one occasion when I wrote a speech for the President on the way to the event. It was Lincoln's birthday, 1975, and I got a phone call from Terry O'Donnell, who was in charge of the President's schedule. He said that the President got a phone call from Bob Hope, a good friend, and Bob asked the President to present him with the award Hope was being given by an organization at one o'clock that same day. I asked, "What kind of an award?" and Terry said, "Well, Hope is being named Comedian of the Century." I said, "One o'clock. All right, that's not so bad. It's about ten o'clock now." He said, "Yes, but the motorcade is leaving in ten minutes for the President to go over to the Lincoln Memorial to do his Lincoln Day speech and then he's going right to the Washington Hilton. So, when are you going to do it?" At this point I grabbed a stack of five by eight cards and some felt tip pens and I ran like mad for the motorcade. I'm in the motorcade and I'm scribbling away, not really scribbling away; I'm printing away because whatever I come up with has to be legible to the President because he may not have a chance to look at it before doing it.

We show up at the Lincoln Memorial and the President is doing his speech, and I'm printing away and I realize that I'm not going to be finished before we leave for the Hilton. So I go up to the Secret Service beside the limousine and they, of course, knew who I was, and said, "I've got to ride over with the President." Now normally this is worked out in advance. You just don't invite yourself into the presidential limousine. I have to give them all the credit in the world; they were not authorized to do this but they realized the emergency when I explained the situation and they let me in. Now the President comes down the long steps from the Lincoln Memorial and he opens the door and gives a little start because he wasn't expecting me. I said, "Please, Mr. President, it's the only way." And we now sit side by side; he's looking out the window and I'm still working away. We show up at the Washington Hilton and they open the door for the President. I said, "Please, Mr. President, one more minute," and he signals the door to be shut and he's making small talk with the Secret Service man in front and I'm finishing my last card, and off he goes. He had one quick moment in the holding room to look at the cards and he went out and did the presentation. One of the things I've always admired about President Ford is he had and has faith in his people. Until you let him down he gives you the benefit of the doubt. He figures you are going to do the job that you were hired to do. And in this case it worked out very well.

I still remember the opening line. He got out in front of this massive audience, two thousand people, and when you are giving an award to Bob Hope you can't do it in a solemn manner. President Ford started out by saying that it was an occasion that was really good news and bad news for him. He said, "The good news is that I'm here today to name my good friend Bob Hope as the Comedian of the Century. The bad news is, how am I ever going to explain this to Earl Butz?"

Let me mention one use of a speech writer that isn't being made. It's based on something that I experienced during the Ford fight for the nomination against Governor Reagan. I feel that a presidential speech writer, or speech writer anywhere, should be part of the acceptance process and they very rarely are. Usually the acceptance of a speaking engagement is determined by a scheduling department and the President—and is then presented to the speech writer. Then the speech writer has to sit down and grind out the words, and that's sometimes unfair because sometimes the words shouldn't be ground out at all.

I think back to an incident that happened in North Carolina when we had just about licked Governor Reagan for the nomination. We had won four primaries, this was the fifth, and it was generally considered that if we won North Carolina the Reagan forces would throw in the towel. We were going like a house on fire and we did three or four very good appearances. And then the President was scheduled to appear at a girls high school to address a group of perhaps 1800 young ladies, fourteen to eighteen years old. I think it was a Future Homemakers of America group. I remember looking at this and thinking, "Why have they scheduled this in the midst of a knock-down-drag-out political battle for the primary? What are we going to say to these kids?" Well, we did the obligatory mom and apple pie in America speech and it went over surprisingly badly. The kids were quiet, they stared at the President; it got a very quiet reaction. I couldn't understand it because it was the right speech for the group, and the sort of speech that political figures have made through the years to such a group. We got trashed by the press. They pointed out that the audience stared at the President, and why would such an inept speech be given at such a point in the President's fight for the nomination? I couldn't understand it either.

A few days later I was talking to one of the advance men about it. I said I couldn't understand why the speech was scheduled but since it was scheduled, I couldn't understand the audience's reaction because normally kids are thrilled to death to be hearing the president of the United States. He said, "You don't know what happened?" I said, "What happened? I only arrived with the presidential party." He said, "Just before the presidential party arrived, perhaps the dean of women, the principal, some school official, stood up and the place was pandemonium. Kids were screaming and yelling 'the President is coming!' and the place was jumping. When she got order she said, 'Look, this is the first and perhaps the only time in the history of this school that a president of the United States has ever come to this auditorium and if I hear one peep out of you, you are going to hear from me about it!" And then the President of the United States walked into this thoroughly chilled auditorium. Toward the end the kids livened up a little but it was a disaster. But regardless of that unexpected curve of the kids being told to simmer down, we should never have accepted that speech invitation at that time.

One thing that I don't know if anybody has really discussed here about working in the White House is the tension. I guess it's not considered macho to talk about the effects of tension but after we were defeated in 1976, President Ford immediately told us that President Carter will be our leader for the next four years. "I want you to help him and his staff as much as you possibly can" and we all did. But nobody came to me, as head of the speech writers, to represent the new writing team. I didn't realize it at the time, but they had really not focused on speech writing and they had not appointed anybody. On about January 15, five days before we were to leave, I got really steamed about it and I tried to reach Jody Powell, couldn't reach him and got Stu Eizenstat, and I put the blast on him. I said, "You know, you people are coming into this operation like you're going to run a peanut stand and it's a lot more complicated than that. We want to help you people but when we go, there won't be anybody else around to help you. There hasn't been a Democrat in the White House in a long time that you will be able to call on. So if you want any help from the speech writing department, you'd better send somebody over."

A couple of days later Jamie Fallows shows up. Jamie was almost instantaneously, perhaps on my phone call, made head of the speech writers. He came over and we talked for about an hour. Finally Jamie stood up and said, "Is there anything else you could tell me?" I thought to myself, "If I, coming in two and a half years earlier, had been told by anybody that I was going to experience more tension and anxiety than I ever realized existed on this planet, I would have thought to myself, 'Good Heavens, I've been in show business all my life; I've worked under

tension, I know what tension is.'" But you don't know what
tension is until you begin to work in the White House.
Milton Friedman, President Ford's senior speech writer,
always characterized it as part of the air there, it's fed in
by the air conditioning. Tension is with you at all times,
and it's very hard to be a free spirit.

A couple of days after I came to the White House we
went to a reception for the press at the White House. This
was about twelve days after President Ford had assumed
office. Milt Friedman introduced me to a reporter as a new
speech writer and the reporter said, "How many speech
writers are there now in the White House?" I don't know
what prompted me to say this. I turned to Milt and said, "I
don't know, Milt, how many are there now? Is it five or
six hundred?" And immediately the pen came out, "What do
you mean?" the reporter asked. I realized from that point
on, you had to be on your good behavior twenty-four hours
a day. And that tension ultimately gets to you. The only
person who didn't seem to be very much affected by it was
President Ford. I saw myself crumble; I saw my colleagues
crumble; but he bore up under it amazingly well. And yet I
feel this tension has to reach any president. What comes to
my mind when I hear of tension is, for example, sitting in
the Oval Office working over speeches in a rather relaxed
scene, and suddenly the buzzer rings and it is so and so
who wants to come into the meeting because there is a
problem. Well, you don't interrupt a presidential meeting
unless it is something quite important, so Secretary of State
Kissinger might come in, and the speech writers are sitting
there while Kissinger outlines some problem of considerable
importance. We are all watching Kissinger and then as soon
as the problem is presented, all eyes, like a moving picture
camera, pan to and focus on the President. The common
thought is, "Mr. President, how do we proceed?" I never
saw any evidence of President Ford feeling this tension but
I feel that he must have.

I'm going to say something on presidential humor and
then I am going to hold for questions. President Ford has
a good natural sense of humor. He likes to use humor.
President Ford used humor a great deal in his speeches and
in his relationships with others—and that's particularly
important when you are president of the United States.
The more powerful you are in a position—if you are a CEO
in a major corporation or you are the president of the

United States—the more important it is that you eliminate the emotional and psychological gap between you and the audience. If you are president of the United States you are standing up at a lectern, high above the audience. The Secret Service always leaves a certain amount of space between the first seat and the president as a reaction space and the last thing a president or a CEO of a large corporation wants is to have that gap. And so it is very important that a president start off a speech with humor that reaches out and communicates on an emotional level with that audience.

I'll give you one example of how President Ford did it. The President had accepted a speech at the University of Notre Dame on March 17, on St. Patrick's Day in 1975. Many of his advisers in the White House felt that he shouldn't do the speech. There was a serious recession going on; there was still a great deal of hard feeling about the President's pardon of Richard Nixon; the Vietnam situation was still a high visibility problem; and there had been a great deal of feeling in the White House that a college campus was the last place that a President should go at that point. There was some fear of actual violence. It was not altogether unjustified because I still remember one of the last bits of campaigning President Ford did in October of 1974, for congressional candidates. The presidential party was actually chased into the field house of the University of Vermont. I was one of the last people to get in before the door was slammed and it was touch and go. There was a crowd of maybe two or three hundred kids. I don't think they meant any violence to the President but they were moving in on him and started to run toward him and we had just this thin phalanx of Secret Service. It could have been a very bad scene. That sort of thing is what we were concerned about.

But the President wanted to do the speech and said that he was going to do the speech. The problem was how could we reach out in this field house, talking to fourteen thousand students, one thousand faculty, and make instant communication with the group? As always, the President wanted to use humor. I spent a much more than normal amount of time working on jokes and I probably came up with perhaps thirty possibilities and finally decided on just a few. We did an obligatory St. Patrick's Day joke and then the one that I figured would do the trick is this joke, which was written for President Ford at the University of Notre Dame. This is the joke as written:

> As your next door neighbor from Michigan, I've always been impressed by the outstanding record of the students of the University of Notre Dame. You've always been leaders in academic achievement, in social concerns, in sports prowess. And now, once again, you are blazing new paths in the development of new concepts in mass transportation. Some communities have the monorail, some have the subway, Notre Dame has the quickie.

Now I see you are underwhelmed. So let me just play a tape of the President doing this joke at the University of Notre Dame, and I'm going to let the audience reaction go to its limit, and then make a few comments concerning it: (Tape was played followed by a lengthy audience reaction of laughter and applause). That reaction was 28 seconds long. The average big joke in show business runs four or five seconds. The place exploded, kids were standing on their chairs, yelling, screaming, laughing, pandemonium! Now, what was that all about?

In South Bend, Indiana, where of course the University of Notre Dame is, the drinking age is twenty-one years or over. In Michigan, just nine miles, the drinking age at that time was eighteen years or over. So the big problem that the students had at the University of Notre Dame was how to get up to Michigan, those nine miles, to do some weekend drinking. And how did they solve it? They bought themselves a bus, and what did they call the bus? The Quickie. It had the four elements of what I call a relevant demand-laugh joke. The first element was surprise.

When the President started to go into that long laborious buildup, and calculatedly so, the kids were convinced they were going to get another long, dull, boring, the future is your pap, baloney speech that they get most every commencement exercise. You could see their eyes starting to glaze. Worse—halfway through that build, if you listened to the tape very carefully, you would hear that one of the kids yelled out "Bull!" Actually, I think it was a two-syllable word. There was laughter around it which indicated that there was potential hostility in that audience.

But at the point where the President hit the Quickie, they were completely caught off guard. So surprise is a big factor. Relevance is another big factor. I saw a videotape of the President doing this and when the place went up for grabs, they had maybe 40 or 50 of the faculty sitting in seats in back of the President on this raised platform, and one of the faculty leaned over and whispered something to one of the professors and the professor looked back and shrugged. What was obviously happening was that the faculty member was saying "What's a quickie?" And the professor was saying, "I don't know." But the President knew, and the kids knew, and the kids knew the President knew, and at that moment the President and the kids were as one. Now that doesn't mean that for the rest of the speech the kids were going to buy, just sop up, everything the President said. But at that point or at any point during the speech, if somebody was going to challenge the President or heckle the President, you could bet that the kids wouldn't stand for it, "Hey, that's my friend, the President. You hear him out."

I'm always asked how many jokes a CEO or a president should use. Well, I had a feeling that this was either going to be a tremendous success or a tremendous bomb. The President is a gutsy performer, a gutsy speaker. If he had gone through that whole build and then hit that punch line and stopped, and we hadn't been right about the impact of the quickie, you can bet that we would have had a side bar in the paper the next day, saying the President told a joke that went into the ground. But it was so effective that in the South Bend paper the next day on the front page there was a box right in the middle of the page, outlining the quickie joke. So it had been enormously successful.

Normally, I feel you do one big joke and get out, but I also felt that, if we were right about this joke, we could take advantage of what in show business is called a roll. Once you get the audience on your side you can almost recite the telephone book and they'll enjoy it. And that was so in this case.

The President did one more joke and I'll just play it for you now and then I'll quit. The audience had come over to the President's side so strongly that they laughed on three straight lines: "This has been a most exciting day. As we were getting off the plane at the county airport (laughter) a rather amazing thing happened. (laughter)

Somebody asked me how to get to the campus of the University of Notre Dame. (laughter) What made it so amazing—it was Father Hesburgh." (long and loud laughter)

So I've burned up an hour of extemporaneous no-notes remarks but perhaps I can answer some specific questions you might have.

QUESTION: I would like to ask about the speech writing coordination between Senator Dole and President Ford during the fight for the nomination in 1976. Senator Dole relied heavily on humor but it seemed to me that it kind of backfired. And I don't know whether the speeches were coordinated with the President's speeches, or your department had anything to do with his?

MR. ORBEN: Well, certainly the humor wasn't coordinated. Bob Dole is a very witty man and at that point I think he was on his own as far as humor was concerned. In those days he got labeled as the hatchet man and that's kind of unfortunate because he likes to use humor and sometimes it is a rather acerbic humor. On the other hand, thanks to his wife, Elizabeth, he has now become much more mellow. He still uses humor a great deal but it is more of the type of humor that President Ford used. I always characterize it as arm-around-the-shoulder humor. It is more affectionate humor than biting humor. Senator Dole has moved in that direction.

As far as coordination is concerned, there was precious little. The Dole writers knew the themes, and we knew the themes, and I frankly don't remember much in the way of either conferring or collaborating with them. They pretty much went their own way.

Once somebody becomes vice president of the United States there is usually a substantial gap in communication between the staffs, not necessarily between the president and vice president. But I would guess that George Bush's staff has precious little to do with the White House. When Ford was vice president, there was precious little communication between the vice presidential staff and the president's staff, and maybe that was good.

COMMENT: I asked that because I felt that Senator Dole's abrasiveness really was a hindrance to the election of Ford, and that may be an important thing.

MR. ORBEN: I personally wouldn't ascribe that much importance to it. But he became aware of the fact that it was not creating an appealing personality for himself and I think he has since learned that lesson.

QUESTION: To go back to your quickie, are there certain advanced methods that you use in order to be wired into the group that you are going to be addressing in order to use humor that is that pinpointed to the audience? You said that the faculty members did not know what a quickie was. How do you get that information?

MR. ORBEN: At the present time, one of my ways of making a living is giving seminars and workshops on communication to corporate speech writers. I spend a lot of time on the procedures to be followed and it takes a lot of time to describe them adequately, but I'll try to shorten it to a few minutes.

In the old days when Bob Hope had a radio show, he would sometimes do remotes. For example, he would come to Charlottesville and do a radio show here. Before he showed up, three or four days in advance, two writers would show up and they would talk to as many people as possible. They'd find out where the hangouts were and how the football team was doing, and all the inside things that you would kid about among yourselves. And then, with that information, they would write local jokes.

How did the quickie come about? Well, my procedure always was: first, you start with calling the people you have on the list as being responsible for the event, members of the faculty and such. I always used to point out that the President liked to start off with some lightness. And what are you kidding each other about in South Bend, Indiana? And you can count on the reaction being, "Oh, there's nothing funny around here." You can count on that. But you can't quit there; you've got to keep talking. And so I say, "How about the football team?" and that usually gets either comments on how good or bad they're doing. You keep asking questions.

On this special occasion I went through most of the faculty advisers that I had on the list and I was getting nowhere. Then I called some of the student leaders, and in a way they are almost as bad as the faculty because the student leaders are not going to make any mistakes. They are going for chancellor or president so they are not going to tell you anything that is going to get them into trouble. So I went through the whole bit without any success. Then I called a student who was more of a free spirit and he told me about the mystery meat in the school cafeteria, and every school has the mystery meat, so you don't want to go with that sort of cliche subject. But then he said, "Well, there is the quickie," and he giggled. So I wrote down the quickie. I said, "What's the quickie?" and he told me it's the bus that they bought. I said, "That doesn't have a double meaning, does it?" My name isn't exactly Neil Simon but it is known somewhat. I was always afraid of some smart aleck kid setting me up. He said, "No, no, it's the bus." All right. So I thanked him.

And now I call up another student and we go through the mystery meat and the football team and all the rest. He never mentions the quickie. And finally at the end of all this, I said, "Have you heard of something called the quickie?" and he giggled. I said, "What is it?" and he said, "It's the bus," and once again "This doesn't have a double meaning, does it?" and he said, "No." So I put a check mark beside the quickie.

Now I call a third student and we go through the whole drill again, the mystery meat, and he never mentioned the quickie but as soon as I mentioned the quickie, he laughed. So I knew what the subject was. And when you have that magic type word, then the whole idea in writing a joke about it is how do you get to the quickie so that the quickie is the very last word of the very last sentence? You do that by just picking up on what it is—it's a transportation mode—and then you construct the whole thing as a description of normal modes of transportation and you end with the quickie.

This incident also illustrates the value of access to the President. If I didn't have a one-to-one personal relationship with President Ford, the quickie never would have been done, because if I were working in the bowels of the old Executive Office Building, sending up material through the chain of command, some hero, half way up the staffing chain, would have looked at it and said, "The quickie—sounds dirty" and he would have eliminated it and I never would have known who did me in. Interestingly enough, when we reviewed the speech in the Oval Office, somebody raised this point, that quickie has several meanings. Is it possible that this would be construed as a dirty joke? And the President looked over at me and said, "What do you think?" I told him the whole drill that I had just gone through and I said, "To my knowledge there is no double meaning to it. It just means the bus," and we never had any problem with it. All it did mean was the bus.

NARRATOR: Is there any way that President Ford could have turned around this ridicule of him that the best athlete in the history of the presidency seemed to be clumsy?

MR ORBEN: That really irritated me, this question of his being called clumsy or inept. Here's the most athletic president we have had in this century. The man was captain of the University of Michigan football team; he was offered two spots on professional football teams; he played in the East-West Shrine game, which is an all-star game. He was a center when the quarterback didn't take the ball out of your hands, he had to pass it back to the quarterback who was on the run and lead the quarterback so that he didn't have to break stride.

One of the interesting things about President Ford at the White House is women used to love to dance with him because he was so agile and such a good dancer. So to have him criticized for being clumsy used to infuriate me. If it infuriated him as well, he never said so.

I had an ongoing battle with some of the White House people about this. The only way you can combat negative image humor is with more humor. If somebody did a joke—Chevy Chase would joke about it every week and you would try to rebut it by saying, "Oh, you don't understand, he was captain of the football team" and all that—you look dull. "What's the matter, can't you take a joke?" is the answer to that sort of rebuttal. The only way we could have overcome that image battle would have been by the use of humor. I had many discussions, if not arguments, at the White House with others who felt we should ignore it. We should look the other way or we should get mad. Well, that's nonproductive. I won a few battles; I lost most. But we did win a few.

When President Ford went to Japan there was a picture taken of him shaking hands with either the emperor or the prime minister and the President had on—I don't know where he got them—the world's shortest pair of striped pants. When he bent over to shake hands they came half way up to his knees, and newspapers ran this picture prominently. So the President came back from the Japanese trip, I wasn't on that trip, and he called me into the Oval Office right away and said, "Did you see that picture?" and never one to put my career on the line, I said, "What picture?" He smiled and said, "You know what picture." He said, "We've got to have some fun with that." And that night he had a speech to do at a "Scouter of the Year" banquet in Washington. So he opened his speech that night with: "They say once a Scout always a Scout, and I can tell you from my own experience that is true. After all these years I still love the outdoors. I still know how to cook for myself, at least breakfast. And as anyone who saw those pictures of me in Japan will know, on occasion I still go around in short pants." That made all three networks and at that point all the cartoons and all the kidding about the short pants stopped. I felt that if we had done the same thing about the clumsiness issue it would have stopped.

One quick example of that: what started this image role were two very unfair, unkind and untrue remarks by Lyndon Johnson about Congressman Ford when he was minority leader. One was he played football too long without a helmet; the other was that he couldn't chew gum and walk at the same time. Actually Johnson's original quote was a little more pungent than that but that's the way it usually appears.

At any rate, one time President Ford went up to Yale University for the Yale Law School's Sesquicentennial Convocation, and he started off his speech by saying "It's a great pleasure to be here at the Yale Law School's Sesquicentennial Convocation, and I defy anyone to say that and chew gum at the same time." And again it made all three networks and it was saying, "Yes, I know what's being said and I feel so confident in myself that even I can make jokes about it." The more he did along those lines, I think the better off we would have been.

QUESTION: Were you ever able to arrange for the speech department to be in on the scheduling sessions so you'd have some input?

MR. ORBEN: Not really. I came to the conclusion this would have been a good thing after the North Carolina event—because that was the first occasion we really suffered from. There were speeches that you would write and say, "Why are we doing this?" But it wasn't a problem. The North Carolina event was a problem. By that time we were in a hard and no-holds-barred struggle for the nomination with Governor Reagan and we were all sort of hanging on by the fingernails just trying to get the product out. But I think that sort of judgment from the speech writers should be part of the speech writing process.

QUESTION: One of the most difficult acts to do well is to deliver a written speech as if it were from the heart. Did you work with Ford or other speech writers on the delivery process?

MR. ORBEN: It's a two-fold problem: the speech has to be constructed in such a way that it comes across as conversation more than essay. Beyond that there was some amount of coaching but the President has a warm personality and, left to his own resources, does the right thing. I've always regretted very much that I wasn't a part of the preparation for the debates. It was interesting that at the very first debate, if you recall, something went wrong with a component of the sound system and for twenty-six incredible minutes you had the President of the United States and Governor Carter standing in back of these lecterns waiting for the sound to come on. That was characterized at the time as looking like two fellows in a tailor shop waiting for their pants to be given back. They spent 26 minutes immobilized in front of a huge national audience.

I have always felt that President Ford, a very natural person, after a few minutes, would normally have said, "Well, this is absurd" and smiled and come down and sat on the thrust of the stage and made small talk with the audience and he would have looked marvelous; instead they both stood up there like mannequins in a store window and they both looked bad. I think they both had probably been so mesmerized by staff with the importance of this debate and not to do anything wrong, and so they didn't do anything natural either, and that was unfortunate.

QUESTION: You sounded as if you use humor at the beginning of a speech. Do you steer clear of it at the end?

MR. ORBEN: No, in fact we came up with one of the best endings for a bicentennial speech. It was for a speech given on July 3rd at Kennedy Center. The President closed by saying:

> Two hundred years ago today, John Adams wrote his wonderful wife, Abigail, that he expected the glorious anniversary of independence to be observed down through the ages 'with shows, games, sports, guns, bells, bonfires, and illuminations from one end of this continent to the other.' So break out the flags, strike up the band, light up the skies, let the whole wide world know that the United States of America is about to have another happy birthday, going strong at 200, and in the words of the immortal Al Jolson, 'You ain't seen nuthin' yet!'

And that Jolson quote made me feel kind of sheepish because I had been in show business all of my life and it was someone from the academic community who thought of it. Oh, well—it was a marvelous ending to the speech—and set just the right tone for the entire event.

I'll give you an example of one of the problems with humor. If the speaker, president, CEO, or anybody, uses humor in the middle of a speech, if you are into heavy stuff and suddenly you go into humor, you have to signal to the audience that now it is fun time because if you don't, it may happen so fast the audience might not immediately recognize it as humor. And worse, what will happen is the audience may react a couple of sentences later when you are back into the heavy thoughts again. This is the best example I can give you: President Ford went to Cincinnati to dedicate an environmental office building and it was an extraordinarily hot day. It was 96 degrees; it was an outdoor event; the audience was hot and uncomfortable. In the middle of the speech he was talking about what our administration had done to clean up the environment. He gave a few examples and finally said, "And as a result of our efforts, fish have once again been seen in the upper reaches of the Hudson River." He said, "They cough a lot but they're there."

When we went over the speech on the plane, I pointed out that the joke came out of the blue. I said, "What you really have to do is at the point where you state that fish have once again been seen in the Hudson River—you've got to smile and sort of kick the dust a little and then do the line. If you don't, it's going to come too fast." It was a hot day, he was perspiring, the audience was perspiring, and he sailed right through it. And the joke itself got next to nothing. But then a sentence and a half later, people started thinking about it and he got a big laugh at that point. President Ford has always been very aware of audience, and as soon as he heard that laugh, he stopped, laughed along with them, and then picked up the beginning of the sentence. So that's always the danger if you drop humor into the middle of the speech; you better make sure that the audience knows it's fun time.

NARRATOR: I'm sure that others have had the same thought I have. If the president of a university or any of our leaders want to get any help with the leavening effect of good humor and goodwill, the first person they ought to turn to is Bob Orben. Thank you very much.

A FOOTNOTE ON FORD AND
THE VOICE OF AMERICA

JAMES KEOGH

NARRATOR: James Keogh was the director of USIA in the Ford administration. He offered this brief comment on one aspect of President Ford's character.

MR. KEOGH: I had one troublesome situation which centered around a Congressman from Ohio named Wayne Hays. He was chairman of a very important House committee that had charge of all the perks, all the offices, cars, parking spaces, stamps, everything, so he had everybody in the House beholden to him, and everybody was afraid of him. He had great power as a result. He also was chairman of a Foreign Relations subcommittee that sat on the authorization for the USIA budget, and this led him to feel that he was the one who was going to run USIA. He particularly wanted me to hire the people whom he wanted to give jobs to. This is not a very pleasant or tasteful thing, but in those circumstances you do hire some of the people that a congressman wants you to hire. But I reached the end of my rope finally. I took some of the people he wanted me to hire but there was one particular individual, a close friend of his, whom he insisted I hire. I refused and I went to see him and told him, "I just cannot do so, there is a matter of morale in the agency. I know the President would want me to take this stand," although by that time the President wasn't focusing on what my agency was doing. I said, "I can't hire him." Well, it so angered Mr. Hays—Mr. Chairman as he insisted on being called—that he held up the USIA budget for several months.

Very early in the Ford administration on a Saturday morning I got a call from a duty officer who said to me, "Mr. Director, have you seen the *New York Times*?" And I said, "Not yet," and he said, "Well, it's pretty bad." As it turned out, the front page of the *New York Times* had a story entitled "President Ford to fire USIA Director." The story went on to say that I had angered important people in Congress and that therefore Ford was going to fire me because it wasn't the way to do things. I thought I knew where that story came from and on Monday morning I sent a note to President Ford saying, "I want to come over and talk to you about the story in the *Times* which says you are going to fire me." The following morning President Ford called me and said, "Well, you know and I know that there is no truth in such a story. It is certainly not true and I've never said that to anyone, but let me tell you who planted that story," and I said "I think I know." And yes, indeed, recently Wayne Hays had been in to see him.

This is an interesting thing about the press. There was a story there. Wayne Hays was trying to get me fired and he had asked Ford to do so. This is what the story should have said, but that wasn't quite enough. The reporter had to go one step further to make it a better story and say that Ford was going to fire me. Here, I think, is a classic example of what happens with the press. There is a story, but it gets escalated and distorted in order to make it a better one. This is the classic case of presenting what makes an interesting story rather than what is actually happening.

Now for months after that I would go back home to Greenwich, Connecticut and I'd see some old friends and they'd come up and say, "Well, Jim, what are you doing now?" I'd say, "I'm Director of USIA," and they'd say, "Oh, well, I thought . . ." and then the conversation would trail off. They were sure I had been fired.

QUESTION: When President Ford pardoned Nixon, you were director of USIA. What problems did that cause for you? How did you handle it?

MR. KEOGH: It didn't cause any problems for us. We had an overseas audience, of course, and we reported it straightaway. We aired President Ford's speech on the Voice of America, reported it on all of our media as a straightforward news story of what was happening. We reported also the criticism that came from those who felt that it was the wrong thing to do. But that did not cause us any problem. The main reaction around the world was surprise that so much fuss was being made.

Problems developed in other ways. There was concern on the part of some on the Hill that we would tailor and present the news on the Voice of America to try to protect the administration. Here, one gets into a very sensitive and difficult argument. There is no such thing as a sacred body of something that is the news. The news in the main is what reporters, writers and editors say it is. We had to establish some guidelines, and these were the ones that I set up: we will report Watergate fully and fairly; however, we will not use gossip, rumor, or unsubstantiated charges. This led some critics to charge that I was trying to censor the Voice of America, but that is totally incorrect. We were a government operation and we had to be extremely careful about how we handled this. Our problem was more difficult than that of other media. We couldn't be an international CBS or "Sixty Minutes." We had to be something else. In the end, it worked very well but it was a sensitive and difficult time. For example, if the *Washington Post* or the *New York Times* printed a story that did not have a named source for an accusation, we used it on the Voice of America and in our other material giving the *New York Times* and the *Washington Post* as the sources. Essentially the material was used anyway in that circumstance. But the pardon did not cause any problem.

V.

THE DEPARTMENTS
AND
THE WHITE HOUSE

DECISION-MAKING IN
THE FORD PRESIDENCY

SENATOR CHARLES E. GOODELL

NARRATOR: Senator Charles E. Goodell of New York was one of two senators—Robert Griffen being the other—who analyzed the Ford presidency in the Ford oral history. References have been made to President Ford's selection of his vice presidential partner in the light of some of the political events that were to follow in the 1976 campaign. Senator Goodell's association with Vice President Rockefeller has a special bearing on our oral history. Senator Goodell, as many of you know, was born in the other Jamestown—New York.

SENATOR GOODELL: Actually, its *one* of the other Jamestowns. Forty-eight states have Jamestowns in them. Only Alaska and Hawaii have managed without one.

NARRATOR: He is a graduate of Williams and the Yale Law School. He was a Ford Foundation faculty fellow and taught in New Haven. He was admitted both to the New York and Connecticut bar. He served in the 86th and 87th Congress from the 43rd district in New York, and in the 88th through the 90th Congress from the 38th district in New York. He was a United States senator from 1968 to 1971. He chaired the Planning and Research Committee in the House. He was chairman of the Republican party for part of New York. He has written *Political Prisoners in*

261

America, and has continued to participate in numerous activities from his position as counsel to King and Spaulding in Washington. It is a privilege to have him here with us to discuss the Ford presidency and any other topics he may wish to address.

SENATOR GOODELL: I thank you very much, Mr. Thompson.

I did have quite a bit of experience with previous presidents, though only a little with Jack Kennedy. I went to the House of Representatives at the age of 33 without ever having been in the state legislature. I went through the town board and was Republican party chairman. I was appointed to the Senate by Governor Rockefeller after Bobby Kennedy was assassinated. I served for two and a half years. Maybe Governor Rockefeller at various times regretted having appointed me. Rockefeller, as many other people do, had a reverence for the institution of the presidency. I probably was most prominent in my career for defying Richard Nixon on his two Supreme Court nominations, Haynsworth and Carswell, and on the war in Vietnam. Governor Rockefeller disagreed with all of my positions in that respect. However, he learned to have some disrespect for the presidency after he became vice president.

If you have read Bob Hartmann's book, *Palace Politics,* you probably understand what I am talking about. I went through a period of being chairman of the Clemency Board which was a no win appointment. There is no way to be particularly popular in dealing with the Vietnam veterans. Some went to Canada, but most just stayed here or served and had their problems with the military and with the disagreements in this country about the war in Vietnam. At any rate in 1974 and 1975, since I was in the Old Executive Office Building I spent quite a bit of time traipsing back and forth on West Executive Avenue to the White House to talk to Jerry Ford, a very close friend of mine. Some may not be aware that Bob Griffin and I originally led the revolt that put Jerry Ford in against Charlie Halleck as minority leader in the House. Jerry Ford had been a very close friend of mine, so when I was chairman of the Clemency Board I walked across the street quite frequently to talk to him about what was going on and how I might be of help.

One of the most interesting and probably most telling things about Jerry Ford was that in the twenty to thirty minutes I would be in the Oval Office and sitting in front of his big desk talking, he would spend the whole time taking notes. I never took any notes at all, and I felt very embarrassed about it. But he did this constantly with his staff people and everybody else. He would sit there and take notes about every comment you made.

At any rate, I did have some insight during this period into the inner workings of the White House and the administration. There has been a lot written about it and I'm not going to repeat what has been written by Bob Hartmann or Jerry terHorst or Ford himself.

Becoming president of the United States, president of a university or president of a corporation suddenly puts you in an entirely different arena. Jerry Ford had been minority leader, so he knew Congress very well. He knew the senators and members of the House very well and the leadership on the Democratic as well as the Republican side. However, he wasn't prepared to be President of the United States. I'm not sure anybody ever is. It is just an entirely different environment than anything else in life. I don't think, for example, that Lee Iacocca is terribly qualified at this point to be President even after what he has been through with Chrysler.

At any rate, Jerry Ford came into the presidency and he brought with him his loyal House staff, which had absolutely no concept of how to run the White House. He kept most of the Nixon people which was, from my viewpoint, his biggest mistake. It wasn't that the Nixon people were not qualified and very capable, but their first loyalty was not to Jerry Ford. It was still to Nixon and the memory of Nixon. There were exceptions to this among the staff people but if I had one major criticism of Ford when he became President it was that he didn't wipe the slate clean and bring in his own people. They probably would not have been any more liberal or conservative or any different in qualifications than the Nixon people, but they would have been loyal to him and accountable to him. Bob Hartmann makes that point very strongly in his book, *Palace Politics* and I recommend it because it is a very honest book. Bob Hartmann lacked some perspective, but he wrote exactly what he saw was happening in the Ford White House.

Bob was fond of calling the Nixon people "the Praetorian guard." They were the people who remained there and were serving Ford after Ford succeeded to the presidency. There are a variety of decisions that I wish I had participated in with Ford but in which I did not participate. I was not part of his kitchen cabinet, but I spent quite a bit of time going over and telling him what was happening in the White House, as I saw it. It was almost an ideal situation for me because I didn't carry any particular responsibility. I could go over and tell him what people were doing wrong and what they were doing right.

I remember one occasion when I went over to see Ford. I told him of an experience I had had three days before. I was dealing with a young member of the Praetorian guard. We were talking and I said, "Don't you realize the President has already made a decision on this? He has been very precise about it. It's a matter of policy." He said, "Our job here is to prevent the President from making mistakes." He was literally overruling the President. Three days later I went in and told Jerry Ford about it. He was writing it all down and said, "What's his name?" I said, "I'm not going to tell you his name. I'm not in that business. You just ought to know that these situations occur." After all, usually when the President of the United States asks a question of a staff person or a Cabinet secretary, the question goes out, and reverberates throughout the whole executive branch. It goes to the Pentagon and the State Department and to the Congress; the fact that the question was asked by the President becomes a very important thing in terms of policy-makers. It means the President is personally interested in this; often it then gets changed. This comes down the line. The President wants this and each one sort of shades it in his own way. There's an enormous possibility of distortion at each level. That's a very dangerous thing.

I've thought many times about how to organize the White House and the Pentagon ideally. I'm not an expert on the Pentagon but I have known intimately a variety of people who are trying to cope with organizing the Pentagon. In terms of the White House, there is just so much power there. One 28-year-old associate can walk out of a meeting, and go down the hall and overrule the generals and the admirals. It is something that Jerry Ford was only beginning to understand when he was running for election against Jimmy Carter.

I believe very deeply that it was sad that Jerry Ford was not elected President because I think at that state in his career he had begun to understand how to cope with all these factors and forces of power that come to play on the presidency and the staff people. It brings out in many ways the best and the worst in staff people.

QUESTION: On whom did President Ford rely heavily and use as a sounding board? How did he operate?

MR. GOODELL: In foreign policy he relied very heavily on Henry Kissinger. Jerry Ford was not really deeply involved in foreign policy issues as minority leader or as vice president. He felt he needed Henry Kissinger in foreign policy. He grew out of that in the later stages but initially he relied almost entirely on Henry in foreign policy matters. He also relied very much on Haig. Haig held the White House together during the difficult period when Nixon was not paying very much attention to the presidency. Haig was making the hour-to-hour, day-to-day decisions. Nixon was consulted of course, but usually he went along and told Al to go ahead. So when he got in, Ford relied very heavily on Al Haig, his own personal staff, and Bob Hartmann. He had Jack Marsh, a good Virginian and very fine person, whom he relied on very heavily and who was very loyal to Jerry.

Ford got to a point where things were coming apart in the White House. He brought Donald Rumsfeld back from Brussels and thereafter relied very heavily on Rummy. He also relied a great deal on Rockefeller. They had a very close relationship, though there were problems elsewhere. I was brought in to try to mediate a variety of situations between Rockefeller and Rumsfeld. This sort of thing happens inevitably at any White House with all the power that's there. Rockefeller and Rumsfeld became rivals within the White House structure. Each of them on occasion would call on me, Mel Laird or somebody else to try to mediate their problems with each other. Ford never had any patience with this kind of situation. He normally said, "Well, you can work this out. There is no big problem." But he relied very heavily on Rumsfeld. When he first came back from Brussels, I visited the White House. I said,

"Rummy, you've got to come back because Jerry needs
somebody to organize the White House." His comment was,
"Well, things do seem to be a little spongy around here."
He came back at some sacrifice, but he also was ambitious
to be president himself. In fact, of the three choices that
Bob Hartmann laid out for Jerry Ford as vice president, the
three choices were Rockefeller, Bush and Rumsfeld. Of
course, he added a couple of other names just so people
wouldn't be offended that they were not included on the
list.

I think Bob Hartmann was perhaps the strongest
influence in the early period of Ford's administration
because Bob was an experienced, knowledgeable cynic. He
had been through the whole process with the White House
press corps and knew the press very well. He was a
realistic person and he was totally loyal to Jerry Ford. Bob
Hartmann was the guy who wrote Jerry Ford's magnificent
opening address as President and authored the line, "Our
national nightmare is over." He wrote a variety of other
important things that Jerry Ford said, not just national
television speeches but some of the things he sent to the
Congress.

There are a whole variety of others that in the early
period were influential. Certainly Mel Laird and Nixon were
to a degree. Ford would call Nixon once in a while and ask
his opinion. There were a variety of other Cabinet members
too. Rogers Morton and Bob Griffin were very important.
Griffin went way back as I did with Jerry Ford. Jerry
trusted Rogers Morton and would call him in and ask his
opinion. I'm sure I've left some names out but these are
people who come to mind that had the most influence on
Ford in the earlier period.

QUESTION: We've heard about the Praetorian Guard but
when it comes down to naming names, people seem to speak
in muffled tones. Hartmann and Marsh were at the head of
the list of loyalists. Who was at the head of the procession
of Nixon carryovers that challenged him?

MR. GOODELL: The whole Cabinet with the exception of
one or two fit that category. Kissinger was definitely of
the Praetorian Guard. He was always maneuvering behind
the scenes. In the White House there were the assistant

press secretaries; there were holdovers in the office of the Counsel to the President.

I hope none of you are really close to Phil Buchen. I love the man, but one of the things that happened that I had to deal quite a bit with was the President's Counsel. Phil Buchen was appointed Ford's counsel. He came from Grand Rapids without any experience with Congress or the political process in Washington and the counsel makes a lot of the most important policy decisions in the White House. He determines what to do on various legislation; what to do on all appointments, whenever there is a conflict concerning which ones are qualified to be in this or that position. He certainly has a tremendous influence on judicial appointments in the Justice Department. Unfortunately Phil Buchen was surrounded by a whole bunch of people that he didn't control. He was running his law firm from Grand Rapids when a whole variety of these people were doing their own thing under Nixon. When Buchen became counsel, they were sometimes running circles around him. I could give you a whole variety of other names but it doesn't serve very much purpose.

The higher-ups were not as important as the middle group who were really doing the work and handing it to the top people. If Ford made one mistake when he came into the White House it was not getting his own people who had some training and background in dealing with Washington, Congress and the press right up there with him. I repeat, it wasn't that the Nixon people were incompetent. Most of them were very competent. But Ford needed people who were totally loyal to him. He didn't have them.

QUESTION: You mentioned two of the failed Supreme Court appointees and I guess you can attribute Judge Carswell's failure to poor staff work. He certainly had nothing in his undistinguished record to make him a qualified applicant for the Supreme Court of the United States. Judge Haynsworth, however, is different. For those of us who continue to practice in his circuit, there is a certain amount of reverence given to him. I'm interested in your political analysis as far as the appointment is concerned and also how the opposition built which led to his defeat.

MR. GOODELL: If I made one mistake when I was a United States senator, it was my opposition to Judge Haynsworth.

I think he is a very fine judge and very well thought of. My opposition to him was based on a series of his decisions on civil rights and civil liberties. He was going through a process of growth when the law was changing rather dramatically in terms of civil rights and civil liberties.

I really didn't take the lead in defeating Judge Haynsworth's nomination. I can tell you a little anecdote about that. When I was in the Senate—this had to be August of 1969—Judge Haynsworth was nominated and I had already made a comment after his nomination that I had misgivings about him. Everett Dirksen had just died and there was a vacancy on the Judiciary Committee. I was the ranking Republican to succeed Dirksen on the Committee. To make a very long and involved story very short, Attorney General John Mitchell came down and made a big case that I should not be on the Judiciary Committee because of my announced opposition to Haynsworth. They went through this whole process including having Senator Hansen, who was not a lawyer, assert his seniority over me to be on the Judiciary Committee. There were no non-lawyers on the Judiciary Committee as a general rule. Bob Griffin came up to me and said, "Charlie, Strom Thurmond is opposing your nomination to the Judiciary Committee and they want me to make myself available." I said, "Bob, please do. I would like you to be on the Judiciary Committee; it's obvious I'm not going to be on it!" So that's what happened. They appointed Bob Griffin and he ended up leading the fight against Haynsworth. The fight was based not on civil liberties or civil rights but on conflict of interest in cases he had participated in involving corporations in which he held stock at the time. That was the biggest issue that undermined his nomination and Griffin was the one that led on the issue.

QUESTION: I would like to ask about President Ford's appointment of his representatives abroad. I'm not thinking of the career foreign service so much as the people he appointed to represent him abroad who were not members of the career service. He appointed an exceptionally good ambassador to London, Anne Armstrong, who was able because of her relationship with him to be a most effective ambassador, or so the British thought. I'd like your comments on the process by which he decided which people would represent him abroad.

MR. GOODELL: Anne Armstrong was among a small group whom Ford knew personally and for whom he had great respect. Most of the other appointments I think were made on recommendation of Henry Kissinger and a variety of other people and Ford just went along with them. Anne Armstrong certainly was an exception because he and I knew her from way back, not just in the Republican party arena but her own involvement in a whole variety of important issues, domestically and internationally. She was a person of great stature. I think he reappointed her primarily because of his own personal knowledge of her qualifications. I don't think Henry really liked to have people like Anne Armstrong who were independent of him.

COMMENT: But she was an exception.

MR. GOODELL: I think so.

QUESTION: I'd like to continue the discussion of President Ford's appointments with a further question.

First of all, could you throw any light on his appointment of Justice John Paul Stevens of the Supreme Court in 1975 replacing William O. Douglas? I ask that because appointments in the Supreme Court are historically personal decisions made by the president. They usually don't delegate them to anyone else. I ask it because in going through Ford's papers I found evidence to illustrate your earlier point, that President Ford was really caught in the cross-pressures of the White House. On the one hand, there was tremendous pressure to appoint Robert Bork, who had been acting associate attorney general under Nixon and, on the other hand, considerable support to appoint a woman. You find Sandra Day O'Connors' name appearing on the list in 1975. I think that illustrates the difficulties that Ford, this accidental president, had. Also it illustrates some of the problems of the modern presidency in those kinds of appointments. That is, as the size of the White House staff has grown, they are subject to known pressures from Congress and to interest groups within the White House itself.

The second question is, could you throw some light on the Senate role with regard to Supreme Court appointments given your experience with Carswell and Haynsworth but also anticipating controversy should one or more vacancies open up on the current Supreme Court before 1988? Particularly in the spring of 1988 one might find the American government in the same kind of controversy that arose when Earl Warren stepped down or actually offered to step down and President Johnson offered to appoint Abe Fortas. Of course there was tremendous controversy over that nomination. So my question is two-fold. I'd appreciate it if you could throw light on the appointment of Stevens and on the role of the Senate in constraining this personal presidential prerogative.

MR. GOODELL: I can't throw much light on how Jerry Ford decided on Stevens. I do know that he was looking for what he considered to be a highly qualified judge who had experience on the bench. Earl Warren was a great chief justice but he didn't want to go with an Earl Warren type; he wanted to get somebody basically from the Appellate Courts or perhaps from the District Courts. He wanted somebody with judicial background and reputation. He wanted a different model. He had guilt feelings about what he had done in proposing to impeach Justice Douglas, and rightly so. He was not about to appoint somebody who would be identified as ultra-conservative or what we now call a right-winger. At any rate, he wanted to have somebody who was thoroughly qualified to be on the Supreme Court of the United States. How he came to Stevens, I do not know and I can't shed any light on that.

QUESTION: Do you think the pending election in 1976 had any bearing on his appointment? If he had opted for Robert Bork, whom others recommended and pushed very hard, would that have been highly controversial and hurt his chance in the 1976 election?

MR. GOODELL: No. Those who know people very well, whether they know them as presidents of corporations or senior partners in law firms or deans of colleges and universities, recognize the foibles of individuals and I certainly recognize a lot of foibles in Jerry Ford. One of the things he was very clear on was he wanted to have no political involvement in these appointments to the Supreme Court. He felt Bork was much too strong on a variety of issues. I don't think Betty Ford influenced him. It's a mistake for me to say that; Betty Ford always influenced him but I don't think she did much on that.

QUESTION: Were you and others aware of Mrs. Ford's drug addictions and problems that she was having with her health and do you think they affected President Ford's performance?

MR. GOODELL: The period that I knew Jerry Ford the best was when he was in the House of Representatives as minority leader and I was part of the Republican leadership and worked very closely with him. Betty had terrible back problems and she had all sorts of medication to try to deal with the pain. I saw her frequently on social occasions and she was often uncomfortable. Beyond that I think she was very supportive but I think she was most supportive after he became President. Let me give you a little background on this.

People say that being president of the United States is the most difficult job in the world. It is in some sense, given the momentous nature of the decisions you have to make. But in many ways it's the easiest job, because everything is taken care of for you. You are almost a monarch. The secret service takes care of everything. You get on Air Force One and you are very comfortable.

Jerry Ford in the six-year period that I knew him particularly well was traveling all over the country on commercial airlines. He was flying into Des Moines or Chicago or Jamestown, New York, or wherever else. He would get on a little one-engine plane and fly for two and a half hours then get back on that plane and come back on an airline at 12:30-1:00 in the morning so he could be back when the House opened the next morning. It was a very, very difficult period. He made 267 speeches in other districts than his own during the first year after he became minority leader. He traveled endlessly to help candidates or incumbent Republicans who were running for Congress, and in some instances people running for the city council. That wasn't too easy on the family and on Betty. He was an absent husband a good deal of the time. He would come back very tired. She was very devoted and very supportive. How she came onto a combination of drugs and alcohol I don't know, except that I know she was in a lot of pain and difficulty and she was raising those kids almost by herself. She was there carrying the burden. I'm sure some of you are aware what it is to deal with children going through their teens. They were having their problems and she had to try to cope with them. I had five sons and my wife did most of the coping.

QUESTION: You mentioned that President Ford took notes on most communications person-to-person and you also mentioned that there was a good deal of distortion in some of the things he said in various areas of government. I wonder first, what happened to the notes? Second, was he aware of the distortions and of the problems that they could present? And third, was he cognizant that a possible solution would have been to take what he said and transcribe it? Did he avoid taping because the bad press taping had gotten under Nixon?

MR. GOODELL: To my knowledge he did no taping. I'm not an authority on that. I never was advised and Jerry would have told me if he was taping a conversation that he and I were having, I'm sure.

QUESTION: I was thinking more of his taping his own comments.

MR. GOODELL: He may have done some of that. I'm not aware whether he kept his personal notes and put them in the Ford Library at the University of Michigan or whether he still retains them. He used to keep prolific notes. I don't know what's happened to them.

QUESTION: Do you see any way that we can change the power of the White House mafia? It seems to me this was not an original part of our government. We have the secretaries who now seem peripheral. Occasionally you know their names and what they are doing. As one authority says, "It's an unelected government that runs the government." With all your experience do you have any feeling as to whether that will ever change or whether Congress could change it?

MR. GOODELL: First, let me issue a disclaimer about my experience there because I didn't have that much experience in the White House, but I did have some.

COMMENT: You saw a lot.

MR. GOODELL: Yes. I was an observer on many aspects. I don't have any simple approach to it. What I think would be salutary at least is to have the Old Executive Office Building occupied by Cabinet members. Henry Kissinger, after he got to be NSC adviser, which was probably most important position, was right down the hall from the president. Access to the president was his main source of power. Cabinet officers such as Bill Coleman, Rogers Morton and a whole variety of other people would come to me asking me to try to set up an appointment with the President.

Haldeman and Erlichman controlled the access to Nixon. Later on Haig controlled access to Ford in the early days and then Rumsfeld took over. Occasionally, I could call Ford's personal secretary and she would get me in because she knew I had a relationship and that he would want to see me. Generally, Cabinet officers had to go through the appointment secretaries or Rumsfeld.

I would start out by having the people who are making the policy decisions close to the president and able to communicate personally with him. That means their deputies would be running the departments. But they would also be going back to their departments and making policy decisions there, too. That's the only approach that I have come up with to keep Cabinet members, appointed by the president and approved by the Senate, at the top policy positions without abdicating decision-making to a bunch of young, inexperienced or experienced cynics or simply idealistic people in the White House staff. Those staff people shouldn't be making decisions that are essentially overruling Cabinet officers, a practice which I witnessed a lot.

QUESTION: Several of your predecessors suggest that a Ford/Reagan ticket would almost certainly have won in 1976. They've gone on to say that that was impossible because of Ford's relationship to the liberal wing of the party and to Rockefeller in particular. They've hinted that Ford and Reagan didn't find much in their relationships that attracted them to one another. What *is* the story about the relationship between the Rockefeller wing and those who felt that a Ford/Reagan ticket might win or was it never really discussed?

MR. GOODELL: It's hard for me to think of anybody of that period who is basically more stable and more conservative in the way I would define conservative than Jerry Ford. His voting record and everything he stood for was conservative, especially in the domestic and economic areas. There was apparently something between Ford and Reagan that didn't work very well. They didn't like each other. That was exacerbated in 1976 not only by Reagan running against Ford and trying to get the nomination but also because Reagan didn't campaign actively for Ford in the campaign. Ford might have been elected had Reagan campaigned for him in a few critical states. Ford didn't lose to Carter by that much and that might have made the difference. Ford did drop Rockefeller and tried to compromise on Dole. Who knows whether Ford would have won the midwest without Dole, but with Dole he did sweep the whole midwest. I think he probably would have without Dole, but that's another matter.

Bob Hartmann was very strong in his views that with Carter being the Democrat's nominee, Ford had to get the middle states, the midwest and the northeast, or at least some of the northeast, in order to win because the south was going to go to the southern candidate, Carter, which it ended up doing. It would have been very interesting if Ford had kept Rockefeller on the ticket. I would say that a Ford/Rockefeller ticket would have carried New York. I don't know whether it would have carried other northeastern states and I don't know whether they would have lost some of the midwestern states.

Ford and Rockefeller had a very close relationship which was somewhat poisoned by a whole variety of things that happened in the White House structure. I'm not sure it would have made very much difference one way or the other. Frankly, I think Ford would have won if he hadn't made the mistake of saying that Poland was not a Communist country.

NARRATOR: In the conclusion of a discussion like this, we ask the speaker to strike a balance sheet. If you had to enumerate the strengths and weaknesses in Ford's political leadership and his presidency, what would they be?

MR. GOODELL: The obvious strength of Ford was that he united the country. He was what he appeared to be, a very honest, straightforward person. He wasn't making any deals and this was important in the aftermath not only of Watergate but also of what we had been through with the Johnson administration where there were all sorts of deals. I think his sincerity was his greatest strength. It was effectively conveyed to the American people and that's what we needed more than anything else at that particular point in our history. Nobody thought he was a fast talker or a slippery character trying to put something over on them. Most of us disagreed with him on some issues, but we knew what he stood for. He had a pretty good sense of what was needed in the country at that point.

As for his weaknesses, I guess the main thing is that I wish he had had four more years. I think he was beginning to understand what he had to do to organize the White House and make it run the way he wanted it to. He was learning about administration generally and how to be tough and keep people in line. Jerry Ford was tough but he wasn't mean. He probably would have developed a little meanness.

QUESTION: Do you believe that Mr. Ford's long service in the Congress with its necessary focus on wheeling and dealing and making compromises in any way limited his ability to make positive, clear and rapid decisions?

MR. GOODELL: In the early stages, yes. I don't think it was a major factor after six months in the White House. Having made some negative comments about Ford, and I made them freely and honestly because he's such a close friend of mine, I have to say that after about five or six months he began to understand his powers as President. After one or two months, he understood that he was commander-in-chief. In terms of the military, his background in the House on the Appropriations Committee with defense appropriations and the rest prepared him fairly well. He was always a leader in that field plus he'd had a military career. He did understand what was going on in the Pentagon and in the military. I don't think he was unqualified very long in terms of his ability to make policy decisions.

In personnel, I think he was disabled. He was a compromiser who in Congress always had a loyal staff of people who were not undercutting him. As president, he was just beginning to understand that in the White House there were a lot of people in the power conflict who were undercutting him, doing their own thing and not following his commands. But that's a different issue. Personnel decisions were very hard for Jerry. Jerry is such a decent person, and he wasn't about to believe that somebody sitting across the table from him was going to walk out the door and not be loyal and follow the President's orders. I think he was beginning to get mean at the end of his presidency. If he had had another term, he probably would have been mean enough to be a Harry Truman, one of his favorite presidents. As you probably know one of the first decisions Jerry Ford made was to put Harry Truman's portrait up in place of Abe Lincoln's and he put Abe Lincoln back in mothballs.

QUESTION: Was the Nixon pardon a strength or weakness? Would he have acted differently if he had been meaner?

MR. GOODELL: That was a strength. He made the decision on his own, just as he made the decision to grant clemency to the draft evaders over protest. The pardon was something that angered a lot of his friends and angered me. He never talked to me or to others who worked with him in political affairs. That was something he did because he felt that it was important for the country. He believed that the country should not go through a year or two of having a president being perhaps indicted, tried in court and even sent to prison. You can name about thirty different things that probably affected Ford's defeat in 1976 and that was probably the most important one. If he hadn't pardoned Nixon he probably would have been reelected.

The longer I get away from that decision the more I think it was a wise decision, not a wise political decision but wise for the country. It was a courageous decision and he made it on his own. He didn't consult John Burns or Bob Hartmann or people closest to him. None of the people closest to him realized that this was what he was going to do. He decided that if he debated this and held meetings with all his advisers around, it was going to leak, which it would have, and then there would have been a big furor.

So he called a press conference Sunday morning and announced it. I have to have respect for him for it even though I wish I had been consulted. I would have advised him not to do it.

NARRATOR: We were told by some of your colleagues you would give us an additional dimension in understanding the Ford presidency. I think they were right and we are all most grateful to you. [**Director's note:** Sadly, Senator Goodell passed away not too long after his visit to the Miller Center.]

THE REESTABLISHMENT OF THE WHITE HOUSE SCIENCE OFFICE

H. GUYFORD STEVER

NARRATOR: Each year, the Stevers retreat, or maybe advance, from June to October to an idyllic summer site in Randolph, New Hampshire. The late James Conant and Percy Bridgman, before their deaths, and now Ed Purcell, and some distinguished theologians and philosophers all have summer places there. On one occasion I had the privilege of visiting this group for a few days, and I was struck how close to the Socratic dialogue the conversation seemed to be. Exchanges were leisurely and meandering but opened up areas of thought as much as any I had known. Guy Stever in an absolutely remarkable way, along with Conant and others would talk about very profound and complex scientific and societal issues with a great clarity and insight.

I'm sure all of you know most of the biographical facts. Guy was born in Corning, New York, and is a graduate of Colgate. Like other renowned scientists, he received his doctorate at Cal Tech. He began as an assistant professor at MIT and rose to become full professor in aero engineering and then chairman of a threefold department, including mechanical engineering and several other units. He has been director and head of the National Science Foundation. From its inception, he has been at the center of the guided missile effort and is a widely respected science statesman. He served as science adviser to

279

President Ford, so therefore knows both the Ford presidency and the scientific framework in which the science adviser must operate. He also served President Nixon. It is a great pleasure to have him with us, and to have Mrs. Stever as well.

MR. STEVER: Thank you very much. The current science advising structure is really due to Mr. Ford, although it, with some changes, much mirrored that which had been before. To give credit more generously, it actually came out of the work of a lot of people in Congress and elsewhere during Mr. Ford's presidency.

My first meeting with then Vice President Ford was arranged so we could talk over the progress of both science advising and the general state of U.S. science. As an outline, I used *Science Indicators*, our relatively new National Science Board publication. It was on its way to becoming a best seller in the science world, quoted widely for its annual analysis of the health of American and foreign science, science education, technology, and comparative analyses of the relative strengths of science in the different countries. We exchanged views on some of the problems that American science was having in the budgeting area. I pointed out two or three of the diagrams from *Science Indicators* which illustrated dramatically the decay in support for research and development in the United States. The most effective graph was the one that showed the percentage of the GNP allotted to science and technology during the past two decades. Support was clearly beginning to drop off in the United States, and, if one subtracted the space and military science budgets, it was particularly poor compared to the research and development budgets of the two countries that were emerging as our greatest economic competitors, Japan and West Germany.

President Ford absorbed quickly all the messages that we were trying to get across. In fact, he already knew the dangers of many of the trends from his work in the Congress. Then our conversation turned to the proper place for the science policy apparatus. I told him that I believed that, even though we could do useful work at the National Science Foundation (NSF), the White House was in the long run the proper place for the science advisory apparatus. He agreed quickly and forcefully saying that his congressional experiences indicated the great value of having the science apparatus in the White House.

Later, at a Franklin Institute gathering of all past and present science advisers, everybody favored the return of science advising to the White House except George Kistiakowsky. He wanted to wait for a new administration, in his case hopefully a Democratic one.

Events moved rapidly. Nixon resigned and Ford was sworn into office. At first, he was busy handling the furor over his pardon to President Nixon for the Watergate events. President Ford saw that his most important task was to get the country to think positively and to move forward. The economy of the United States was stagnating and morale was low due to the Vietnam War and the Watergate affair. I believed that the pardon was necessary to help the public to forget Mr. Nixon and Watergate. In fact it did, for I recall that around the fifth day after the pardon, in spite of the furor that had occurred, the front page of the *Washington Post* had no mention of either Nixon or Watergate. That was a remarkable turnaround.

Another important move made by President Ford was to call a major conference in Washington, D.C. on the economy. I led a group that examined science and technology and its possible contributions to the resuscitation of the economy. Most of the activities in scientific research and development don't have an immediate effect on the economy except in the expense column. There is, of course, a vitally necessary long-term contribution that arises from research and development. We described it as best we could. I noticed that the other groups in finance and business didn't come up with any knockout blows for the recession either although the economists did point out that this was a very unusual situation because there was stagnation in the economy at the same time there was inflation. 'Theoretically that was impossible, so they felt they should invent a new term, "stagflation." Perhaps that was a contribution to recovery.

At the receiving line at the White House reception for the members of this conference, President Ford seized my hand and said, "Now Dr. Stever [it took him a long time to begin to call me Guy], we've got to talk over the issue of restoring science advising to the White House." We talked a short time and since the line was piling up behind him, he turned to one of his aides and told him to arrange a meeting with me to discuss the subject and asked me to bring him some recommendations. The White House minion did not respond to that directive and some time passed. At another White House reception, Ford said, "Why haven't you been over?" I said, "I haven't been invited." This time we made a date for our meeting, which was the beginning of what finally led to the Science and Technology Policy Act of 1976. At our White House meeting, the President made five points very clearly:

- First, he wanted the White House science apparatus to be reconstructed, though not necessarily as an exact replica of the past one.

- Second, he believed that it was very important for the establishment of science in the White House to be legislated by an Act of Congress as a sign of legitimacy.

- Third, he wanted the Office of Management and Budget to begin to work, with my help, on the proposed legislation.

- Fourth, he wanted his newly named Vice President Rockefeller to lead the effort with Congress.

- Finally, he wanted me to continue as science adviser and director of the National Science Foundation until a new bill could be passed.

We immediately began to work on those instructions. We had some exchange in New York with a small private group established by Rockefeller. As you recall, there was a delay in getting Rockefeller confirmed, so this slowed our effort somewhat. When he was confirmed, he was also asked to head the White House Intelligence Committee which had some high priority matters on its agenda. Therefore, science matters continued to move slowly, though we began to work with the Office of Management and Budget and to draft some legislation.

Ford requested me to maintain my two positions at the NSF and as science adviser. This allowed us to keep the operation going and by then it was running at a pretty good clip. However, we expected that this temporary assignment

would only last for a short time but it actually extended
from the late summer of 1974 until the spring of 1976 when
the Act was finally signed.

The appropriate committees in both houses of Congress
began the hearings on the restoration of the science
apparatus at the White House.   Scientists, engineers,
industrialists, and others gave numerous testimonies on the
matter; in fact, some of them had started before Mr. Ford
became President.   The OMB, other White House units and
the NSF science advising office began to coordinate drafts
of the administration's proposal to Congress.   Though Mr.
Rockefeller was the focus of the politicking for this
operation on the Hill, I was the principal point man in
defending various administration proposals.   We finally
introduced a specific bill to the Congress.

Although most of the staff in our science advising
office at the time kept on with their work, a few of us
spent a great deal of time on the relation between the
administration and the Hill.   Needless to say, not all
elements of the administration agreed on the concepts of
the role of the restored office.   For example, the OMB
wanted a relatively small, invisible role for us.   They did
not want the original President's Science Advisory
Committee (PSAC) or anything similar to it restored.   They
did not give a very high priority to getting anything
through.   This position reflected the opinions of the
remaining Nixon people on the domestic policy staff.   We
ultimately had to develop our program around their
objections by going through Vice President Rockefeller's
office.

At one point during these activities, Mr. Ford asked
me to discuss progress with him.   He was particularly
interested in my views on the desirability of reestablishing
the PSAC.   By then, he was aware of the opposition from
OMB and others in the White House who didn't want it.
My point was that I thought the President needed a broadly
representative body from the science community which would
meet regularly.   He needed to be well-briefed in order to
study a number of important issues, as the former PSAC had
done for earlier presidents.   To strengthen this point, I said
that Congress was establishing an Office of Technology
Assessment, ostensibly to assess technology, although I
thought that it would become a very strong advisory center
for Congress.   He said abruptly, "I believe that too."

However, as things worked out the administration never did include in its proposed legislation any support for a strong PSAC.

The best work on the proposed bill was done by the Science and Technology Committee of the House, chaired by Representative Olin Teague, a conservative Democrat from Texas, who was a genuine admirer, friend and supporter of President Ford. In the Senate the subcommittee chaired by Senator Edward Kennedy was very active in putting forth their ideas as well. But the two committees, House and Senate, were often at loggerheads and fought over details which were unimportant, and resulted only in delaying passage of the legislation.

The final form of the bill was, in my view, excellent. The Science and Technology Policy Priority Act of 1976 established a President's Science and Technology Adviser in the White House. The inclusion of the words *engineering and technology* in the bill was very important for some members of the engineering community since they wanted to make the point that the President's science adviser should cover fields related to engineering, technology and industry, not just science in its pure forms. Of course every science adviser had worked in the broader arena from the beginning, so there was really no change except in the title. In fact, the advisers are still called "Science Advisers," although officially they are "Science and Technology Advisers." Even more important concerning science, engineering and technology, the bill presented a clear picture, sometimes a beautiful one, of the relationship between the entire spectrum of science, engineering and technology and the economy, national defense, and the quality of life of the nation. It was a job well done.

In addition to the President's Science and Technology Adviser, the Federal Council on Science and Technology, which we had nurtured during the interim, was renamed as the Federal Coordinating Council on Science, Engineering and Technology (FCCSET). Again, it was essentially the same apparatus which had existed for more than a decade and a half and an organization which had some successes whenever there were important problems that involved the cooperation of several agencies on matters related to the science and technology field. Of course, it was ignored if a strong agency wanted something its own way. The new FCCSET has continued with that kind of up and down activity till today. FCCSET, like its predecessor, did well in coordinating large scale research in atmospheric sciences, oceanography and other areas. It performed less ably in policy areas, such as patent policy.

The Act included a President's Commission on Science and Technology (PCST), which had some major differences from the former PSAC. This Commission had a charter to look at any science and technology issue or problem and was now forced to operate under "sunshine" rules, limited executive sessions, and open general meetings. This was a handicap to PCST. There was also a provision that PCST was to operate for two years and at the end of that period recommend whether it should be made a permanent commission. William Baker and Si Ramo, two exceptionally talented scientist-engineers served as co-chairmen. They developed a superb list of priority problems for the science adviser and the OSTP which was used by the science adviser right through the Carter administration.

The Act also established a committee of state and local authorities to address the science and technology issues of great importance to those governments. This was a good thing at the time because participation of the states and the cities in the use and support of science and technology for their own special needs was growing. Thus, the Intergovernmental Science Council was started.

The Act clearly had more to it than the OMB and some other White House offices wanted, but it was such a good job that the President signed it without delay. We immediately began to move on implementation, even though there was no officially appointed White House science adviser. I was still continuing in the dual role until one was appointed and confirmed. By then, less than a year of President Ford's first term was left, and we faced the impending uncertainty of an election year. A vigorous manhunt was started and a large number of names were suggested by a large number of movers and shakers. In the end, I was invited to do the job, although there were some stirrings against my nomination.

Certain NSF activities, particularly in the social sciences areas, generated antagonism from the extreme right of the Republican party. We had incurred the wrath of some right-wing Republicans. Many of them were against President Ford's renomination and his moderate Republican attitudes. Their quarrel with us focused on an NSF supported science education study program in the social sciences. It was called MACOS, *Man a Course of Study*, and had been conceived by some respected sociologists, psychologists and other social scientists. Not only did some conservatives claim that the course content was anti-family, anti-religion, anti-American, and anti-anything else they could think of, but also, they discovered, and I give them credit for this, that the NSF project officer violated some of our own principles of peer review and circumvented required administrative approvals by the National Science Board. After Congress discovered our poor performance, we compounded the problem by setting up an internal investigating committee, which also did a weak investigation job.

The conservative group of senators or, at least some of their staff people, thought they could make a big case against me as President Ford's proposed nominee for Science and Technology Adviser. They carried their opposition to an extreme, causing me great discomfort. I finally told President Ford that he could withdraw my name to get rid of that noise against him in a vital election year. He laughed and said, "Oh, that nonsense." But the senators did exact their pound of flesh by holding up my confirmation.

Ford's reaction to this whole situation obviously endeared him to me, but by then I knew it was characteristic of him. He was very supportive of the people who worked for him, as well as very understanding of the vicissitudes of the political process and political life. He was very human and a very fine person to deal with. I would like to give you one example of this aspect of his character which did not bring him any publicity but helped the science world. It concerned the selection of the awardees for the National Medal of Science. Professor Linus Pauling of the California Institute of Technology had had a very distinguished career in science. One of his main accomplishments was the discovery of the nature of covalent bonds, the bonds which hold organic molecules together. It was a tremendous leap forward in science and he received the Nobel Prize for it. He also made major contributions to research on the structure of DNA and in other fields of chemistry as well. He was a brilliant scientist, teacher and recognized world leader in peace movements. He received a Nobel Prize for the latter, but many thought he was too much of an activist. The night that John F. Kennedy had invited the Nobel Prize winners to have dinner with him, he was one of the marchers in front of the White House. At dinner time he put down his protest sign and went in to join the other Nobel laureates. His activism didn't help his relationship with either the Republican or Democratic administrations, often overly sensitive to criticism, but certainly he was a hero to others for his convictions.

Early in the history of the National Medal for Science, Linus Pauling was listed among recommended awardees. But for several years, his name was rejected by the White House. During the Ford administration, I was also an *ex officio* member of the nominating committee for the Medal and discovered that the committee was no longer nominating Pauling, because even though then ranked him very high, he was ignored by the White House establishment. However, when Ford was President, I suggested that we ought to nominate him once more. The committee agreed and Pauling was once again high on the list of twenty recommended nominees.

Soon after, I got a call from White House staff and they told me about Linus Pauling and why people had objected to him in the past, all of which I knew. Then, they asked why he was nominated. I gave a long defense of the fact that, as a scientist, he greatly deserved this recognition and that we should not take into account a person's liberal or conservative bent for the award of the National Medals of Science. Later, we got back the list of nominees from the White House with the ten winners ticked off by President Ford. (He was left-handed and his check mark was a reversed check mark, which was easily recognized.) He had checked Pauling's name as a nominee. It was not that Mr. Ford didn't know about the objections; he had been thoroughly briefed on both sides of the issue. For me, it was another example of his desire to heal the wounds of our society.

A marked characteristic of President Ford was to receive briefings on both sides of the issues involved and to give everybody a fair chance. The budget discussion on the number of space shuttles was another example of this. The Challenger tragedy reminded me of a related incident. At the beginning of the Shuttle Program, NASA wanted to build five complete shuttles. The OMB only wanted them to have three. President Ford asked for our opinion, so we studied the matter. We made a strong case for four shuttles and the critical parts of a fifth one without its assembly. I may have leaned toward NASA's position, but knowing the budget situation and OMB's attitude, I believed that NASA would not get their full program, so we tried to present an effective compromise. In any case, Mr. Ford called the heads of NASA and OMB and me into his office. He listened carefully to all presentations and took some notes. He told us to come back after an hour for his decision, and when we returned, he selected my compromise. I do not want to imply that he always selected my position, but in this case he did. The point that I want to make here is that once he took his decision, he made it clear to the three of us at the same time. We did not have to spend more time on it. Some politicians I know would have patted us each on the back individually and separately, praised us each excessively, and almost encouraged us to continue the battle. But he let us know that the issue had been decided in no uncertain terms. We were free to go back and focus on our other business and not continuᵛ to squabble over the shuttles.

In 1976 there were many celebrations and activities pertaining to the Bicentennial. My wife and I were often invited to parties and events as the leaders of the world came to wish the country, "Happy Birthday." The very positive outlook toward America and what it stood for presented by Ford always pleased me and made me proud. His book entitled *A Time to Heal* says it all. He was a very fine *human* being and I think he did a great amount for the country at that time.

I will never forget the morning after the election. As you know, the Republicans hoped for bad weather across the country because there were clear statistics about the stronger determination of Republicans to vote in inclement weather in comparison to Democratic voters. The Republicans figured that bad weather would definitely move the election towards their candidate. The one time I strongly wished that a flood had inundated Ohio was after we realized that, if President Ford had received additional votes in that state, he would have won through the electoral college process. In the 8:00 a.m. staff meeting as the group sat around in the Roosevelt room and reminisced, Bill Seidman commented, "Well, we're turning over a truly strong economy to the new President. We have really battered it back into shape." That didn't mean that it had fully recovered, but it was coming along. We were then instructed to cooperate fully with the incoming administration, which we all agreed to do. Then, as I walked back to the Old Executive Office Building with Alan Greenspan, President Ford's economic adviser, he said to me, "I've won some and I've lost some in my life. It's more fun winning." I wish President Ford had won.

President Ford left an excellent legacy to science and technology. The Act that reestablished the science adviser's apparatus in the White House was a positive advance. His final two budgets, which stopped and reversed the slow decline in federal support for basic science were another positive advance. This was something which I was always pleased to point out on the graphs published by the NSF in *Science Indicators*. Those budgets and OMB support paved the way for an important development: the successive administrations' reaffirmation of the role of basic research as an investment in the future, rather than merely an annoying expense of the present. In all of my contacts with President Ford, he has been very understanding and supportive of the importance of science and technology to the country and to the world.

NARRATOR: You have surely given us another dimension of the Ford administration that we didn't have. Do we have questions?

QUESTION: Can we go very far without pushing science education a great deal more?

MR. STEVER: No, because that's a crisis now and it will continue. It is hard to figure out where support for science education should be located. Most of us feel that our universities are the strongest in the world for basic research. But support for university-based research is not keeping up with the demand. The universities also have to compensate for poor education in earlier school years. So science education—except for that in a few excellent schools—is not being pursued properly. The environment in which many people are brought up often doesn't give them a background for the study of science. As a result, we have a problem getting enough American-born young people into science and convincing them to negotiate the early tough humps of study in science so they can attend good universities where they can be introduced to good research.

QUESTION: Let's take the example of the deterioration of the ozone layer. It is way off in the future somewhere and it is going to create some problems. How does the science adviser deal with that? Does he send a task force out to work on it? Does he go to see the President? Does he wait for the President to come and see him? What is the process?

MR. STEVER: I think it depends partly on the times, on whether the President has time for science, and on the science adviser's personal relationship with the President, the OMB and others. A good science adviser is in very close contact with the science world and he knows the ups and downs as scientists approach a research issue. This whole business of the ozone layer has had its ups and downs. In my time it surfaced but we had insufficient data to make decisions. There were many people who believed, and still do believe, that this is going to be a serious problem. In our time we sponsored research.

QUESTION: The NSF funded it?

MR. STEVER: Yes. And studies have shown more and more deleterious effects on the ozone layer. There are two problems which stem from the interaction between the sunlight and the atmosphere: one is the ozone layer weakening and the other is the greenhouse effect, that is, the trapping of the sun's heat due to carbon dioxide in the atmosphere. I think the greenhouse effect is a worse threat in the long run, because expected temperature increases in the next century and beyond will change many patterns on earth such as the distribution of fertile areas for agriculture, the sea level (affected by melting ice caps), etc.

As more studies have been made, the object has been to inspire the administration to support more study of the problem. The case of the greenhouse effect may require very expensive actions such as putting precipitators on power plant exhauststacks and handling exhaust from all sorts of combustion. Work on such scale will require big political action. It is really beyond the science adviser's muscle power, but he can help by convincing more and more people.

The electorate will use good information when it is properly presented to them and I think such science information is being presented better.

If a science-based issue came from a crisis like Three Mile Island, it can go to the President quickly. However, I believe that most of the long-range science issues are better treated slowly over time. Sometimes scientists overestimate a phenomenon and if we act too quickly we would make serious mistakes. There should be moderation here.

QUESTION: You referred to at least three interlocking components of the position: advising when advice is sought; to some extent, presenting initiatives without their being specifically requested; and an advocacy role, although of course they are all interrelated. I have two questions. Are there any capsulated guidelines for the appropriate mix of these components? With an eye to the future, do you see or recommend any change in that mix, any change in the nature of the function of the office?

MR. STEVER: No, I think that is a pretty good tried and true mix. It has changed with time and different science advisers, but I think the three roles are all very important. Since the President is so locked into the immediate, it is very important for him to have somebody to remind him constantly of the long-term effect of strong science. That is a very important role but it has to be performed carefully and wisely. One cannot quickly demand a large budget for every emerging problem. There must be a good case and it must have a steady thrust.

By the way, Congress recognizes the long term payoff of scientific research and has done a good job of supporting it in recent years.

The second role, the constant contact for scientific advice on problems that come up, is very important because quite often an issue or problem is presented in the White House and its scientific relationship is not immediately recognized or properly weighed.

The third aspect deals with new initiatives that come out of science. They usually are long term, but should be advanced by the science adviser early on. The best example I have is in the energy field. I mentioned earlier the study of alternative energy sources which PSAC started in the late 1960s which began to affect budgets in the early 1970s. When the oil cutoff arrived and emergency action was needed, there was a road map to follow. We also started early initiatives in the new biology as applied to agriculture. There were others, as well.

NARRATOR: I'm sure I speak for all of you in thanking Dr. and Mrs. Stever for taking time out to be with us. I'm sure conversations like this went on in his office when he was president of Carnegie-Mellon. They certainly went on in the NSF and the office of the President's science adviser. They also went on in Randolph, New Hampshire. If Guy Stever can explain science to ordinary people like me, he can explain it to anyone. The same clarity ran through everything that he said today. We are ever so grateful.

MR. STEVER: I want to thank you. It is so important for this country to have people who think broadly about the responsibilities of our top leaders. We are still the most powerful country in the world and the quality of our leadership is immensely important. So I appreciate the opportunity to join you briefly in your program.

HIGHLIGHTS OF A BRIEF TENURE, 1975-76

JOHN T. DUNLOP

NARRATOR: When we contacted Professor John T. Dunlop at Harvard University he kindly agreed to share a paper he had written for another purpose.* His paper is important not only for what it conveys about his own position in the Ford administration but for the light he throws on the relationship between the White House and one of the large departments of government.

MR. DUNLOP: I was the first tenant-secretary of the new Labor Department building, except for one week, that previous secretaries had dreamed and planned. But the larger environment was not strange. I had first worked for the Bureau of Labor Statistics in 1938. I had known each secretary beginning with Frances Perkins, and I had often worked directly with them before they held office on particular problems of labor-management-government relations. I had been chairman of the tripartite CISC (Construction Industry Stabilization Committee) starting March 29, 1971 and director of the Cost of Living Council for President Nixon starting January 11, 1973, attending cabinet meetings and serving as a member of the Economic Policy group meeting daily at the White House and weekly with the President. I had also been chastened by

---

* A version of Professor Dunlop's paper is scheduled to appear in the spring of 1988 in the *Monthly Labor Review*.

congressional committees and the press. Shortly after he took office President Ford asked me to recommend a labor-management committee that he announced on September 28, 1974, at the end of the Conference on Inflation; I was to serve as coordinator of the committee[1] which continued through my period as secretary.[2]

When President Ford on January 16, 1975 invited me to be secretary, I asked him what was the job as he saw it, and what did he want in the post. He responded that he had two particular concerns: (1) he wanted to improve the communications between the labor movement and himself and his administration, and (2) he recognized that the economy was entering a serious recession, and he wanted the best advice and judgment of labor and management as to how to deal with this situation. At its December 1974 meeting, the Labor-Management Advisory Committee had unanimously recommended a precise form and distribution of a tax cut that was later accepted by the President and the Congress.[3] In the swearing-in ceremony of March 18, 1975, President Ford said, "The Labor-Management Committee he chairs told us that what we most need is a tax cut even before I asked for a tax cut in my State of the Union Message in January."[4]

My response to the President at the swearing-in ceremony formulated major elements of a philosophy of the assignment publicly undertaken. The major themes were a strong collective bargaining system with labor and management working together with government, the limitations of regulation, and the short-term concern to get the economy moving and the related long-term need for attention to structural problems. A few paragraphs express the spirit and philosophy:

> The group here this afternoon, Mr. President, is symbolic of the diversity of our country—labor and management, academics and practitioners, old hands and young specialists, both sides of the legislative aisle, and active minority groups—and no one can neglect the historical tensions of geography.
> Mr. President, we are a 'can-do-people.' Again, as you said Thursday night, Mr. President, 'our people cannot live on islands of self-interest.' We must build bridges and communicate

our agreements as well as our disagreements. Only then can we honestly solve the Nation's problems.

A corollary of that theme is that a great deal of government needs to be devoted to improving understanding, persuasion, accommodation, mutual problem solving, and informal mediation. . . . I have a sense that in many areas the growth of regulations and law has outstripped our capacity to develop consensus and mutual accommodation to our common detriment.

It is my hope that business, labor and government, working together, can address the immediate problems of the Nation while having a deep appreciation of our longer run necessities and opportunities, not only for the economy as a whole but in individual sectors and industry and regions as well.

With the general assignment of President Ford, the statutory policies and the expressed themes, it is appropriate for the present purposes to comment briefly on what appear to me to have been some of the major activities of the period.[5]

(1) The regulatory responsibilities of the Labor Department had increased rapidly in recent decades exposing quite a different posture to management, labor and the public and creating a different internal spirit from its traditional role as compiler of data, preparer of reports, stimulator of training and convener of labor and management representatives. In 1940 the Department administered 18 regulatory programs; by 1960, the number had expanded to 40; in 1975, the number stood at 134 including recent complex programs such as ERISA and OSHA. Even manpower programs which contained the large bulk of the appropriations were significantly and excessively regulatory in their approach. I prepared a paper, "The Limits of Legal Compulsion,"[6] presented at the visit to each regional office expressing concern with the "limitations on bringing about social change through legal compulsion." The paper closed with the following:

The development of new attitudes on the part of public employees and new relationships and procedures with those who are required to live under regulations is a central challenge of democratic society. Trust cannot grow in an atmosphere dominated by bureaucratic fiat and litigious controversy; it emerges through persuasion, mutual accommodation, and problem solving.

To effectuate this approach I took the lead in developing labor standards under Section 13(c) of the Orban Mass Transportation Act and convened labor and management representatives to seek agreement on standards to be written into the Federal Register for comments and for subsequent formal issuance. I also became directly involved in seeking to mediate the complex Coke Oven standard under OHSA. In the administration, generally, I advocated "negotiated rule-making" where appropriate and feasible.[7]

It is a source of considerable satisfaction that negotiated rule-making has come to be recognized as an appropriate means of establishing regulations, supported by the Administrative Conference of the United States, and its use is growing by EPA, OSHA and other federal agencies. It needs to be made clear that negotiated rule making, when properly applied, does not constitute a dimunition of government responsibility, nor does it represent the privatization of public functions. But such means may operate faster, reduce subsequent litigation, engender better compliance and better serve both private parties and the public weal. Would that the Labor Department made greater use of these means.

The Regulatory Management developed by the White House and centered in OMB by Executive Orders 12291 and 12498 raise serious questions for me as to the centralization of such authority.[8] No White House or OMB staff is ever going to know as much about a subject or have as direct understanding of the affected parties as the secretary should have. In 1984 and 1985 OMB made changes in 48.6 percent and 26.3 percent of all Labor Department proposed rules.[9] Concerns of the White House and OMB are appropriate, and consultation and raising serious issues to higher levels has always been appropriate, of course, but such centralization for me is obnoxious to constructive industrial relations, efficient labor markets and participatory labor-management-government relations.

(2) From the outset I was interested in a greater degree of procedural cooperation and professional reinforcement among the labor relations agencies dealing with private parties; the objective did not focus on substantive decisions. Accordingly, I met periodically in a group with the heads of the Federal Mediation and Conciliation Service, the National Mediation Board and the National Labor Relations Board. There are a number of things that a secretary can do informally for these agencies with respect to budgets, staffing, access and with respect to appointments. Moreover, these officials have a perspective on labor and management and their interactions that is of considerable interest to a secretary. These agencies help to shape the labor-management climate of an era and the consequent quality of economic performance that has to be a priority of any president. The labor-management arena as a whole must be the concern of the secretary of labor.

(3) The President's Labor-Management Committee, created by Executive Order 11809, was given a broad charter to advise and make recommendations to the President. The Committee met regularly with a prepared agenda; the secretary of the treasury and other economic officials also attended, and the President regularly met with the Committee at each meeting. In the 15 months of activity, the Committee held 8 meetings and the President took part in 7 of them. The Committee also concerned itself with national energy policy, housing, financing public utilities, unemployment and labor-management committees in private sectors. At each session with the President the Committee also provided its individual and group views of the economic outlook, often more immediate than permitted by government data.

The Committee provided a significant opportunity for direct communications between the President and his administration and the labor-management community. Both groups interacted with each other. Other business groups were consulted separately.

(4) A significant illustration of the interactions among industrial relations developments, economic policy and foreign affairs is afforded by the U.S.-U.S.S.R. grain agreement of 1975.[10] The possibility of a longshore strike communicated in advance to the secretary alerted the

administration to serious problems, including the consequences of further significant Soviet purchases for domestic grain and meat prices, shipping usage, and to the potentials of significant agricultural and foreign policy opportunities. A cabinet level group was enabled to follow developments, advise the President and secure his approval to negotiate a five-year agreement, assist farmers, and to resolve the longshore stoppage.

The centrality of industrial relations and their complex interweaving with other vital issues of the nation are well illustrated by these events in which the Labor Department had a major role.

(5) The international labor-management arena has long been a concern of the Labor Department including representation in the International Labor Organization, the only U.N. agency in which both labor and management are directly represented. The United States had a growing series of difficulties with the ILO prior to 1975 related to the selection of top associates of the director general, the representation of the Soviets in the labor and management members of the Governing Body, the budgetary levels and allocations among countries, the uneven treatment of reports on violations of human rights and conventions made by committees of experts, and the use of the annual conference in June as a political forum for attacks on Israel and U.S. policy. In close consultation with labor and management, and with the full collaboration of Secretary of State Kissinger, a letter of notice of intent to withdraw two years hence was developed, approved by the President, signed by Secretary Kissinger, and sent November 5, 1975.

In order to improve governmental policy-making on ILO matters and to enhance participation of management organizations and labor, a cabinet-level committee was established involving the secretaries of State, Commerce, Labor and later the National Security Advisory with labor and management members to be regular attendants. This committee still operates.

Subsequent events and negotiations helped to create desirable changes in ILO structure and policies, and I was particularly pleased that in 1977 President Carter assured the continued membership of the United States. I have had close ties to the ILO over the years, having spent the year 1957-58 at the ILO—but not on its payroll—at the invitation of David Morse, then the director general, writing my

Industrial Relations Systems. I came to have deep respect for the organization and its potential, and then came to know Francis Blanchard, the D.G. in 1975 and since.

(6) Brief reference should be made to a few other efforts in the 1975-76 period. I experimented to develop new approaches to the congressional oversight function, both by regular visits with key committee members and a comprehensive presentation, on manpower and training, rather than to await specialized hearings on politically sensitive issues or administrative problems. Seldom do congressional committees get a comprehensive view of a topic developed by a cabinet officer.[11] I organized a weekly seminar with prepared papers on future or underlying questions for the press and media before a regular press conference and passed out diplomas at the end of my tenure. A special staff unit assisted in my participation in the general economic policy-making of the administration.

It probably would be inappropriate not to include some comment on the situs picketing legislation, the more so since a view in some circles has developed that I privately lobbied the President and obtained his promise to support the legislation if enacted.[12] Good staff work at the White House, it has been said, would have prevented the subsequent problem for the President. [Editor's note: See Cheney's chapter.]

The reality is that at the earliest meetings with the President on the topic he stated he wished to support the legislation; he said he had become familiar in detail with the issue after 25 years in the House. I insisted that any political arrangement for support in the 1975 elections be directly arranged with labor representatives, particularly the Building Trades. At meetings on the topic on May 21, 1975 and June 4, 1975 with the President, OMB director Lynn and senior White House aides including Donald Rumsfeld, William Seidman or Richard Cheney were present. The President met with President Robert Georgine of the Building Trades Department on April 22 and July 8, 1975, on the later date the President announced his intention to run in 1976. My approved testimony on June 5, 1975 followed, but with more restraints, the testimony of Secretary Shultz of 1969 on the same subject. The draft legislation was significantly modified from June through November and made more responsive to the concerns of contractors; and a new dispute machinery for all labor-management disputes in the industry was added in Title II with the agreement of virtually all parties to collective bargaining in the industry.

The reality then as now seems quite clear. The President was anxious in his quest for election to secure the endorsement of a number of unions, particularly the building trades as President Nixon had done in 1972. He sought the invitation and spoke before the Building Trades convention in San Francisco in September. But the politics of the Republican party changed from May and June to December when the bill sat on the President's desk. President Ford was now concerned that Ronald Reagan would use the bill if he signed it into law to defeat him in the Republican primaries and caucuses. He told me on December 11, 1975 (with Richard Cheney present) that it was a good bill, and that I had done what he had asked, but he would have to veto it because otherwise he would be defeated in his quest for his party nomination as he explained the politics of various states.[13]

I responded that I respected his decision, but it would not be the first time in American politics that positions taken to secure nomination precluded subsequent election success. As I stated in my letter of resignation, his veto has destroyed my capacity to perform the duties the President had invited me to do. I retain a high regard for President Ford.

ENDNOTES

1. *The Conference on Inflation*, held at the request of President Gerald R. Ford and the Congress of the United States, Washington, D.C., September 27-28, 1974, pp. 291-92.

2. Subsequently, the labor and management members decided to continue their joint meetings as a private group and asked me to continue to serve as coordinator. The Labor-Management Group continues to the present. See, John T. Dunlop, *Dispute Resolution, Negotiation and Consensus Building*, Dover, Mass., Auburn House Publishing Company, 1984, pp. 252-66.

3. On January 10, 1975 the White House released the recommendations of the Committee. This was the first occasion on which organized labor had supported an investment tax credit.

4. *Weekly Compilation of Presidential Documents*, Monday, March 24, 1975, pp. 281-82.

5. Also see, *Unfinished Business: An Agenda for Labor, Management, and the Public*, Abraham J. Siegel and David B. Lipsky, Eds., Cambridge, Mass., The MIT Press, 1978, pp. 29-36.

6. John T. Dunlop, "The Limits of Legal Compulsion," *Labor Law Journal*, February 1976, pp. 67-74.

7. For a discussion of the historical background to negotiated rule-making, see Henry H. Perritt, Jr., "Analysis of Four Negotiated Rulemaking Efforts for the Administrative Conference of the United States," *The Georgetown Law Journal*, 1986, pp. 1627-1717; Administrative Conference of the United States, *Sourcebook: Federal Agency Use of Alternative Means of Dispute Resolution*, Washington, D.C., 1987.

8.   See National Academy of Public Administration, *Presidential Management of Rulemaking in Regulatory Agencies*, A Report by A Panel of the National Academy of Public Administration, 1987.

9.   *Ibid.*, Table 3, p. 14.

10. For a detailed internal account, see Roger B. Porter, *The U.S.-U.S.S.R. Grain Agreement*, Cambridge, Cambridge University Press, 1984.

11. "Comprehensive Employment and Training Act—Review and Oversight," December 5, 1975.

12. See Frederick V. Malek, *Washington's Hidden Tragedy, The Failure to Make Government Work*, The Free Press, 1978, p. 26; Richard Cheney on TV, January 1986, referred to the decision of the President to support situs picketing as "Oh By-the-Way Decisions."

13. See Jonathan A. Kantar, "The Ford Administration and the 1975 Common Situs Picketing Issue," Thesis Submitted March 29, 1985 to the Department of History, University of Michigan, Ann Arbor, Michigan.

FORD VIEWED FROM AGRICULTURE:
A NOTE

SECRETARY OF AGRICULTURE EARL BUTZ

NARRATOR: Earl Butz was secretary of agriculture from 1971 to 1976. He was born in Indiana in Noble County. He did his undergraduate work at Purdue on a 4-H fellowship and got his degree there in 1932. Two things of unequal importance happened in 1937: he got his Ph.D., which was of minor importance, and he married his wife, Mariam Emma Powell, who had been a home demonstration agent in North Carolina. That was very important. He was head of the Agricultural Economics Department at Purdue from 1947 to 1957. He served in the Eisenhower administration as assistant secretary of agriculture. He returned to Purdue as dean of Agriculture and then vice president and dean of continuing education.

When he became secretary of agriculture in 1971, his primary goals were to keep America the best fed nation, to improve the farm economy, strengthen rural America, and support the free market system. He carried that message to all fifty states and around the world to more than fifty nations and a million and a half people. That is one of the reasons that we hoped very much that we could have an opportunity to talk a little bit today about the Ford presidency and any other matters that he may want to discuss. It is a pleasure to have Earl Butz here today.

SECRETARY BUTZ: Ford is a gregarious man who likes people. He was easy to get to. He had been a minority leader in the House of Representatives and was used to crafting a consensus from conflicting opinions. You had to watch yourself so that you protected Ford's time. Ford was probably the right man for post-Watergate when the importance and prestige of the presidency had to be reestablished. Ford did that as well as anybody could have done. Because he was a gregarious chap he wouldn't put you down the way a person who is overly intelligent sometimes will. That was essentially the difference between Ford and Nixon.

I recall an incident involving Jerry Ford and the issue of tobacco price supports. The tobacco boys had gotten away with bloody murder. As a matter of fact, they had drawn a blueprint for self-destruction, because they always wanted higher price supports. At that time, they had an important item that they managed to have tucked in a bill. If it had passed, it would have changed the formula for calculating the parity price on tobacco and essentially would have raised the price about ten cents a pound. Of course, they didn't say it increased the price of tobacco, because at that point the anti-smoking league was very active too.

They had very cleverly hidden this change in the method of calculating parity. Nobody knew it was there. Ultimately, it came to our attention. We decided that it just would not do because the price of tobacco was too high already. We were losing our export market and encouraging production elsewhere. We were fighting that thing vigorously on the Hill. I recall I went up there and met with some people from the tobacco states, including Virginia, the Carolinas and Georgia. In the course of the meeting, I said, "If you put this thing through it is going to hasten the death of tobacco in this country." One of the congressmen replied, "Butz, I know you are right but I face opposition in the primary next spring. I've got to take this position." We thought we had pretty well stopped the thing until the night before they were to pass this bill. Somehow, they changed the number on the House Resolution and attached it as an amendment to something else. It was near the end of session and we had our man sitting there on the House floor to make sure that they didn't call it up for a motion for a unanimous vote. He had to take a telephone call. While he was gone, the twenty-two people on the House floor passed it unanimously. There it was—an amendment to a bill that they had to have.

I recall we argued about that bill when it came to the White House. I was sitting there with the President and he had his staff there. He also had somebody from the National Republican Committee there. They said that the politics of this were such that he didn't dare veto the bill. I said that the Congress was absolutely dishonest in the way they did it. Jerry Ford understood it because he had probably done the same thing himself when he was up there. The rest of them said, "If you veto this bill you are going to lose something else. You are going to lose those Southern Congressmen." Now Ford was a man of tremendous principle. I recall him sitting there and finally he said, "If I don't veto this bill, I can't live with myself. I'm going to veto it." He was that kind of a chap. It turned out that the veto was politically right too. Even the *Raleigh News and Observer*, once they found out the shenanigans those characters had played, said it should have been vetoed.

In a case like that, you saw a man with real principles. Jerry Ford was and is such a man.

NARRATOR: Would you say a word about something that people who have talked about Ford have emphasized, namely, that he is a wonderful fellow but that his administration, at least in the beginning, was torn by conflict between the Nixon carryovers, the Praetorian Guard, and the Ford loyalists.

SECRETARY BUTZ: There was some of that obviously. The vice president is never prepared to take over the presidency. Al Haig told us, "I've had the vice president in, trying to brief him and bring him up to speed." Then of course Ford took over the Nixon staff and at the same time, the Watergate uproar continued. Then came the Ford pardon of Nixon, which I think had to be. At that time, trauma gripped the whole White House crowd even though the Democrats were about to carry that thing on to its bloody conclusion. They were after the president.

I think the pardon was absolutely essential. The administration could go ahead then on a positive, constructive basis. In retrospect I think it had to be done, but it should have been done even before it was.

VI.

THE FORD PRESIDENCY:
FOREIGN POLICY AND DEFENSE

FORD AS PRESIDENT
AND HIS FOREIGN POLICY

GENERAL BRENT SCOWCROFT

NARRATOR: We are very pleased to welcome General Brent Scowcroft to today's forum at the University of Virginia's Miller Center. General Scowcroft's service to the nation's highest executive—as assistant to the president for national security affairs, 1975-1977 and as deputy of that position, 1973-1975—was the fulfillment of the vision that Secretary James Forrestal had when he prescribed that the national security adviser should be the person who would "buckle up all the separate strands of policy that comprise foreign policy." And Forrestal added he should do it with a "passion for anonymity."

Among other things, General Scowcroft is a highly decorated military leader, the recipient of the highest honors that this country has to give its servants in military affairs, including the D.S.M. with two oak leaf clusters, the Legion of Merit with oak leaf cluster, and the Air Force Commendation Medal. In public affairs, the fact that he was called upon to be a member of the Tower Commission, that he was chairman of the President's Commission on Strategic Forces, and was a member of the President's Advisory Committee on Arms Control testifies to the respect in which he has been held over the years by successive administrations, both Republican and Democratic. It is an honor to have him with us.

GENERAL SCOWCROFT: Thank you very much, Ken, for that exceedingly generous introduction. I have been talking with Ken for a long time about the oral history on Ford, so why don't I just say a few words about Ford and his presidency and then we'll talk about whatever you like.

One of the interesting things to remember about Gerald Ford is that he was perhaps the only president and certainly the only president in modern times who achieved the office but did not seek it. He became Vice President and President by accident, and is therefore perhaps unique in the sense that he doesn't have whatever it is that makes people want to be President of the United States. Gerald Ford does not have that hunger, ego, or that insecurity—whatever you want to call it—that is now called "fire in the belly." Gerald Ford didn't have that; his ambition was to be speaker of the House. If I had to describe him in one word it would be "normal," and that says a lot because I think his presidency will be known in future years as a presidency which returned us to normal.

President Ford was not a great intellect but that is not a prime requisite for being president. A great president needs to possess two qualities: the first quality is courage, the courage to make a decision and then stick with it. Gerald Ford did that perhaps better than anyone else. When he made a decision he did not worry about it. The decision had been made and he could move on to the next problem or issue.

The second quality a president must possess is the ability to pick good people and to know when to listen to them. This is extraordinarily difficult. President Ford inherited a completely staffed administration and this posed difficulties and problems that he never resolved. He disliked having to deal with the problem of squabbles and quarrels between people he respected. In fact, he did not deal with this problem very well at all. He was unable to be what FDR called "a bit of a butcher." A president cannot afford to have those kinds of personal feelings for people with whom he deals.

When we look at the Ford presidency, especially in foreign policy, we notice that it has no great peaks or valleys. The high point for me was just before the fall of Saigon. Gerald Ford refused to pull American troops out of Saigon until the very last minute. This decision involved enormous risk, some to the American troops involved, but especially to his own political popularity. The outcry, the demand to pull American troops out immediately was tremendous. But one must remember that thousands and thousands of Vietnamese had staked their very lives on American support. President Ford's courageous stance enabled a large number of Vietnamese to get out of the country without the loss of American lives. This was perhaps Ford's finest hour. It was a tough, lonely decision made with great courage.

Perhaps Ford will not go down in history as one of the greatest presidents, because to be a great president one must be the kind of aberration from the norm which generates the energy to do the things that the presidency demands. Gerald Ford was, however, ideally suited for his primary task. He was a man for his time because he restored the United States to normality following a time of great internal turmoil.

QUESTION: How much responsibility does an adviser feel for giving a president all of the information that he needs to have?

GENERAL SCOWCROFT: It's a great responsibility and presidents and advisers have handled it in very different ways. When I was part of the National Security Council, we would handle big decisions by doing a substantial study in which we would include the recommendations of the interagency groups, etc. As national security adviser, I would attach to that a memorandum of no more than three pages in which I summarized the issues to the extent that I knew them, the views of his other senior advisers, and then my own judgments regarding the pros and cons of the different options and recommendations. I tried not to give the President lengthy reading materials. I summarized everything I sent to him with the documents behind the summary in the event that he wanted to go over them.

Other people have done it differently. Zbigniew Brzezinski, for example, told me that he ordinarily gave President Carter between one hundred and one hundred and fifty pages of reading every night. I think that is a burden one cannot impose on a president; he doesn't have time to do things like that. He should focus on the forest and not on the trees. This consideration puts a very great burden on people who want to present things as accurately and as honestly as possible.

It reminds me of what I once heard a man say, "I wrote a long letter because I didn't have time to write a short one." That's the nature of the problem. But again, different presidents like to get information in different ways. Ford liked to make his decisions after listening to his advisers argue the issues back and forth. He liked the give and take of personal debate. He was a voracious reader but he rarely made decisions based only on his reading of the documents.

Nixon was just the opposite. Nixon didn't particularly like meetings; he didn't like listening to oral arguments. Instead he preferred to take all the papers into his office, study them and then just ask questions. Advisers must learn to respond to the way in which a president wants information; otherwise they will either frustrate the president or the president will go around the system to get his own information.

QUESTION: Would you care to comment on the Ford decision to grant the pardon of Nixon?

GENERAL SCOWCROFT: I wasn't involved in the decision. I think that the decision as much as anything else cost Ford the 1976 election. I also think that he made the right decision and that he made it in the interest of the country. Had Ford not pardoned Nixon, and had Nixon been brought to trial, I think the whole country would have been thrown into a time of great turmoil. Ford would have found it extremely difficult to govern the country had Nixon gone to trial.

QUESTION: Gerald Ford had a long career and a great deal of experience in Congress. Did this experience affect in any way his understanding of the presidency?

GENERAL SCOWCROFT: Yes, his experience in Congress certainly did affect the way he performed the duties of his office in the White House. First, he was not a good manager. Congressional experience does not enhance management skills. As I mentioned, he had trouble managing his staff, though not his time. His experience gave him enormous skills in dealing with Congress. Even after the election of 1974 when the Republicans were a relatively minuscule part of the Congress, he was able to do much more legislatively than one would have anticipated. He was constantly on the telephone with members of Congress and accomplished a great deal with them. One of his carry-over habits was that when he faced a controversial issue, whether the issue divided Congress or Congress and the White House, his first thought tended to be, how do we reach a compromise on this problem? While that is a way of life on Capitol Hill, it is sometimes better as president to go down in defeat than it is to win only half of your goals—it all depends on the issue. But he definitely brought the legislative approach into the White House with all of the good and the bad attached to that attitude.

QUESTION: What kind of intellectual and personal qualities should a president have?

GENERAL SCOWCROFT: I think they are implied in the second of two conditions I listed earlier: to know how to pick good people and to know when to listen to them. A president needs a kind of feel for what is right, for the mood of the American people, and for how much one can lead without getting too far out in front, which would be counterproductive.

I think Gerald Ford has it; I think Ronald Reagan also has it, or had it until recently. It is knowing exactly how to do things; it's a resonance with the American people. It's hard for me to define. Intelligence you can hire; you can hire the smartest people in the world when you are president, but that's not the necessary quality; it's knowing how to put the pieces together and when to listen to the experts; to know in your bones when they are wrong and that you have to go a different way. It isn't necessarily being a Rhodes scholar or Phi Beta Kappa.

QUESTION: As a member of the Tower Commission you had an opportunity to review and to study in depth President Reagan's style. I would be interested if you could contrast the President's style with that of Senator Muskie, in terms of their effectiveness. Could you comment on their effectiveness as president or as potential president?

GENERAL SCOWCROFT: That's an interesting question. Let me take President Reagan first. His own description of his management style is to pick outstanding people whom he can trust, then trust them to do their job and come to him if they have any problems. If they don't come to him, he assumes there are no problems. He is too trusting. Reagan is an incurious President; he is not fundamentally interested in foreign policy; he is not at all interested in details; he deals in grand schemes with broad policy implications and assumes the people whom he has appointed will take care of all the details. It is a style which puts an enormous burden on the people around him.

In the case of Iran, and even at the Reykjavik summit, the system failed him. One might say that with the National Security Council system, by and large, the President gets the kind of system he deserves because it is his creature. That's really not a fair judgment, however, because in a presidential government, unlike a Cabinet government, a president at the outset of his administration must put together a team of staff members even when he has only the dimmest notion of what his own job really is. If he had previously been vice president, then he would of course have a clearer notion. Yet at that early stage he must select the people on whom he is going to rely. Even if he knows them all personally, he can have no real idea how they will work together. He will not know whether he is putting together a closely knit team or a bunch of people who will spend most of their time fighting each other rather than constructing and managing his policy. It is a very difficult system. In a parliamentary system, there is a shadow cabinet with people who have been together for years and years. Everyone knows what the other person thinks and it is easier to put the team together and have them work together.

I didn't know Ed Muskie well before we worked together. I found that he has a very penetrating mind, that he was able to see pitfalls that were not readily apparent in various approaches to problems. He didn't ordinarily get bogged down in minutia. He had a sense of inner direction and a sense of what it was we were about and how it had to be done for the good of the country. Ed Muskie is a very philosophical man. His costly tears in New Hampshire demonstrate more than anything else the perils of the electoral process in this country. It is unfortunate that our judgment could not be on the whole man but rather on a particular moment at which he was experiencing a great deal of personal stress. In my opinion, Senator Muskie possesses outstanding qualities.

QUESTION: How would you contrast your experience among military leaders with your experience among civilian leaders like President Ford in terms of their effectiveness in cutting their losses? There is a body of thought which suggests that presidents are at times unwilling to let those people go who are closest to them. Military persons must also cut their losses, but they seem better able to accomplish that task.

GENERAL SCOWCROFT: I think military officers are impressed with the need to make decisions early, especially when information is very inadequate and when instinct tells you to temporize until you know more about the issue. A part of the essence of the military profession is the need to make firm decisions in the face of inadequate information. In combat, that is how they must operate. A good operating rule of a politician, on the other hand, is never to close a door behind you. Keep all options open and try to judge and respond to the way the situation is going.

I think that one of the President's major problems in the Iran-contra affair is how long it took him finally to understand how significant it really was. When we first talked to him he was convinced that his only real problem was the possible diversion of funds. It our second meeting, we told him that, in our judgment, the impact on the country of the diversion of funds issue was almost incidental in comparison to the political fallout from the President's apparent betrayal of his own ideals. President Reagan had come into office declaring he was going to make American stand tall again, that no longer were we going to kowtow to terrorists and hostage takers. Those words struck a very resonant chord. He adopted a position that was not only right, but was also very popular. Then he turned on that policy in secret and did the very opposite. That was the most damaging aspect of the Iranian issue.

In the beginning, I believe the President simply did not realize that. In the sense of cutting losses, the way Irangate proceeded from the point at which it was first disclosed was hauntingly similar to the way the Watergate crisis proceeded. There is an element of Greek tragedy in both in that each one took a series of steps to try to stem the tide. Each was, however, never quite sufficient actually to turn the tide. Watergate is a classic case, the inexorable move toward disaster with the President each time thinking that if he did just one more thing, he could stop it. One sees a little of that in the Reagan reaction. To get back to the heart of your question, had either one of them at the outset of the crisis gone farther than they had to go at the moment, they could probably have turned it off. But hindsight gives one a wonderful perspective.

QUESTION: In looking back over the last twenty-one years of the National Security Council, do you think it should be restructured or redefined or reduced in some way?

GENERAL SCOWCROFT: The Tower Commission made a point of contacting all the living former presidents, all the secretaries of state, secretaries of defense, national security advisers, several chairmen of the Joint Chiefs and directors of central intelligence. We asked each one of them what they thought the strong and weak points of the NSC system were when they were involved with it, and if they were to come back into the government, what changes they would most like to see. The consensus of views about what it should and should not be was remarkable. We also looked at some twelve crises that presidents from Truman to Reagan have faced to see how the system behaved and whether there were any common points of failure. As a result of those efforts, we put together what we called a model of the NSC system. The model was not structurally precise but showed, in general, what the system must do in order to serve a president properly. How it accomplishes its purposes can vary according to the president's own style.

When we began my personal view was that we couldn't be that specific because the style of our presidents has been so different. After all, one can't change their style; they are elected by the American people. The NSC system is a vehicle by which the president transmits his creative urges, his instincts for policy to the permanent departments of government. It has to be his instrument. We have presidents such as Ronald Reagan who do not want to become involved in the specifics of policy; or Jimmy Carter who immersed himself in detail; or Lyndon Johnson who was uncomfortable when a paper clip dropped and he wasn't informed about it; or Dwight Eisenhower who wanted the system to run as a military staff system did. We've had a range of presidents from the most intrusive, domineering and demanding to the most relaxed and incurious. So we need a system that is broad enough to accommodate those various personalities. I am comfortable that we have described in the Board report a system which will serve future presidents well, as, by and large, it has served previous presidents. But it has failed before and it will fail again. In our system we cannot prevent presidents from stepping off a cliff if they are determined to do so.

As decision-maker in the executive branch, the president has enormous power. Everybody around him is there simply to help him make decisions and run his executive branch. What the system must do is to make very clear the dangers when a president is disposed to step off a cliff. It should make it crystal clear what the consequences of a particular move are likely to be. If then the president insists on following through with his initial decision, the Constitution permits him to do it. So the system must not only help him make decisions, but also warn him of the dangers of decisions.

The Tower Board, I believe, is the first formal group ever to look specifically at the operation of the National Security Council system. I would hope that all presidential candidates would read that report, not only as a case study of the way things can go wrong when people of good will, trying to do their best, ignore certain fundamentals, but also as a stimulus to their thinking on how they can best use this system to mesh with their own style in decision-making.

QUESTION: What policy areas are covered by the National Security Council staff? Does it play a role in the formulation of economic policy?

GENERAL SCOWCROFT: The National Security Council staff is composed of—and it varies over time—between thirty and fifty professionals in various fields, which may change according to the president's needs. They are managed by the national security adviser. They work for the Council itself, but the Council works for the president so they all basically work for the president. There are no other people on the present White House staff who have that kind of function. International economics, however, has never been generally a part of the NSC structure itself. The subject that we perhaps have the most difficulty in dealing with in our government structure is economics. Almost every Cabinet officer and agency head thinks that some portion of our economic policy is his responsibility. Each president has set up some kind of council or similar grouping to try to deal with economic affairs, both domestic and international. These groups have met with varying degrees of success. There are people in economic areas who deal with foreign affairs, a special trade representative, for example. But for national security itself there really isn't anybody on the White House staff other than the national security adviser.

NARRATOR: Over the years, General Scowcroft has displayed a genuine and sincere interest in the Miller Center almost from its beginning. We've been able to hear from him and learn from him throughout the history of the Center. Perhaps more important and less ethnocentric is the fact that the nation has heard from him and learned from him at the times when we needed his counsel the most. He has helped us in this discussion understand why the nation trusts him so much. We thank him and we look forward to the next public service that he performs, a contribution for which we all shall be grateful.

FORD, KISSINGER AND THE
NIXON-FORD FOREIGN POLICY

JOSEPH J. SISCO

NARRATOR: It's a pleasure to introduce a man who has been a close, personal friend for many years. Joseph Sisco is scholar Joseph Sisco and we labored together as long suffering graduate students at the University of Chicago. He was a legend there and he remains a legend in his present work and activities. Others have been tapped as potential leaders in foreign policy almost from birth, but Joe Sisco made his way and achieved his success through dint of hard work mastering and sticking with the subject. As graduate students at the University of Chicago, we used to comment about the fact that he as one of the brightest students in the graduate group had spent two years at a junior college and then finished his degree at a very fine liberal arts college, Knox College in the midwest. McGeorge Bundy and others followed different paths through private schools and Yale and Harvard. Joe Sisco was at the top of the graduate student group, not only in international relations but in the Soviet field, where he did a good deal of work and mastered economics as well.

Joe Sisco was associated with the Department of State from 1951 to 1976. I remember a recurrent phrase that was used when people were talking about what we were doing in the U.N. or in the Near East or wherever it might be, whether it was the Rogers plan or strategy in the General Assembly or the Security Council. My friends and his

319

friends, leaders like Joseph Johnson used to say, "If you want to know what we are trying to do, ask Joe Sisco," and that continued through his career. He held high positions in the government beginning as deputy assistant secretary, assistant secretary, and then finally undersecretary for political affairs, a position for which four respected diplomats were considered and every one of them—Phil Habib, Walter Stoessel, David Newsom and Sisco—ultimately fell heir to that position. However, from that group Joe Sisco emerged as undersecretary in 1974.

He has won numerous awards: the Rockefeller Public Service Award, the Civil Service League Award, and many others. He was president and chancellor of American University in Washington. He serves today on five corporate boards in his consulting agency work, and that consulting work is a story in itself. Today he is involved in the leadership of an agency that provides economic, political and social advice to groups that are working in China, the Soviet Union and other countries all over the world. It is most fortunate in this oral history that we can have Joseph Sisco as our final speaker.

QUESTION: Because of the overlap between the Nixon-Ford foreign policies, you may want to say something about the *dramatis personnae* in the two administrations.

MR. SISCO: Let's begin with Henry Kissinger. One of the reasons for Henry Kissinger's success during the Nixon administration is that he had a hands-on style and President Nixon did not. However, while Nixon was not involved in all of the major decisions, he didn't leave decisions to others, with no follow-up. He didn't exhibit the kind of monumental disinterest that we find in the current president (Reagan).

QUESTION: Did you observe moments when, because of his forcefulness and his ability to maneuver, Kissinger was in some danger of losing his own position?

MR. SISCO: He was very careful in front of other people. I never saw Kissinger do or say anything *vis-a-vis* President Nixon in his presence that would have embarrassed him or would have made the President look small. At meetings, with only Henry, the President and myself present, he was very deferential. He avoided any overt manifestation of his dominance over the President. He was very careful in those situations. It tells you something about the man.

QUESTION: Yes, it does. We've had people in the oral history who have ridiculed and joked about Kissinger. How widespread was that?

MR. SISCO: Very widespread. They used that as a vehicle against one another. There was a lot of backbiting in the White House. Kissinger sought to assure himself unimpeded access to the President. Haldeman was trying to be overly protective of Richard Nixon, and there were jealousies between top advisers. There were a number of people with clay feet.

QUESTION: Who were the people most willing to stand up to Kissinger from time to time?

MR. SISCO: On several issues, Hal Sonnenfelt, who was a senior member of the National Security Council (NSC), stood up to Henry. On certain issues, the Special Assistant for National Security Affairs, Winston Lord stood up to him. Ted Elliott of the State Department did, but very indirectly through Secretary of State Williams Rogers. Ted wasn't in a substantive position. Larry Eagleburger, one of the most able people, was a total ally.

QUESTION: What about Bill Hyland?

MR. SISCO: Bill was very able but he was very much a satellite. Bill is soft-spoken. Henry respected Bill, and gave him the opportunity to voice his opinion.
Basically, Henry operated with very few people. He worked with William D. Rogers [not Secretary of State Rogers] on the Latin American side. Rogers was a very good man. He worked with Philip Habib on Vietnam in Paris. Because we were working toward the conclusion of the Helsinki Accords, Walt Stoessel did quite a bit of the work on European affairs. Kissinger considered Walt a good and able man, but he was not one of the inner group. There were about eight or ten people with whom Henry worked, and that was all.

QUESTION: Was Alexander Haig part of that group?

MR. SISCO: Haig was Kissinger's deputy for a period of time in the NSC. Haig was a high level expediter. I don't mean this in a negative sense. Haig was a good organizer, a follow-up man for paperwork. Henry had little respect for Haig, substantively.

COMMENT: I've always been puzzled by the fact that Haig was associated at all with someone like Kissinger.

MR. SISCO: One reason that Henry started the process of utilizing military people on the NSC is because he knew that they were no challenge to him intellectually or otherwise, and that they were used to carrying out orders. They also could give him a sense of Pentagon thinking. They were also good organizational people and were good at monitoring. As far as Henry was concerned, however, he did not rely on them for intellectual input. He relied on Peter Rodman, for example, as his assistant. Rodman is a bright fellow. He is now on Carlucci's National Security Council staff. Larry Eagleburger is a bright fellow. He had enough intellectual cannon powder on any issue, whatever the issue was, and these military men were absolutely no challenge. On the inside, there was a great deal of maneuvering that occurred largely for personal aggrandizement.

COMMENT: Kissinger must have a great deal of personal charisma.

MR. SISCO: Kissinger is a lot of fun. One of his positive attributes is a wonderful self-deprecating sense of humor. We never stopped laughing. Likewise, we never stopped shouting at one another. He'd say to me, "You can't talk to the secretary of state that way," and I'd say to him, "Henry, when you start acting like a secretary of state I won't talk to you that way." It also isn't true that he didn't consult. He wanted advice, and he talked to people. He brought in many people who had considerable knowledge about an issue. Granted, he tended to look down on the young kids at the desk level in State, and not many got a chance to get into his office. There were times when we brought one of them in to give the experience of being in a discussion in the secretary's office. He'd become angry that the group was too large, and he'd break off the meeting, citing that there were too many people. Then he'd call us in for a harsh reprimand, saying, "Damn it, you can't trust them, it's going to leak. I've already told you I don't want these guys in here." That would happen often.

QUESTION: What about people like Roger Morris who wrote the book about his experiences with Kissinger and the NSC? What did he think about people like Morris? He recruited a number of them for the NSC in the beginning, but they eventually left for other positions.

MR. SISCO: Yes, Morris was recruited in the beginning as was Morton Halperin. The dropout phenomenon was related to the whole issue of tapping telephone conversations. Sonnenfeldt was one whose phone was tapped.

COMMENT: He said he was the most tapped person in the NSC.

MR. SISCO: He very well might have been.

COMMENT: He said he was tapped even after he left.

MR. SISCO: Dick Pedersen, who was in the State Department and was our number two man at the UN mission, suffered under similar circumstances. The court case on the tapping has still not been concluded. The suit against Henry is still there.

QUESTION: I'd like to ask a couple more detailed questions about President Ford. Will you describe your first associations with President Ford? What were your impressions of him as a leader? When did you first meet him? Did your initial impressions change in any way?

MR. SISCO: I had known Ford as a congressman and had briefed him on various matters. I felt that as a congressman he was a solid and personable man. He didn't have a deep knowledge of foreign affairs. His interest was primarily domestic and his experience had been primarily legislative. Yet I felt that he was the kind of politician who was open-minded and a man with whom one could talk.

That was my initial image of Ford before he came into the presidency.

After he became President, my interaction with him was twofold. First, I was a participant in a number of National Security Council meetings over which he presided. I was then undersecretary of state and therefore dealt with a variety of topics, from arms control to the Middle East. Second, I traveled with him. We went to the Middle East together where we met with Middle Eastern leaders. I went to China with him where we met with Mao and a number of others. We went to the Philippines and met with Marcos and danced with Immelda.

I've come to the conclusion that the image that many hold of President Ford as an individual of very modest intellect is the wrong image. I sat in at least two NSC meetings where intricate dimensions of the arms control issue were being discussed. He not only asked the right questions, but also had absolutely no trouble whatsoever understanding the complexities of it all. In contrast to President Nixon's style, he reacted to the issues right there in front of us. While he was basically a modest and self-effacing man, he was really a man of considerable self-confidence. He came in saying "I'm going to hold on to Henry and others because I need all the help I can get," and that was the right approach. I also liked Ford personally.

The Ford White House was well run. It wasn't brilliant nor was it bright and particularly impressive. There were few new initiatives but that was more a reflection of the circumstances surrounding his takeover and the fact that we were in the last phases of many policy initiatives than it was any deficiency in either the system or the president himself. He made a good impression on foreign leaders at a number of meetings in which I participated. Therefore, I see Ford as most nearly resembling President Truman in the conduct of his presidency.

COMMENT: Truman was his hero.

MR. SISCO: Yes he was. Ford was a man who would not have backed away from any hard decisions if indeed there were critical decisions to be made. His tenure as president was short and the image of Ford as the man with the trick knee who fell off the steps of the airplane or the man who stumbled in a comment on Poland in the campaign with Jimmy Carter is a very wrong view. What we can say about President Ford is that he was a seasoned and pragmatic politician whose experience was primarily legislative. When we pick a legislator as president, however, we never quite know what we'll get because they haven't had experience in administration.

I think if President Ford had had another four years he would have been a solid president, a stable president, a reliable president, a predictable president, but not necessarily a brilliant president. He made no bones about being an intellectual giant. He was not a huge conceptual-framework thinker of the stature of Nixon, but he was open-minded about continuing the detente with the Soviet Union. He was willing to focus seriously on arms control and was not unwilling to put a damper on the Pentagon. I've got to say my pulsations about Ford are quite positive.

COMMENT: We've hosted many of the people on his staff, and they bring up a common point. I wonder if you observed it from the standpoint of its impact on foreign policy. They say that one of the tragic aspects of the Ford administration was the clash between the Ford loyalists, people who had known, worked with and admired him in the Congress—some of whom he brought into the White House—and the carry-overs, the people from the Nixon administration.

One argument is that Ford allowed too much infighting to take place. It has been noted that he was a very fine person but had great difficulty knocking heads and that was one of the major problems of the Ford administration.

MR. SISCO: Yes, much of that went on, and we all knew that. It really didn't manifest itself, however, in the narrow frame of the issues about which I'm talking. When Henry Kissinger was there, he was the field general in foreign policy and related issues. Late under Nixon Haig had become *de facto* president, and he did a remarkably good job during that transition period. Therefore, I forever am perplexed by how obtusely he handled his position as secretary of state. He was unable to fathom that he was in a different environment. Haig must be given due credit, however, for his actions in that very, very difficult transition period. One could see that he knew where the power was and how to put it together. So he played a very useful role.

There were a variety of people who had been working with Ford, and these loyalists helped Ford in that immediate political transition. The focus was not specifically on foreign policy. Instead, they simply concentrated on taking over from Nixon. The loyalists comprised the inner group on which he relied. From the outset, he had to integrate the whole organization and run the government. When he shifted from the Executive Building to the White House there were frictions between the staffs. There was jealousy of Kissinger. Haig, although seen as having played a useful role, eventually had to step aside and allow others to take over. That was essentially the attitude. There was a tremendous amount of backbiting, particularly in that early period. Happily, it wasn't reflected in most of the substantive issues in which I was involved. We reached a midpoint between the two extremes in the NSC meetings. These meetings were not the kind of superficial show that Johnson often held, and they didn't follow the restricted approach of Nixon. They were somewhere in between. Inevitable backbiting between two staffs took place, but I saw no serious adverse impact on the pursuit of American foreign policy.

QUESTION: Would you have seen evidence of it, however, if it had affected domestic and not foreign policy?

MR. SISCO: I worked on both sides, I would have had to. If there is anything I learned from that period it was that you really had to touch base with the power leaders, because one of the weaknesses in successive White House organizations has been that the domestic side doesn't talk to the foreign policy side and vice versa. Remember, that Kissinger believed in linkage between foreign policy issues, but one of the problems has been that over the years, we've never had sufficient linkage between the external and the internal issues.

QUESTION: How would you describe the relationship between Ford and Kissinger?

MR. SISCO: Their relationship was good. Ford relied heavily on Henry. He was secure enough and modest enough to ignore the fact that his personality was being dwarfed by Henry's huge personality. That didn't seem to bother him.

I had the impression that Henry acted reliably. He did a good job throughout the transition. It was a blow to him when Ford decided that he couldn't wear the two hats, but Henry had become a liability with the Congress over the many Vietnam issues. The foreign policy of the administration was also beginning to disintegrate. Ford had to put his own stamp on foreign policy. He was already carrying the political liability of the previous Nixon administration from which he couldn't be totally divorced.

QUESTION: Did Kissinger communicate with Ford in the same way that he did with Nixon? One of the things historians are puzzled about is that unhappy reference Ford made about Poland during the second presidential debate with Jimmy Carter.

One of the stories has it that Kissinger briefed him, but that he did it quickly and that Ford didn't grasp the whole analysis Kissinger was trying to convey.

MR. SISCO: That could very well have been the case, I don't know. Ford was not inclined toward perceiving a lot of the complexities of foreign policy issues, and it could very well be that there was a vacuum. I have no way of knowing that. Those who are looking for a scapegoat on this would tend to blame Henry. I think that's probably a bum rap. That would be my own judgment, but I don't actually know.

QUESTION: What about the kinds of problems that occurred with regard to detente? Effectively, the word was expunged from the vocabulary. Was there anything that Ford or Kissinger could have done to retain the principle, or had the reaction in Congress gone too far politically, and had Reagan's attacks from the right wing led to such uneasiness that there was no way they could have supported or defended the earlier policy?

MR. SISCO: Henry was very reluctant to see the word detente expunged from the administration's vocabulary because he felt that he was detente's architect. Moreover, he held the view that it was, after all, the Nixon-Ford administration and that it was unwise to reverse gears. For Kissinger, continuity is an important objective reality of American foreign policy, as indeed it is. He gave all the good reasons one could give for maintaining the concept of detente.

On the other hand, the speech writers in the White House, and the people who were looking at it from the point of view of getting Ford elected, had recognized that detente had become a dirty word. It had become political and negative and, therefore, they tended to eliminate the word or to phrase it in such a way that the whole concept was wrapped up in campaign ambiguity. Moreover, it was generally recognized that there was no new push that could warrant further serious progress with the Soviet Union. Above all, what had happened was that Henry's support on the Hill had eroded. No matter where the President went on the Hill, he was told about the massive mistrust of Kissinger.

QUESTION: Is Kissinger resilient enough that when the criticism becomes as intense as it did for him, as it did for Dean Rusk or for Dean Acheson, he can handle it in the way they did, or does he handle it differently?

MR. SISCO: Dean Acheson was a model of decorum— almost painfully controlled; he took criticism and persevered. Rarely have I seen Dean Rusk fly off the handle in a very serious way. Henry would allow his temper to blow up from time to time. He was emotional. He saw in front of his very eyes the dismantling of much that he and Nixon had put together. Moreover, Henry did not have a high regard for Ford's intellect.

QUESTION: Did he say that to some of you?

MR. SISCO: I can't give you a direct quote but I know that he felt it. He felt Ford was a decent man, but he didn't give him very high grades intellectually. That was very clear.

QUESTION: What happened to Kissinger's leadership in the

State Department when his colleagues and subordinates were forced to endure his daily emotional outbursts?

MR. SISCO: He worked with a very small group; therefore, it was up to this small group to try to bring in the rest of the Department to the extent that they could be brought in. There were very definite limits on what could be done in this regard.

The obverse of this is that people in the Department saw Henry Kissinger come in the aftermath of all this preponderance of executive leadership and saw in him a possible vehicle for a reassertion of departmental responsibilities and power. That, of course, didn't happen. In the last phases of the administration he was forced to deal with things on an issue-by-issue or more tactical basis. These efforts were largely designed to hold operations together rather than to embark in new directions.

QUESTION: You have described the relationship between Dean Rusk and George Ball as being virtually unique. How would you describe your relationship with Kissinger during the period when you were undersecretary?

MR. SISCO: I was not his alter ego. He relied as heavily on Larry Eagleburger as any officer in the Department. But he was careful in assuring free access to others including me.

QUESTION: Is there any lesson to be drawn from Kissinger's experience that will stand up in other administrations? Was Kissinger's role in which he was the premiere intellectual, the conceptualizer, the paramount strategist best employed as NSC adviser? Did that role begin to become a liability when he had to speak as the responsible constitutional officer and secretary of state, or is that interpretation a distortion? Were there too many other variables?

MR. SISCO: I think that's a distortion. I think any perceived difference occurred because of a contrast between the accomplishments of the earlier part of the Nixon administration, prior to the adversities of the later phases of the Vietnam War, and the political fallout that resulted from the later period.

The lessons I draw are all relatively positive. It is very important to have an NSC adviser who thinks conceptually and strategically, because it is at that coordinating point that all of the arguments, resources, and intelligence assessments have to be put together and synthesized and, on that basis, one has to make a recommendation. This dimension, however, is less important in a secretary of state. There isn't any question that a department such as the State Department can plan strategy, although if you read Kissinger's two books he would say that that is an impossibility, that any bureaucracy is much more interested in its own self-perpetuation and is more concerned with the tactical than the strategic aspect. That assessment is true in the sense that the department has to address issues on a day-to-day basis of building peace. Therefore, the majority of the decisions are tactical decisions. Objectives, on the other hand, are created within the broad framework of a strategic approach.

Henry would argue that strategic thinking can't be done any place other than in the NSC. I don't accept this. I accept that it can be done effectively at the NSC level, where all resources are brought into focus, despite the fact that the State Department might have a different view than the Defense Department. Each department can and must do its own strategic planning.

The job of a secretary of state is more tactical. It involves public presentation. It is diplomatic representation. It is the implementation of the broad strategic goals of the administration on a day-to-day basis. It is day-by-day negotiations. The secretary of state is at a great disadvantage when compared with the NSC adviser. He does have to appear before Congress and defend the policy in numerous Hill appearances. The NSC assistant focuses on briefing the president, advising him on issues, and making recommendations based for the most part, on documents that have been produced by various departments. He has a big task of coordinating, facilitating, monitoring, and of pulling various Departmental views together.

If we have someone who can synthesize strategy like Kissinger, we are very fortunate. The propensity is, however, to neglect that role and become so heavily enmeshed in the day-to-day implementation and operational aspects of strategy that it defeats the whole purpose of the system. That was Henry Kissinger's vulnerability. The NSC duplicated State in a number of activities. It got into the day-by-day diplomatic process. There was competition between the NSC adviser and the secretary of state. That's the way it really worked, or didn't work.

I think it would have been a much easier relationship if Henry had cooperated more fully with Bill Rogers and if there had been much greater sensitivity about the personal relationship. Henry admits this in his book. He had a tremendous substantive background. He also had good people around him and he had the confidence of the President—all the things that anybody would possibly want in that particular job. As far as the NSC system is concerned, we need someone who is knowledgeable and someone who will coordinate. We need someone who will ensure that the information goes through to the President and who recognizes that it is the secretary of state who is the principal adviser and the principal voice. Above all, we need someone who does not want to use that job as a platform for becoming secretary of state.

QUESTION: It is often said that leaders go under when their greatest strength becomes their greatest weakness. Reagan's supposed great strengths are as a communicator and as a hands-off administrator; yet in his November 1986 press conference on the Iran-Contra issue, he couldn't say anything about the Israelis or about what he did, and the public discovered that he had been practicing such a hands off policy that he may not have known what was happening.

It was sometimes said of Ford that he trusted Kissinger too much, that he therefore allowed Kissinger to be a lightning rod and that he became the prime target for attack. Politically that might have been right, but it backfired, and it seems that that hurt him in the end.

MR. SISCO: That's a valid judgment. Ford was very deferential to Henry. He was in awe of Kissinger's breadth and knowledge. I saw signs of that. This is where some of the friction emanated.

Ford's immediate staff tended to see Henry as someone who was bigger than life and as someone who dwarfed the President as a personality. Secondly, they saw Henry as a self-serving man. They also saw him as a political liability and as a residue of Richard Nixon. The inner group of private advisers resented Henry's relationship with Ford.

When President Ford said publicly, "I need Henry," he meant
it.   He was a modest man reflecting his own feeling of
shortcomings.

QUESTION: Is it possible to outline in broad terms some of
Ford's strengths and weaknesses?

MR. SISCO: Ford's strengths are integrity, decency, and a
commitment to the country and to its institutions.   He left
us with the feeling that the country may not have been in
the hands of a brilliant man, but that the country was in
good, reliable, and stable hands.   He possessed the strength
of the experienced legislator, the strength that flowed from
ninety-eight percent of the members of Congress saying, "I
like Jerry Ford, I've worked with him, and I find him a
decent and honest man."   Ford had credibility.   He
communicated an almost indescribable element—confidence.
We felt that this man would not do anything that was shady
or dishonest.   In other words, he possessed the virtues of
middle America, the virtues of how America wants to see
and likes to see itself in its true moral dimensions.

I hesitate to use the term weakness, because I don't
believe that Ford had any fundamental weaknesses as I
define weaknesses.   Certainly, there were limitations.   Even
though he was knowledgeable, he was limited in his
background in foreign affairs.   He had the inherent
limitations of a man who never expected to become
president and yet was thrust into the most awesome of
responsibilities.   He was there too short a time to make a
real mark.   He also had great modesty, which in my
judgment is both a strength as well as a possible limitation.
He was solid.   We will never know what kind of a President
he would have made and where we would be if it had been
four years of Gerald Ford as opposed to Jimmy Carter.
That would be a very interesting scenario to ponder and
discuss.

FORD, FOREIGN POLICY AND
THE BUREAUCRACY

MICHAEL RAOUL-DUVAL

NARRATOR: Michael Duval is managing director of the First Boston Corporation, an international investment bank with headquarters in New York. He is responsible, with the firm's executive and management committee, for policy for the commercial real estate business of First Boston. Both the general counsel and the governmental affairs staff of First Boston report to him. Michael is a graduate of Georgetown University whose Jesuit faculty he describes as his first mentor. His second mentor was the United States Marine Corps. He has said both brought something into his life that he has never outgrown and that remains essential in his development. He has a University of California law degree. He joined the Department of Transportation as an attorney in 1967, came into the Nixon White House in 1970, became associate director of the Domestic Council in 1972, and served in that capacity until 1974. He became special counsel to President Ford in 1974 and continued in that position until 1977, when he was appointed vice president for industrial products activities and later senior vice president of Mead Company.

MR. DUVAL: Thank you, Ken. I'm somewhat intimidated by that introduction. I didn't think anybody could remember that much about someone other than themselves. I'm having a hard time now remembering all that about me. I commend you for it. As you said, I think back and I guess maybe there are four great educational experiences I've had in my lifetime: the Jesuits, the Marine Corps, Haldeman, and Rumsfeld; and they were all about the same!

I spent seven years in the White House, about half that time in the West Wing, and the balance in the Executive Office Building. That's a long time. I can sort of understand what Sakharov and others have gone through in their lives—that's a long time to be in such a position. Fortunately, I was young and single, and I think that those are the two most important factors to surviving that long in the White House, particularly at the time when I was there. At least for a portion of that time it was literally open warfare, and the only good news was that you knew if you got the grenade out of the foxhole it would hit an enemy, no matter what direction you threw it in.

In fact, I can remember going to work when they surrounded the White House with buses. It was during the Vietnam riots. They would take the old D.C. transit buses (they finally found some good use for them) and parked them all around the White House, bumper to bumper. That sort of became the outer wall and then the Secret Service and the White House police were the inner wall. It was an interesting way to go to work each morning.

I have discussed elsewhere my impressions of the Nixon presidency. The transition from Nixon to Ford was filled with pathos including Ford's assuming the office. At eleven o'clock, I walked back through the same passage on my way to the East Room for the swearing in of Gerald Ford and the delivery of the famous "Confirm me with Your Prayers" speech. The walls were completely bare of any photographs. Once again, on my way back after the speech, the Ford pictures had already been put up in the West Wing.

My involvement with Ford began instantly because he was directly involved in energy issues. I thus had a first hand view of his efforts to restore the moral authority of the office. That was his greatest legacy. The process was already beginning. The fact that Ford made it easy for the American people to put Watergate behind them was a measure of his integrity and character.

The problems he faced were substantial. Number one, we were in the last days of losing, for the first time in our nation's history, a war. The policy decisions we made in dealing with the Soviets, with the Chinese and with others were compromised by our failure in Vietnam. Allies such as Iran, South Korea, and others wondered if they could trust the United States. Iran found out the answer and South Korea may yet. The fact is that that was the major foreign policy issue: the balancing act between Vietnam and our other foreign policy goals.

There were two domestic issues, one really domestic-international. We were in the worst recession in the nation's history at the time and an energy crisis; the result of the formation of OPEC was deadly. Ford picked that as the issue to attack first. His first State of the Union message, delivered in January of 1975, was devoted exclusively to energy. I was the Domestic Council guy on energy, the only person in the White House that Ford could rely on concerning that issue. He had some very strong staff people on energy, but they had their respective constituencies. I spent hours with Ford, very often one-to-one, and I saw a man who came to office with no idea and no expectation that he'd be in that role. It was extraordinary to see how he adapted to it. Some incidents were very amusing and some were very sad.

I remember that I was in the Oval Office with Ford the first time his telephone rang. We were both sitting next to the fireplace, and he'd obviously never gotten a phone call there before. This was the Saturday after he was sworn in, and I'd never been in the Oval Office when the phone rang. When it did he looked at me, and I looked at him. He said, "Mike, will you answer it?" because I was closer to the desk. "Will you answer it for me?" and I said, "I don't know if I'm supposed to do that, but there is a phone right next to you." I still don't know if I should have said that, but he picked it up. . . . "Yes, dear. Yes, dear," and then he says, "Just a minute, dear." He put his hand over the receiver and said, "Mike, Betty wants to go down with come congressman to so and so. Can she take an Air Force plane?" and I said, "Yes sir." I thought I'd better be decisive and the President said, "Betty, Mike says you can." I'm sure she had no idea who Mike was. "Mike says you can go ahead and take the plane and take the congressman with you." So after the meeting I ran out of the office. Haig was still around. Rumsfeld hadn't come in yet. I ran into Haig's office and said, "Al, I just authorized the wife of the President of the United States to take an Air Force plane. I told the President that," I said, "and if

I'm wrong, take it out of my salary, but you are not going back in there and overrule me." Apparently it was all right!

There are some other Ford anecdotes which I can get into if you want. His decisions on energy, of course, were embodied in the State of the Union message. There is a lot that went into that and a lot about how that affected his style, but it tells you something about his style of decision-making.

The next crisis was the emergence of the abuses that had occurred in the foreign intelligence agencies (CIA, NSA, etc.). There were the Church and Pike committee hearings and all that happened in the aftermath of Watergate. They escalated very quickly into a witch-hunt and into a serious overreaction on the part of the Congress. I'm not saying that there were not abuses, but there was a serious problem in the way Congress approached it. As a result of coming in the aftermath of Watergate, and because of the nature of that reaction, we very nearly lost the capacity as a nation for foreign intelligence. Ford asked me, at the suggestion of Don Rumsfeld and Jack Marsh, to take over the management of that problem, both in terms of containing the congressional investigations and dealing with the question of executive privilege. Then we sorted out what the function of the intelligence agencies should be. For the first time since the late 1940s there was a broad look at how we should conduct foreign intelligence. I spend six months and one hundred percent of my time doing that and prepared a major decision book for the President. He issued an omnibus executive order that resulted in the first comprehensive codification, if you will, of the ground rules for intelligence, and it still exists. It has been revised a couple of times, but it is the basis for the command and control structure of the intelligence agencies.

I might add that while I was in the process of doing that, and as Hartmann put in his book with glee (I assumed he heard it from Jack Marsh and others), a not exactly shrinking violet vice president of the United States and former governor of New York, and a not exactly shrinking violet secretary of state and former national security adviser, waltzed in together into the Oval Office with the purpose of asking the President of the United States to fire me, Mike Duval. This may have been the high point of my career, and maybe the high point of my life. Fortunately, the President stood up for me at the urging, I think, of Jack Marsh and rebuffed them.

Once the intelligence crisis was over, I turned my attention to the question of President Ford's reelection and at Dick Cheney's request sat down with some colleagues in the White House, Foster Chanick and Jerry Jones particularly, and Bob Teeter from the outside, and in absolute secrecy we wrote a strategy memorandum of two hundred pages that detailed what Ford should do in order to get elected. It was a very critical assessment of Ford—critical in the sense of constructive criticism, but honest. In that memo we clearly said to the President, in straight English, that "your most serious problem is that the American people think you are dumb. Here's why and here is what we think is the reality; and here are the steps you can take." That was a no-punches-pulled memorandum. When we wrote it in July of 1976, he was twenty-five to thirty points behind Carter in the polls, and on election day he lost by about three-quarters of a percentage point. The most significant factor in his defeat was simply something we ended up not being able to do anything about—the seven percent of the vote that was centered strictly on one issue, the Nixon pardon.

Let me wrap it up by saying that I worked with the Ford-Carter transition, one of the most unpleasant jobs I had while working for Ford. A week before the January 20th event, I walked into the Oval Office and said to the President, "I quit," and he said, "You can't do that, Mike, you've got to wait until next week." I said, "Mr. President, for the first time since we've worked together I'm disobeying an order and I'm leaving in half an hour to fly to the Bahamas."

QUESTION: You spoke briefly about President Ford's energy plan that was outlined in his 1975 State of the Union Address. What do you think should have happened so we wouldn't face the lack-of-assets situations that we face now?

MR. DUVAL: There is a simple answer to that question which can be very misleading to people who do not understand the economics of energy. I give this simple answer knowing the risk that I can be misinterpreted, but I don't want to get into a long discussion of it. I don't think it is what you all want to talk about.

The energy crisis was not caused by running out of oil or by any shortage of a natural resource. The cause of the energy problem was that for several decades United States politicians, through price controls on gas, subsidization of nuclear energy, the oil import policy, and control through the Texas Railroad Commission of oil prices in the United States, kept the price of energy artificially low in order to confer what they thought was a benefit on their constituencies. That resulted in the economy, otherwise free, substituting energy in place of labor and in place of capital, creating a huge demand for energy, and reducing the supply of available oil. OPEC took advantage of that at a time when they had the power to do so.

The solution, the clear solution in 1974, 1975, 1976, and today, was and is to take the government controls off, provide some transitional help for those people who would be hurt by it, and to put a floor on the price of energy, not a ceiling. Through a mechanism of import quotas or tariffs, you could make sure that those monopolists who at that time had control of energy could not drop the price below a certain threshold. All of that was the essence of the Ford plan that was presented to Congress in 1975, and no one in Congress even had the guts to introduce it. Not one Republican in the House or the Senate would introduce it. Not very many of them understood it, but none of them worked for it because what everybody was yelling about was lower energy prices and ceilings, when the problem was there wasn't a floor. That was the right answer then; it's the right answer now.

QUESTION: Did Ford give any consideration to the effect on his reelection of his pardon of Nixon?

MR. DUVAL: There is only one person, with the possible exception of Mrs. Ford, who is qualified to venture an answer to that question, and that's Jack Marsh.

I will tell you what Jack and the President have told me, together and separately over time, and that is that Ford did not see himself as really having an alternative. If he had not pardoned Nixon there would have been no chance whatsoever for him to restore the presidency to its previous dignity and proper function of governing the nation and getting on with the business of the country, dealing with the energy problem, dealing with the recession, and dealing with Vietnam. The nation would have continued in its trauma with every state prosecutor and every federal prosecutor and every member or committee of Congress continuing to go after the carcass. As long as that process was continuing, whether it took a year or five years, the business of the government at least for the Ford presidency could never get back to doing what it should be doing. Ford said, "If there is one thing I have to do it is to eliminate that burden." Short of Nixon's death or a pardon, there was nothing that Ford could do to stop it, put it behind him, and go forward. So he felt he had to pardon Nixon.

Was it in his political interest to do that? Yes, don't kid yourself. He and others have made the case that it wasn't in his political interest to do that because then everybody would blame him for it, and therefore what he did was an unselfish act that was against his political interests. The reality is if he hadn't done it, we would have been in the middle of a Nixon trial during the election and the Republicans would not have gotten ten percent of the vote, much less the forty-nine percent they did get. So it probably was in his political interest to do so, but not surprisingly, it was the single thing that denied him the presidency. It was just the reality of how he got there and who his predecessor was, not so much the pardon itself.

QUESTION: Would you like to comment on why you decided to leave so abruptly and not stay the final week into the Carter transition?

MR. DUVAL: Yes, I finally got a reservation to go to the sun! No, I was tired. I was terribly tired, and I had not had a chance to think about what I was going to do. I was essentially out of a job. I didn't have any money, so I wanted to get out and start looking for work. But there was also an emotional aspect, after having gone through the Nixon resignation and the Ford presidency and all of the emotion involved in the 1976 election and the loss, I had no stomach for sticking around for the inauguration. I didn't much like the Carter people, so I just decided to get out.

QUESTION: I've often wondered about what sort of person should be chosen for the office of the president. Should it be a man who has been a governor of a state or a man who has been in the Congress, either as a senator or as a congressman? As I understand it, the chance of being elected President from the House is almost nil—they have almost all come from the Senate.

MR. DUVAL: Don't tell Jack Kemp that.

QUESTION: From your experience, is there any advantage of a man coming in who has had no connection whatsoever with government?

MR. DUVAL: I think there are two ways to try to get a handle on that question. I think the quality of leadership matters a great deal as does the wisdom of the leadership. I don't think it has mattered too much, except during periods of war, over the last fifty years because the United States was so powerful relative to any other nation—economically or militarily—that the margin for error was enormous. A president couldn't mess things up to the point where real peace was threatened or the quality of life was threatened. You can now. You really can.

The quintessential example of experience leading to the chief executive slot is West Germany, for when Helmut Schmidt ultimately became Chancellor, he had been defense minister, finance minister, foreign minister, and I think a member of the Assembly. You see the same thing happening in France.

NARRATOR: And Britain.

MR. DUVAL: Britain, yes, but I think a little bit less, at least in terms of a ministerial portfolio, but certainly in terms of leadership there is no question.

I don't know that Schmidt versus Reagan, for example, proves you get a better leader. Schmidt sounds better. He is very learned and all that, but as for the policies and directions that he took for West Germany, I'm not sure that what his experience counted for was all that important.

I think the single most important quality for the President of the United States that I learned about in watching Ford and Nixon closely, and which is reinforced by what Carter lacked and doubly reinforced by what I see in Reagan, is that inner tranquility that comes from knowing what you are good at and knowing what you are not good at, and being comfortable with both. Ford had it and Reagan had it; Nixon did not have it (but may now) and Carter did not have it. If I may offer a simple definition it's the importance of that inner sense, that gyroscope that no matter how many times you spin that person around or walk him around he suddenly comes back on track and keeps going. It is being at peace with yourself, liking yourself, and being comfortable with yourself. You get there by experience and by doing things. I think that is part of it, but I wouldn't give much credit to going through the House of Representatives or the Senate *versus* being the chief executive of a state. I don't think it matters too much.

NARRATOR: One final question. In these oral histories, we've asked everybody how do you think history will judge your president?

MR. DUVAL: I think the Ford presidency will be a winner, if in fact history does judge it. The mistake that history is likely to make is to treat the Ford presidency as a footnote. I think that would be a mistake because he was successful at defining some of the qualities we most need in that office.

NARRATOR: We thank you for a most illuminating discussion.

FORD AND THE
SONNENFELDT DOCTRINE

HELMUT SONNENFELDT

NARRATOR: We're pleased to welcome you to a Forum with Helmut Sonnenfeldt, one of the country's most experienced authorities on foreign policy. He began serving in the Department of State in 1952 and concluded his work there in 1977. During the mid- and late 1960s, he was director of the Office of Research and Analysis for the U.S.S.R. and Eastern Europe. He left the Department to serve as a senior member of the National Security Council staff from 1969 to 1974, and returned in 1974 to serve as counselor of the Department of State until 1977. He is currently a guest scholar at the Brookings Institution. His mastery of the Soviet East European area has not only earned him recognition among specialists in the field, but he is also the author of the Sonnenfeldt Doctrine.

We're especially pleased to have him with us to discuss a single issue in the Ford presidency and foreign policy which is identified with his name, the Sonnenfeldt Doctrine.

QUESTION: Was it a good thing or a bad thing that the Sonnenfeldt Doctrine was vented publicly? Was that idea an idea that would have been better to keep within the government?

MR. SONNENFELDT: Well, the Sonnenfeldt Doctrine was really nothing new. It was a free, rather unstructured discussion at a chiefs of mission meeting about our interests in Eastern Europe and how to go about pursuing and dealing with them. This wasn't essentially different from what government policy had been all along. What went wrong was that the very discursive seminar-style conversation was written down very elegantly by a very gifted State Department foreign service officer long after the event. He took several people's notes and condensed them into a very elegant *précis* which tightened up some things that had been loose and had some catchy phrases in it that should have been left out and left out some other catchy phrases that should have been there. This was then sent out to the field in a very contentious political period, and somebody inside the government happened to see this telegram and find in it three or four sentences that he thought could be used to damage Kissinger. He peddled it to a couple of journalists who were equally interested in doing that. That's what really created the furor.

There wasn't any great mystery or secrecy about American policy toward Eastern Europe. Nor was there any dirty secret about the fact that we wished the East Europeans would be freer and more autonomous than they were, but that there was not much we could do about it at acceptable risk. What pained me about the episode was not the notoriety it brought me, or even that it caused President Ford some grief in the second debate with Carter. What pained me about it particularly was that it caused so much pain and bad blood in communities in this country which have East European roots and ancestries. Moreover, in those parts of Eastern Europe where we had actually made a little bit of headway in opening some room for maneuvers during Nixon's and Ford's visits to Poland, Rumania and Yugoslavia, there was a sense that they had been betrayed, that we really had toyed with them and that we didn't give a damn. I have to add that our ubiquitous friends in the KGB picked this up very quickly and used it in Eastern Europe to try to disorient and demoralize people who had placed reliance on relations with the United States. Those aspects of it pained me much more than anything I said in regard to the policy, which I think to this day remains essentially valid, as indicated in Secretary of State Shultz's current travels in Eastern Europe where he's essentially saying and doing the same thing, i.e., we do what we can to increase independence.

QUESTION:　　You raised the possibility of an organic relationship between Eastern Europe and the Soviet Union. I don't know whether you used the word but if you used it obviously the word organic means something that is capable of growing together.

MR. SONNENFELDT: The whole thing started because the lead that appeared in an Evans and Novak column said that a close adviser of Secretary of State Kissinger recently advocated permanent organic union between the countries of Eastern Europe and the Soviet Union in order to prevent the kinds of instabilities that might lead to World War III. They manufactured a phrase.　The term "organic relationship" did appear in the telegram and it was in fact a term that I used, but in the context in which I used it, it was very clear.

I explained at great length in a congressional hearing that I was not using the term "organic" in the Hegelian sense but was using it in the dictionary sense, namely "as between living organisms."　That is to say, it was a relationship that does not constantly involve the use of force to prevent a natural evolution. That was in the flow of words what that phrase meant. It had nothing to do with the term organic as meaning "part of a whole" but rather organic as a relationship between living organisms, as the dictionary says in meaning number two. But I promised the Congress at the time that because of the confusion of the meaning, and because of this special sensitivity in Eastern Europe to the word organic, and because of its use among Hegelians, I would not use that term again to make the same point.

I would make the same substantive point today but I wouldn't use the word organic because it has become a code word for exactly the opposite of what I was advocating and talking about, namely that our goal should be to help bring about natural relationships in Eastern Europe which would not be repeatedly subject to Soviet repression and force.

VII.

HISTORY'S JUDGMENT

A PRESIDENT WHO BROUGHT HEALING

LOU CANNON

NARRATOR: On behalf of the Miller Center for Public Affairs, I am pleased to welcome you to a Forum on the Ford presidency with Lou Cannon of the *Washington Post*.

Charles McDowell said recently that perhaps columnists had reached the point of diminishing returns because more and more they seem to be answering one another rather than addressing the subject. Lou Cannon is a notable exception to that trend. He best described the purpose of his columns in a reaction to a review. In a review of *Ronnie and Jessie*, Lou Cannon's book on Ronald Reagan and Jessie Unruh, one reviewer had referred to the deeper contest that underlies all political competition. Cannon responded, "It is to this contest that my interest is addressed. I care a good deal, or I think I do, about our political system, and my intention is to write books that contribute to the understanding of that system and those who inhabit it." That's an objective that has inspired his writings from the days when he covered Ronald Reagan and the State Capitol in California for the *San Jose Mercury-News* to his current writings on the President, Ronald Reagan. More than he knows, those of us who follow the presidency and politics in general draw upon his writings as a source of understanding of the political system.

Perhaps this can be explained by the fact that his career was broader than that of most writers. He was a truck driver for two years after college; he wrote for three smaller papers in the first three years of his career; he was

349

a copy editor before becoming bureau chief in Sacramento for the San Jose paper.

There is a thrust in his writings that political scientists could well do themselves proud in imitating to try to understand the nature and the functioning of the political system. It is an honor for the Miller Center and quite appropriate in this place that we listen to and discuss with Lou Cannon the topic, "A President Who Brought Healing."

QUESTION: It is often said that Gerald Ford was a nice guy. Some of you criticize him for being clumsy but he was an all-American football player. The main criticism heard in these sessions has been that his administration suffered from a split in the White House staff. He couldn't bring himself to fire anybody and had difficulty disciplining a warring staff. With that in mind, how would you characterize his political leadership and presidency?

MR. CANNON: I have a picture on the wall at home taken at the first Ford news conference soon after he became President. There was a huge crowd around him in the picture and I was sitting next to Ford talking. That kind of picture was not an accident. Ford was very much aware of what was going on, and he deliberately stayed after his first news conference and after subsequent ones to show people a different image. Here was a president who was trusted again; here was a president who was not afraid to take questions; here was a president who had respect for the people who covered the White House.

I often think that history will be very kind to Gerald Ford. I think Ford accomplished something. When Ford took office, a number of distinguished people were writing about how long it would take to heal the torn fabric of the American political system and how difficult it would be. However, within a very, very short time everything improved quickly and seemingly without effort. We returned to a condition of equilibrium because Ford was such a trusting and good person that people gave up the sackcloth and ashes. However, he got almost no credit for having accomplished that. In fact, he accomplished it all in spite of the things that overexposed him and subsequently hurt him.

Ford made one monumental miscalculation, the presidential pardon. Anybody who knows Gerald Ford knows that's exactly the kind of miscalculation that Ford would make because Ford epitomizes the phrase "trusting to a fault." He forgives. To have a person as unforgiving as Nixon select Ford was no small feat. You remember that Ford was not Nixon's first choice. Connally was Nixon's first choice. That sounds much more right, much more comfortable. Connally is an operator. But Nixon needed someone he could get through to Congress because of Agnew. I think Ford had a lot of leadership ability, but it was something of an accident that he was selected.

My lead after the Ford loss was that "They say that close only counts in horseshoes and hand grenades." I then proceeded to dispute that idea. I have great affection for Ford. I think he also picked some very good people. He had the disability of not being president in his own right. I've had discussions with a lot of his people about this, and I think Ford realized what he was up against. He understood the political system so well that he knew the virtue of "throw the rascals out," which works in our system. It was almost inevitable that after a Republican president had done what Nixon had that the country was going to elect a Democrat. Not until the heat of battle in 1976 did Ford think he had much of a chance to win.

It was as though Ford was a caretaker. He came in to accomplish something and did that very well, but there was a sense of impermanence. I also think that what is in the top person's head conveys itself to the people remarkably well. I think that is why Reagan transcends a narrow appeal and says things that give people a sense of his assuredness. I think they had some sort of sense of that with Ford but there was a greater perception that Ford was on stage to perform a particular act.

Ford, like the rest of us, was surprised at the speed with which this Watergate drama moved. It was like going to an opera with five acts when all of a sudden the king quits in the middle of the third act. Ford really wasn't prepared in terms of staff or procedural knowledge. The congressional staff he brought with him was not terribly good for the White House even though it had been fine for the Congress. He had a Nixon holdover staff, and he had a new staff that was kind of a shadow staff, waiting to be born. The people who had been there and had worked for Nixon and remained, were mostly people who had not been involved with Watergate. Most of them never knew anything about it and felt, with some justice, that they kept the government going and did good things while Watergate was unfolding. The congressional people were people who had the sort of perspective you tend to get in Congress, which is that they could do anything. Of course, they usually can't. They can usually do what they are used to doing but not anything more. Ford also had some other very sharp people. If he had been elected the second time, he would have selected Dick Cheney as his chief of staff. Cheney underwent on-the-job-training under Rumsfeld and became one of the ablest of presidential chiefs of staff.

In one sense, the Ford presidency is always identified with an asterisk. It can't be compared to anything else. That's both it's value and it's defect. If Ford had been elected, my guess is that he would have had a very good staff. He would have had many of the same people now in government, but they wouldn't have been apologizing for Nixon antecedents. They would have been Ford's people. He probably wouldn't have had Kissinger. I don't think Kissinger would have stuck around anyway. I think that probably was good. I do think that Ford did suffer from being a creature of Congress who thought that you could roundtable everything. Nixon didn't want to meet with anybody; Ford would have met with the world if it would have solved the problem. You sometimes got the feeling that a great mush was coming out of that place.

I remember the Whip Inflation Now (WIN) campaign, with the attendant WIN buttons. What is interesting about that is that a lot of people in the Ford White House thought it was idiotic before they did it. Any White House, because it's hierarchical, tends to think that whatever is going to be done—invade Nicaragua, burn down the University of Virginia, whatever they want to do—is terrific and everybody will give you good reasons for doing it. But in the Ford White House a lot of people gave him reasons why WIN shouldn't have been done. But he didn't quite know how to be an executive and resolve those things.

He could take a lot of criticism very well. His staff prepared a mock up of a picture of Ford saying, in a classified ad, "I got my job through *The Washington Post.*" Ben Bradlee wanted me to get Ford to sign it. Ford cheerfully signed it. He had this absolutely wonderful sense of himself. He balanced a seriousness of purpose with not taking himself too seriously. He was very conscious that he had not been elected. He was extraordinarily conscious of the constitutional process. He knew he was in there on a pass, and it hobbled him in ways that it shouldn't have. He was not decisive. I thought that he was indecisive, not for reasons of his character, but because of the circumstances. It was probably good for my own career that he got out of the White House, but I was sorry.

I thought the Carter election was interesting and as people they are both highly moral. You felt the country was going to be okay no matter who was elected. I certainly did. But I regretted that Ford didn't win only because I wanted to see what he could do. I was just curious to see how he would do with his own mandate. Of course, the Carter presidency turned out to be very interesting in its own right.

COMMENT: I'd like to make a point partly for the record and partly for other presidents and see if you agree with it. You were saying that Ford doesn't get credit for the healing work that he did. I thought that when Jimmy Carter was elected and was inaugurated, he turned to Ford in the first sentence of his inaugural address and thanked him for healing the wounds of the nation.

MR. CANNON: That's true. I absolutely agree with that. I meant he didn't get credit in a sense that Joe Dimaggio never really got credit for the way he fielded a fly ball. He did it so easily and naturally that people didn't realize how far he ran for it. I wasn't saying that because the press didn't write it or because his opponents didn't do it. I'm just saying that it didn't happen. People were focused on the future. The consensus was that the presidency is okay again, now we can go back about our business.

There was an enormous interest in the presidency during Watergate. People who never got involved in politics watched those hearings. I have no scientific basis for this other than my own observation. I had friends who never paid any attention to what I was doing unless I was covering an assassination or something, but they were just glued to the Watergate thing. I think part of it was the drama, but part of it also was that people were really concerned about it. They were concerned in a way rarely witnessed in this country because our system wasn't

working.   Once the system was working again they went
back to their normal worries.

QUESTION: Would you agree with what Cheney and three
or four others said when they were here and talked about
Ford and Reagan, that is that Ford would have won with
Reagan? They also talked about the fact that Ford never
asked him and there was a pact that he wouldn't ask him,
just as later on there certainly was when it was the other
way around. One of them said that Ford's answer when
Reagan was mentioned was: "I don't understand him. I
don't feel right about him." Could you say a little about
the relationship between the two?

MR. CANNON: If you look at the Ford autobiography, the
chapter that opens with Reagan is one of the most blunt
and for me most significant. Ford takes up the notion that
Reagan's challenge didn't hurt him and then he just says,
"How could it have not hurt me?" He goes on and writes
about it in a polite, but very direct and wonderful way
which I couldn't begin to duplicate. I've written about and
talked about the subject of Reagan being the vice president.
I talked to Cheney about it.   Everybody sort of
misremembers or remembers that scene. I covered that very
closely, and I knew the political figures on both sides.
Sears was afraid that Reagan would say yes if he was asked
directly; if Ford had made the appeal, he would have said
yes.   So they set up an agreement that he wouldn't ask.
Where I part company from a lot of analysts on that one is
I don't think it was remarkable that Ford kept his word.
He usually kept his word. I think that Ford is a person
who, if he said he wouldn't ask, wouldn't ask. The reason
that you would set that up, and the reason Sears wanted to
make sure it was set up, was because he suspected that if
Reagan was appealed to he would take it. But I don't think
that tells us anything about either the character of Reagan
or the character of Ford that we didn't already know.   I
think it is sheer conjecture to say what would have
happened if Reagan had been on that ticket because we
know what happened with Dole on the ticket.   All the
information is inconclusive. The data is very unreliable at
telling whether the person in the second slot helps or hurts.
I'm skeptical of that notion. That's something you have to
prove.   You have to prove that Dole or Ferarro hurt or

helped. In the absence of being able to prove it, the assumption should be it didn't do much.

I think having Reagan on the Ford ticket had all kinds of problems of its own. One is that Reagan is not good at second billing. He would have been out there and probably would have been very easy for the opposition or the press corps to pick off. The press assigned to vice presidential candidates are always people who are trying to make names for themselves. Sometimes they do. I'm sure that Reagan would have felt like a prisoner and the first time he expressed himself differently than Ford there would have been fireworks. The race would have had a different kind of dynamic. It would have been a question of which candidate to believe. There is no way to know how that would have turned out.

Ford had one besetting characteristic that was a product of having served in Congress. He was forever roundtabling things. It was the safe course. You were certainly not going to get great bold ideas out of the Ford administration, no matter how many times he had been elected. That could be a great advantage in some situations and a great liability in others. I'm not sure that bold new ideas are what is needed in the presidency, but if that's what is needed it wasn't going to come from Ford. Dole was perceived as the safe choice, though he really wasn't. Again, we look at that through the prism of that disastrous debate that Dole had with Mondale.

In selecting a vice president, Stu Spencer was arguing for Anne Armstrong. Bob Teeter was on the side of William Ruckleshaus. I happened to think that if they had picked Ruckleshaus it might have worked because he would have brought some additional strengths to the ticket. He was Catholic, a skilled politician and a pretty good speaker. He probably would not have gotten into trouble. If he had gotten into the kind of trouble that Dole got into, he would have extricated himself. Unlike Dole, he would have succeeded with the press.

In any case there were essentially four candidates, and three of them were gambles. Reagan was a gamble. Rucklehaus had been involved in the solution of the problem. It might have looked like a payoff, and that could have been a problem. Obviously putting a woman on the ticket for the first time was a gamble. These were all gambles. He did what he thought was safe. It turned out to be the least safe. But it was something Ford would have done anyway.

I think Ford suffered more than most people did from understanding Reagan because he had been in politics all his life. Reagan was least appreciated, least valued, and most underestimated by the very people who are the analogues of Gerald Ford in California political life. When Reagan was elected governor there was a cadre of very able Republicans led by Bob Monagan, the speaker for two years during Reagan's term, the late Jack Veneman, who worked under Bob Finch and for Richard Nixon, Bill Bagley and a couple of other people. These people had no use for Reagan. They had spent all their lives toiling in the vineyards. They were the Republican ascendancy, like the Protestant ascendancy culture in Ireland. They couldn't understand that this interloper could come in and capture mass attention, the public's imagination, and be elected when they all thought they could make a better governor.

Ford is very much a part of that school. The people who have the most success in understanding Reagan politically tended to be people who are, themselves, accidental or who are products of the system or are like Cheney, who has been in the White House and understands the difference between that place and the Congress. If you have worked all your life in Congress or in a state legislature, your horizons are defined by that. I think even if Ford had not been president he never would have understood Reagan.

QUESTION: Would you go so far as to say that the Congress isn't good preparation for the presidency?

MR. CANNON: That's too sweeping for me. I think Congress and particularly the House—you're running half the time you're up there—does not prepare you to understand politics in the Marshall McLuhan age. It doesn't prepare you for people who come in from outside the system and maybe see it in a larger perspective. I don't think it is impossible to be a member of Congress and have that perspective. I think Senator John F. Kennedy wasn't considered a very terrific senator, but he had a broad view of the presidency.

I probably have a positive bias towards Johnson. I think Johnson saw more and was in some ways more of a renaissance man than any of these other figures we're talking about. He was "larger than life." His flaws were as large as his virtues. I think he was really done in by this huge flaw we saw in Vietnam, believing that American power could answer everything. But I think that Johnson was a transcendent figure. Did he make the leap from being senator to president? Sure he did. Anybody who saw that wonderful speech of "We Shall Overcome," knows what an effective, emotional, powerful orator Johnson was. Johnson understood the power of the presidency. He was done in by other things, it seems to me.

COMMENT: He also had executive experience.

MR. CANNON: That's right. The senator who does well as president either has had executive experience or, like Kennedy and Nixon, was essentially using the Senate as a way station. But, it's hard to find an example in the House. There is no modern example. I could cite John Adams but there we're dealing with an entirely different century. It seems to me that in modern times, it's hard to become a president directly from the House.

Still, I don't think Ford was done in by that. I think it affected his understanding of Reagan, but I think Ford was really affected most by what I said at the outset: the fact that he was not fully president. I think if he had ever gotten elected to the presidency he might have surprised some people.

QUESTION: Wasn't there a peculiar fitness about his seeing himself as a caretaker rather than as a full-fledged president?

MR. CANNON: Yes. I think we should be grateful, in a constitutional sense, for that attitude.

I've argued the other side of the coin with people like Dick Cheney, Don Rumsfeld and Stu Spencer. They believe that it can't be argued that Ford was benefited by being defeated. On the other hand, his peculiar mission, purpose or role may be highly valued by historians a half century from now. If he had been elected and his policies had proved disastrous or unimaginative, it would be a different story. He did have a wonderful sense of the constitutional limits, though. I think that is the point of your question.

He did know what that amendment said. He knew what he was in there to do. He expressed the limitation that he had not been elected, and this says to me that he also had what Nixon did not have, a healthy respect for the rule of law. This is a good thing to have in a president at any time.

NARRATOR: There are ten times as many questions than we have time for answers. One way or another, we've got to get you back so other people can ask all their questions. Thank you.

MR. CANNON: I've enjoyed this. I usually talk about Reagan and it was nice to talk about Ford and his place in history.

CONCLUDING OBSERVATIONS

A volume such as this drawing on the resources and experiences of twenty-two close associates of former President Ford has at least three notable virtues as oral history. First, it provides a window to greater understanding of Gerald Ford as a political leader with the various strengths and weaknesses which others call up in their assessments of him. Second, the twenty-two observers help us find our way through the thickets of historical analysis and interpretation. Solid and responsible as President Ford may appear in contrast with other more controversial American presidents, friends and critics alike contest certain points about him. Third, an evaluation of his presidency is confounded by the issue of whether or not it is an unfinished presidency. Staunch supporters of President Ford contend that what was unfinished and incomplete in his fraction of a presidential term would have been fulfilled in a full term growing out of his election. Such a term would have been fully representative of Gerald Ford as President rather than a continuation of the Nixon presidency.

First, the evidence on Ford as political leader points strongly to qualities that somehow were obscured from large segments of the American public. These include his knowledge of the American political system and comprehension of the budget to a point he could review it in its entirety before the Cabinet and the public. Why such strengths failed to gain recognition is a subject of discussion by the contributors. In part they attribute it to the aftermath of Watergate and the miasma of suspicion that surrounded all political leaders. They all suggest that

Ford's pardoning of Nixon may have done him irreparable political damage. Finally, some of the narrators accept the blame for never succeeding in presenting a true image of Ford through the media. They acknowledge that they allowed the public to continue to see the President as a stumbler and bumbler when the opposite was true.

Second, the careful reader will note that different associates view President Ford in different ways. Some assert he was ineffective in resolving conflicts that arose within his staff. In common parlance, he was too good a fellow to knock heads. Others question whether this was true. He suffered the less than loyal performance of certain Nixon carryovers in the White House and the Cabinet. One Ford loyalist refers to this group as the Praetorian Guard. But these differences are perhaps less sharp than those of a former New York senator who condemns the President's counsel, a man who has been especially generous to the Miller Center. As editor, I thought long and hard about including this material but remembered the advice of my former boss, Dean Rusk, who insisted that the people must have access to the full historical record and then judge for themselves. An especially poignant example of differing historical interpretations is that which divides Richard Cheney and Labor Secretary Dunlop on common situs picketing. They differ on the background of Ford's decision on a specific policy issue and the relation of Ford's reelection prospects to the role of labor. Whatever such differences an oral history worth its salt must let the record speak for itself and future historians and the people must judge.

Third, it may seem a distortion to suspend history's judgment on the broader question of the Ford presidency but peculiar circumstances may require it. Ford followed a President who left the office disgraced and rejected. He carried out the duties of his office in the aftermath of Watergate. Ford was an unelected President. His mandate as some saw it was to administer the Nixon-Ford presidency and conduct the Nixon-Ford policies. Is it not fair then to argue that only in a second full term which was truly Ford's could one have discovered the elements for a true historical evaluation of the Ford presidency? Yet that opportunity was never to be his and we can therefore not strike a responsible historical judgment and balance sheet.

Whatever can be said on these three questions, the substance of this rather modest oral history of the Ford presidency may help to place that presidency in American political history. It may point us to institutional principles and political lessons on which to base future study. In other words, the volume's chief value may be in the resources it provides for those who would continue the study an honorable and of a healing presidency.